JOHN
EVELYN

Books in the RENAISSANCE LIVES series explore and illustrate the life histories and achievements of significant artists, intellectuals and scientists in the early modern world. They delve into literature, philosophy, the history of art, science and natural history and cover narratives of exploration, statecraft and technology.

Series Editor: François Quiviger

JOHN EVELYN

*A Life of
Domesticity*

JOHN DIXON HUNT

REAKTION BOOKS

For Jo Joslyn and Alan Choate

Published by Reaktion Books Ltd
Unit 32, Waterside
44–48 Wharf Road
London N1 7UX, UK
www.reaktionbooks.co.uk

First published 2017

Printed and bound in China by 1010 Printing International Ltd

A catalogue record for this book is available from the British Library

ISBN 978 1 78023 836 4

COVER: Studio of Sir Godfrey Kneller (1646–1723), *John Evelyn*, n.d., oil on canvas. Whereabouts unknown (sold at Sotheby's, London, 1993) – photo Sotheby's/akg-images.

CONTENTS

ABBREVIATIONS

Celebration
Mavis Batey, ed., *A Celebration of John Evelyn: Proceedings to Mark the Tercentenary of his Death* (Goldalming, 2007)

Correspondence
Diary and Correspondence of John Evelyn, ed. William Bray, 4 vols (London, 1857), vol. III

Darley, *John Evelyn*
Gillian Darley, *John Evelyn: Living for Ingenuity* (New Haven, CT, and London, 2006)

Diary
The Diary of John Evelyn, ed. E. S. de Beer, 6 vols (Oxford, 1955)

EB
Elysium Britannicum; or, the Royal Gardens, ed. John E. Ingram (Philadelphia, PA, 2000)

Evelyn DO
Therese O'Malley and Joachim Wolschke-Bulmahn, eds, *John Evelyn's 'Elysium Britannicum' and European Gardening* (Washington, DC, and Dumbarton Oaks, 1998)

Keynes, *Bibliophily*
Geoffrey Keynes, ed., *John Evelyn: A Study in Bibliophily* (2nd edn, Oxford, 1968)

LB
The Letterbooks of John Evelyn, ed. Douglas Chambers and David Galbraith, 2 vols (Toronto, 2014). Pagination continues throughout the two volumes

Memories
Geoffrey Keynes, ed., *Memories for my Grand-son* (London, 1926)

MW
Miscellaneous Writings, ed. William Upcott (1825)

1 Francesco Bartolozzi, *John Evelyn*, 1776, engraving.

Introduction

Happy the man who lived content
With his own Home and Continent.
EVELYN AFTER CLAUDIAN

To know men one must isolate them. But after a long experience,
it seems right to put back such isolated reflections into a
relationship.
RILKE, TRANS. WILL STONE

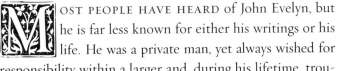OST PEOPLE HAVE HEARD of John Evelyn, but
he is far less known for either his writings or his
life. He was a private man, yet always wished for
responsibility within a larger and, during his lifetime, troubled England. His Diary, published in a modern annotated
edition, tells us much about his public life, little about his
private one. The diary of his friend Samuel Pepys is more
widely used, more fun, and more in tune with what we assume
were the mores of the Restoration: intimate, gossipy, occasionally racy. Little of Evelyn's considerable writing is available,
but much of it is intriguing; yet it has to be found mostly in
collections of rare books. He wrote about urban planning,
fashion, London weather or what we would call climate change

(and that small book has been reissued in modern times). For those in the know he was an accomplished gardener and a specialist on trees. He is, then, if not wholly unnoticed, not really known.

Yet he was somebody to be reckoned with during a heroic period of English intellectual culture. He was a devoted follower of Francis Bacon and applied that master's rigour to a wide range of ideas and materials, augmenting much of the Baconian agenda. As a young man he travelled widely in Europe, attended carefully to everything he saw, found important books to translate for English readers, became an accomplished, if somewhat withdrawn and modest, personage around the court, was a prominent member of the newly formed Royal Society, and knew some of the most exciting virtuosi and scientists of his age (Christopher Wren, Robert Hooke, Wenceslaus Hollar, Robert Boyle); he also advised his contemporaries on the two matters that always mattered most to him – gardening, arboriculture – and their role in a new and Enlightened England. Yet his monumental manuscript on gardening was only transcribed and published in 2000, while the garden he created at Sayes Court in Deptford no longer exists; the wonderful tree book, *Sylva*, went through so many editions, and confusingly changed its title to *Silva*, so that his concern with arboriculture has perhaps lost its edge today.

He also lived through one of the most troubled times that England ever encountered (until the Great War in the twentieth century), with a king executed, a failed republican experiment, military dictatorships, forms of religious belief and practice challenged and changed, another king banished for trying to govern autocratically, to be replaced with a foreign statesman from the Netherlands, confronting wars in Europe, and a developing colony in North America, all driven by and driving a profoundly transformed economy. He found himself living and sometimes serving under five monarchs, yet all the while keeping both his own counsel and a level head, and a firm conviction that his faith in the Church of England and in the probity and usefulness of family life mattered above everything else.

While he was a person who focused upon his family, he also sought to play a role in an England that, once the Commonwealth was abandoned and the monarchy resumed in 1660, was to be a community of promise. He wrote that he was content to exist in 'his own home and continent', but that inclination saw him travelling widely and at length in Europe as a young man. On his return, he nourished ambitions within the state and culture of England to bring home ideas that he encountered abroad, translating important foreign works that he wanted his contemporaries to read, and raising an awareness of European building, town planning and landscape architecture. He worked outward from his own enthusiasms, his own commitments, not wholly given over to a full participation in a country where he found both religion and politics sometimes uncongenial. Yet he also recognized how much he wanted to put his own individual experience into fruitful contact with his contemporaries, for he himself knew that in the late seventeenth century 'isolation' was not an option, though many others did take that path.

Evelyn was caught on the cusp of a society and culture that was developing rapidly, if never smoothly; he contributed to some of its important changes, yet held back from others. While he grew more conservative as he aged, more pious, and sceptical of things around him, he also encouraged younger men to push ahead in what he considered the essential concerns of place and country, learning and knowledge. He was above all an alert, even obsessive, observer of things, a model member of the Royal Society's determination to review, annotate and understand what was happening in the world. Yet his energy and enthusiasm for collecting information on so many fronts, most obviously in matters of garden design, managed to overwhelm his desire to publish new ideas and theories of place-making and garden design. If he had lived beyond his eighty years, he would have encountered thinkers like Joseph Addison, Stephen Switzer and even Alexander Pope. In their world, his own visions of place-making might have prospered.

His considerable range of interests, not particularly unusual at that time, has also meant that his modern biographers have found him difficult to pigeonhole, when specialization today is prized and the boundaries between disciplines have been radically altered. Besides his published diary, there is a wealth of information on Evelyn's various activities. But it is also a vast and sometimes heterogeneous mass, with the Diary itself, the most visited of his writings, often an agenda and inventory of activities with little need to provide any meaningful structure. He was engaged throughout his life in many enterprises and projects, not all of which are relevant to 'seeing him whole'. Maybe he found this same difficulty himself, for he seems to have wished retrospectively to construct a meaningful pattern or narrative for his own life

– revising and rewriting his Diary after the events it first described and compiling a careful collection of his own letters in a compendium of letterbooks, also recently published.

When the large archive of Evelyn materials arrived at the British Library in March 1995, it presented Evelyn as a person of endless curiosity but with little clear sense of what really mattered to him. My own book relies upon some of his earlier biographies, like John Bowle's *John Evelyn and his World* (1981), which is clear, straightforward, sympathetic; Bowle's was preceded by Arthur Ponsonby's *John Evelyn* (1933) and W. G. Hiscock's *John Evelyn and his Family Circle* (1955), and then followed in 2006 by Gillian Darley's much bulkier *John Evelyn: Living for Ingenuity*, where she was able to draw heavily on the Evelyn collections now at the British Library.

My own, slimmer account, while necessarily following the outline of Evelyn's life and contacts, focuses upon what my subtitle terms his 'Domesticity'. I explain this in my first chapter, but it has to do with a double meaning of domesticity in the seventeenth century: that, which we retain today, of living in families with the support and trials of home life; but domesticity also emphasized, in the new world of the early English Enlightenment, accommodating or domesticating foreign ideas, new theories, new resources and technologies, as well as learning to live with a rapidly changing and expanding world. In the face of many of those changes, Evelyn was attentive, concerned and by turns frustrated and uncertain.

While it is hard to isolate one particular theme for him, domesticity offers a fresh perspective on this quintessentially seventeenth-century figure, whose life and career took him through a variety of political, religious and social upheavals which he witnessed and in part contrived to influence. To facilitate this focus, and given his multifarious endeavours, it seems useful to avoid 'the gridiron of chronology' and accept the responsibilities of both a diachronic and synchronic narrative; this allows me to cluster some of his activities around central moments and places of both his family life at Sayes Court and his larger concerns involving the Royal Society, and gives some priority to isolating the man without losing our sense of his intimate relationship with his age.

ONE

Domesticity

All wise Men, should have two Religions; the one, a publick, for
their Conformity with the People, the other, a private, to be kept
to their own breasts.

THOMAS SPRAT

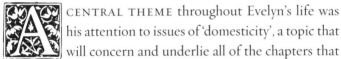CENTRAL THEME throughout Evelyn's life was
his attention to issues of 'domesticity', a topic that
will concern and underlie all of the chapters that
follow. But it is worth a preliminary explanation of what was
involved in domesticity at that time. Today, this means essentially life in the home, or *domus*, attending to near and extended
family members, to visitors, personal faith and domestic tragedies, household and dwelling place, to family finances, and
to children who cannot choose their parents. Yet for Evelyn
in the seventeenth century, that mode of domesticity would
have extended to his close friends and colleagues, like Thomas
Henshaw, Samuel Pepys, Christopher Wren, Sir Thomas
Browne, John Beale or John Aubrey, for whom letters often
took the place of visitation.

Yet this sense of domesticity was not as simple as, and
perhaps more robust than, it can be today. This younger son
was deeply attached to the family estate at Wotton in Surrey,

which Evelyn assumed he would never inherit (though he did so towards the end of his life); even so, it was still a place that always mattered. Not having such a home – an estate with its roots in the countryside, political connections within the county and obligations to the neighbourhood – Evelyn took over elsewhere a property belonging to his father-in-law, leased first from the Commonwealth and eventually from the Crown. It was nonetheless a house and land where he could install a family and indulge himself in the making of a garden, which was a prime ambition in a nation that he felt lacked good and up-to-date garden design. So at Sayes Court he made a dwelling place, together with what became, and remained historically (after it disappeared), an important garden. To Sayes Court in 1652 he brought his wife, Mary, and there she bore him six children over sixteen years; some died young, some succumbed to smallpox or other disease. It was the location to which his family, friends and notables – including Charles II and his queen – would be welcomed and entertained. But it was a lease that constantly involved him in issues both financial and legal, and even territorial, as it was adjacent to the busy, growing and intrusive Deptford dock-yard. Nor was it readily anything like a home: when his young son Richard died at the age of five, he was buried at Wotton rather than in Deptford's churchyard. It was to Wotton that he took Mary to comfort her when her mother died soon after accompanying her daughter to England. It was the place he took his family to during the London Plague of 1665, and during that retreat one of his daughters was born, in the very room where he himself had seen the light of day. Wotton was also the house and home to which he would return to solace himself, where he went (as he put it) to 'refresh himself' or to recuperate from illness, as he did on the eve of the Restoration. And even before he obtained Sayes Court he was proposing and designing garden features for his brother at Wotton, a site that he had hopes of improving even as a younger brother. When chance gave him the ownership of Wotton, he would counsel his grandson on the regime that he envisaged for Wotton and its estate after his death, which for Evelyn came in 1706. It is interesting that while we possess plans of Evelyn's gardening at Sayes Court, we have very few images of it, while Wotton was sketched on many occasions with a loving concern for how it appeared, its complex of buildings, terraces, waters and surrounding woodland (illus. 2 and 3).

While a modern household will usually have one or two family members working outside the home and sometimes bringing work back with them, in Evelyn's case there was no such 'outside' place of work. Though he was constantly active beyond his dwelling place, he had no formal employment, not wanting to practise the law, not wishing to serve in the military, and not obtaining, despite seeking it, any government post, such as that of the Historiographer Royal. He was, nonetheless, a prominent member of the important Royal Society, founded in 1660, and a virtuoso and 'amateur' (in the best sense of that word) in architecture, numismatics, painting and sculpture; but he excelled himself in the art of garden-making. He did engage in what today we call the civil service, but he had no permanent post and therefore no steady financial income; indeed, he sought to obtain employment in government not only for himself, but for his

father-in-law, who had served as ambassador to France before the Restoration, and for his two sons and grandson. All that activity did involve him constantly in work for and at the Court, to which he could journey back and forth from Sayes Court, though on occasions and during winter months he sometimes took lodgings in town. But the Court was not, for this principled and pious man, a very congenial place, and its culture increasingly appalled him.

Ironically, it was to a person in this court that he was drawn, when he became friends with a young maid of honour, Margaret Blagge. The basis of this relationship, about which he later wrote in *The Life of Mrs Godolphin*,[1] appears to have been his need for, and indeed skill in, pedagogy, joined to a pious wish to advise a young woman who sought his friendship in the first place. His early education had been, by his own confession, not particularly useful, and he found the years travelling and studying in Europe were worth more than what he had learned at Oxford. So an instinct to instruct others

2 John Evelyn's drawing of the house and surrounding woodlands at Wotton, in Surrey.

emerged from his own self-instruction and found expression in and outside the family.

One of his first compositions on family matters was the private admonishments, or *Instructions Oeconomiques*, addressed to his young wife, 'to be kept under *lock and key*' (not the wife, the instructions).[2] It was inscribed in gold to 'the present mistress of my youth, the hopeful companion of my riper years and the future nurse of my age . . . M[istress] Mary Evelyn, my dear wife'. He advised his bride of thirteen years on the duties of wives and the requirements of a happy union, on 'Society Paternal', and on county life, all the while sustaining his remarks with a cluster of *sententiae* and cultural allusions to Hesiod, Plato and Cyrus, among others. It must have been

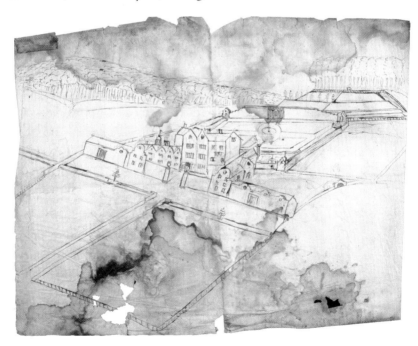

3 Evelyn's rough sketch-cum-plan of Wotton House and its surroundings.

a touch intimidating for even this accomplished young woman, but she clearly rose to the occasion, and later in Evelyn's life he would salute her as 'the best wife in the world, sweet, and (though not charming) agreeable and as she grew up, pious, loyal & of so just a temper'. Later in life Evelyn also composed 'Directions for the Employment of your Time' for his daughter,[3] which begins with advising some devotions, listening to her mother's commands, walking in the garden for exercise, practising writing, playing on the harpsichord, 'more solemn intercourse between God and your soul', family prayer time and special instructions for Sundays. Mary seemed to have honoured those instructions in making her own little book of 'several designs and thoughts of mine for the regulating my life upon many occasions'.[4] Late, he penned a small volume for his son, John, on John's departure in 1692 for a post in Ireland, with advice on religion, 'profitable Entertainment' and what would have to be done to 're-edify' Wotton, which by then Evelyn knew he would inherit from his brother and pass to his son (though the latter never occurred). And in 1704, after John's death and thinking of how his work and values, and Wotton itself, must be maintained after his own death, which occurred two years later, Evelyn wrote *Memories for my Grand-son*.

So he had always been an engaged and careful family member, teaching his sons, acquiring tutors for his nephew and recommending others for his friends' families. A brief acquaintance with any of his lengthy letters will signal how easily he took to the task of instructing and guiding the young. It was a habit that emerged in his deep, pious and sometimes misunderstood friendship with Margaret Blagge.

But for Evelyn the truer home, if not the household, was his country. 'Home and continent' was how he rendered the words of Claudian on contentment. It was, at the very least, an interchange between, on the one hand, Europe and its intellectual heritage and, on the other, whatever can be considered 'home', which comprised Wotton, Sayes Court and the potential of a new England after the Restoration. A pious household was a private religion, to be carefully nurtured, but the public religion was the nation, and conformity to it by its people required at once a commitment to the English religion, to its arts and culture and to its intellectual role in the larger world. In 1671 he wrote to James Hamilton that the religion of the Church of England is a 'sublime, and noble service, comely, and adequate to its glorious object, and would be envied and admired, if the great ones did it honour, and would bring piety into reputation' (*LB*, 1.513–14). And Evelyn chose to serve his country and his faith by what he could do well – through translation, by writing about architecture and horticultural matters, and ensuring that his exile in Europe during the unhappy years of the Interregnum was harvested and conveyed to his countrymen.

So beyond that immediate circle of family and friends was a need to domesticate himself in the larger European world of politics and culture. In his private and domestic life Evelyn was attentive and generous, while also firm and principled. In the larger and public search for domestication, he found the opportunity to travel, which as a younger son without the obligation to oversee the family home at Wotton he could do by absenting himself from England during the more troubled upheavals that preceded the Commonwealth. That brought him into contact – in person and through books – with a circle of both European thinkers and those who had also fled from England in those years. This first-hand knowledge of European experience decisively impacted his thinking, his publications and translations as well as his enthusiasm for garden-making – itself both a personal inclination and one he deemed crucial to share with his English contemporaries. Thus he translated and broadcast, 'for the benefit or divertissement of our country', treatises on French gardening – *The French Gardiner* (1658) and *The Compleat Gard'ner* (1693) – and given that no Italian treatise presented itself to be rendered into English he added his own observations on Italian design in various comments on garden-making. It was due to those projects, wrote Stephen Switzer in 1718, 'that Gardening can speak proper English'. On the basis of both that French expertise and his first-hand visits in Italy, Evelyn built his own English corpus of gardening, horticultural and arboricultural writings as well as practising the making of gardens.

For this 'chameleon',[5] speaking proper English was crucial, whether about gardening, architecture, politics, engravings, fruit trees, arboriculture, navigation and commerce, medals and coins, painting, national characteristics, earth or vegetation. Englishmen without sufficient language skills needed to read important foreign works in their own language, and see how ideas could be accommodated in England and be presented clearly in English. The title of John Ogilby's *The Works of Publius Virgilius Maro* in 1654 acknowledged a famous Roman authority, politician and poet, but 43 years later, the very title of John Dryden's *The Works of Virgil* made them seem

already more English; while Ogilby's edition glossed the text
with elaborate marginal annotations, Dryden's translation
stands alone on the plain page.

Translation was itself a constant effort at domestication.
John Oldham in the 'Advertisement' to his *Ars Poetica* of 1681
argued that his job was to put 'Horace into a more modern
dress, than hitherto he has appear'd in, that is, by making him
speak, as if here living and writing now. I therefore resolv'd
to alter the Scene from Rome to London.' Altering the scene,
literally and metaphorically, was a constant theme of writers:
in the early eighteenth century Alexander Pope's translations
were urged on by Sir William Trumbull, who knew they would
make 'Homer speak good English'. Evelyn himself engaged
largely in such translations, and he encouraged his son John
to do the same: John junior would publish in 1673 a version
of the Latin of René Rapin's *Hortorum Libri IV* (1665), itself
modelled on Virgil's *Georgics,* which was hailed on its title page
as 'And now made English'; the son's *Grotius His Arguments* was
also 'rendered into plain English verse' in 1686.

Thus the nation saw that 'domestication' (on the somewhat invidious analogy of domesticating wild beasts!) was
not only making foreign ideas available and hospitable to
the nation, but was to be done in good and clear English:
what Thomas Sprat in his *History of the Royal Society,* with
which body Evelyn was much involved, termed 'a domestic
plainness'. This concern for plainness, at once domesticated
in England and readable in the study of one's own dwelling,
sustained much of the Society's business, and Evelyn himself
contributed to it by finding good English for Lucretius,
Chrysostom and a cluster of other foreign writers. Yet it was

not a Presbyterian plainness, for Evelyn at least applauded the Laudian character of English Church services; rather, he chose to do everything that seemed useful and proper to enrich the English character with a domesticated Europeanism.

The presiding genius and inspiration for members of the Royal Society was Francis Bacon, and he specifically emphasized the need for domestication in his *New Atlantis*, published in 1627, the year after his death, when Evelyn was yet seven years old.[6] In the fable of Solomon's House in *New Atlantis*, as well as in Bacon's *Sylva Sylvarum* (a title that Evelyn would partly echo in his own *Sylva*, as well as echoing Statius' *Silvae*), he would find much encouragement for his own various activities. The lengthy discourse given by the 'Father' of Solomon's House that ends Bacon's *New Atlantis* covers every possible field of study that the Royal Society and its members collectively would strive to emulate, and to which Evelyn himself contributed: such matters as weather, care of the sick, experiments, 'mechanical arts', furnaces and heat-producing mechanisms, engines of all sorts, the manufacture of gunpowder, flying machines and 'curious clocks', representations of things near and far – from worms and small flies to rainbows and the heavens – and 'perspective-houses, where we make demonstration of all lights and radiations', including the production of 'feigned distances'.

A long section in *New Atlantis* on 'large and various orchards, and gardens', and parks or 'enclosures of all sorts, of beasts and birds, which we use not only for view or rareness, but likewise for dissections' must have struck Evelyn in particular:

Wherein we do not so much respect beauty, as variety of ground and soil, proper for diverse trees, and herbs: and some very spacious, where trees, and berries are set, whereof we make diverse kinds of drinks . . . In these we practice likewise all conclusions of grafting, and inoculating. As well of wild trees, as fruit trees, which produceth many effects. And we make (by art) in the same orchards, and gardens, trees and flowers, to come earlier, or later than their seasons; and to come up and bear more speedily than by their natural course they do. We make them also by art greater much than their nature; and their fruit greater, and sweeter, and of differing taste, smell, colour and figure, from their nature. And many of them we so order as they become of medicinal use . . . We have also means to make plants rise by mixtures of earth, without seeds; and likewise to make diverse new plants, differing from the vulgar; and to make one tree or plant turn into another . . . (p. 38)

The customs and politics of the New Atlantis that in their turn clearly sustained the agenda enunciated at Solomon's House were evidence of two kinds of domesticity: love and care of the family, described in an elaborate description of a quasi-ritualistic family gathering (pp. 26ff.), and the rewards of careful and focused travel. If the society is 'wholly bent to make [this] kingdom and people happy' (p. 21), then travel, though strictly limited, brings news of foreign places, 'knowledge of the affairs and state of those countries . . . and especially of the sciences, arts, manufacture, and intentions'

(p. 24). Travelling 'doth commonly know more by eye' (p. 16); but those less able to travel and see, those that 'stayeth at home', can learn by perusing published accounts of those who do travel, as they bring home 'books, abstracts, and patterns of experiments' from other countries, and are called 'merchants of light' (p. 45). In short, the 'end of our Foundation is the knowledge of causes, and secret motions of things; and the enlarging of the bounds of human empire, to the effecting of all things possible' (p. 35).

As early as 1592 Bacon had told a correspondent that 'I have taken all knowledge to be my province'; from which he wished to purge both 'frivolous disputations, confutations, and verbosities' and 'blind experiments and auricular traditions and impostures', to which end were required 'industrious observations, grounded conclusions and profitable inventions and discoveries'.[7] Evelyn would have appreciated that determination, and in the published works of Bacon he found constant encouragement, even if he himself lapses into 'auricular' conclusions from classical writers. Yet he was also, far less than Bacon would prove to be, possessed of only 'moderate civil ends', less willing to participate in political affairs. But the scrutiny of natural and artistic phenomena and an interest in asking questions and seeking empirical understandings were as fundamental to him as his family, religion and nationality.

Evelyn's sense of family was strong, and during his European travels he was constantly in touch with his brothers and sister. It was to the former that, later in 1659, he prefaced his translation from the Greek of St John Chrysostom's *Golden Book concerning the Education of Children*, when seeking consolation for the death of his five-year-old son in 1658. Geoffrey Keynes rightly says it was the most attractive and personal of his publications. Evelyn's understanding of his pedagogic role in the family was modelled on his concern for the state, which he served loyally as a royalist and an Englishman and where his private conscience in matters of religion (or what moderns would term consciousness) was cultivated. Michael McKeon, in his book on *The Secret History of Domesticity*, quotes John Dryden to the effect that 'Conscience is the Royalty and Prerogative of every Private man' – thereby neatly allowing a connection of royalty with the individual.[8]

Domesticity in the seventeenth century had a far richer significance, as McKeon demonstrates, for the link between private conscience and public deportment was intricate. These involved a more and more complicated negotiation between private and public worlds, between the household (the Greek *oikos*) and the state or *polis*. As McKeon sees it, the 'relation between polis and oikos was understood both metaphorically and metonymically: the polis was conceived and arranged on the model of the family'; while he cites Aristotle's *Politics* ('the state is by nature clearly *prior to* the family'), he misses Aristotle's historical point that *oikos* did proceed *polis*. McKeon also quotes John Locke's understanding that 'the power of a Magistrate over a Subject, may be *distinguished* from that of a Father over his Children, a Master over his Servant, a Husband over his wife, and a Lord over his Slave.'[9] That is an understanding of what home and family mean strikingly different from today's.

A great deal of Evelyn's efforts and achievements in 'domestication' came both in the form of letter-writing and writing for publication and (not always the same thing) the publication itself. This was true especially in the area with which Evelyn was most concerned – the promotion of horticulture and arboriculture. As Elizabeth Yale has shown, naturalists collected their information on the basis of a Baconian observation, then wrote up notes, sketched items, shared their information in correspondence and eventually, perhaps, fixed their ideas in printed form, though with a frequent interest in undertaking revisions, as Evelyn did with his *Sylva*.[10] Correspondence and shared notes were certainly how Evelyn communicated with Samuel Hartlib, John Beale and John Aubrey, among others; equally, the masses of their notes, documents, drafts, sketches and manuscripts did not always result in publication. Yet, as Yale also shows, in this huge and elaborate effort to observe and understand the natural world, the wild, cabinets, herbaria and florilegia were used to gather this somewhat fragmented knowledge into a portrait and representation of the natural riches of Britain itself.

But for many virtuosi it was – long before they turned to publication – the writing and communication in correspondence that established a network of intellectual exchange. Evelyn's correspondence was considerable, and it was through his letters that he sustained and advanced many of his ideas. It was typical that he engaged in correspondence with Samuel Hartlib, a key broker of intellectual ideas across a universal range of disciplines throughout Europe, but this was an epistolary exchange of the kind that he conducted with many others besides Hartlib. This larger correspondence (and his own determination to keep copies of important parts of it in his letterbooks) show that staying in contact with a wide range of contemporary thinkers was essential to him personally and to his hopes for advancing ideas in England. If his much-relied-on Diary reflects the contacts he made and maintained throughout his life (though it is sometimes brief, elliptical and not always accurate), his letters are more eloquent of his sharing of ideas at once scientific and artistic, religious and political, public and personal. Indeed, his letters also reveal that his dedication to domestication was bifocal: to deal with a wide circle of friends and correspondents reflected on his family, and his family implicitly and explicitly was but a metaphor, a metonymy, for the public state.[11]

But Evelyn, as were so many of his contemporaries, was hugely conscious of living through a revolution in print culture, not just of books that were distributed through bookshops and by itinerant booksellers, but of pamphlets and journalism that were widely circulated. Ideas could now be more quickly consumed, communicated and denounced; political animadversions could be quickly promoted or discounted; and science, as Bacon envisaged, would no longer be floated on traditions of folklore, word of mouth and old wives' tales. John Aubrey, also a great compiler of materials, was grateful for this new medium:

> since printing came in fashion, till a little before the Civil wars, the ordinary sort of people were not taught to read: nowadays books are common, and most of the poor people understand letters: and many good books and variety of turns of affairs, have put all the old fables out of doors; and the divine art of printing and

gunpowder have frightened away Robin-Good-fellow and the fairies (illus. 53).[12]

And the home is where language is transmitted, taught and nurtured so that books may be read.

If the gunpowder industry of the Evelyn family had much declined by the Civil Wars, a point Evelyn himself noted in responding to Aubrey's remarks on the county of Surrey and

4 William Faithorne (d. 1691), undated drawing of John Aubrey.

Wotton's woods and streams in particular, then bookmaking indeed was or could be more powerful than the cannon. So Evelyn continued to produce pamphlets, reports to the Royal Society, books and translations – an essential way of communicating foreign ideas to English readers now that books could be widely available. He also found, like Aubrey, that to accumulate facts and observations meant constant revision was needed; yet it led nevertheless to a frustrating failure to complete his magnum opus, 'Elysium Britannicum'. In that, he had hoped to bring together everything that the British gardener needed to know – mechanically, horticulturally, philosophically – in a book worthy of inclusion in a Baconian library of a newer Atlantis.

TWO

Early Life in England

HEN EVELYN CAME to write up his Diary in 1660,[1] he began by noting the domestic situation into which he was born in 1620, recording the ages and characters of his father and mother: his father 'low of stature, but very strong . . . exact and temperate' (*Diary*, 11.2), his mother 'of proper personage, well timber'd, of a brown complexion . . . inclin'd to a religious Melancholy, or pious sadness; of a rare memory, and most exemplary life' (11.4–5). He also acknowledged the house and estate of Wotton, in Surrey, 22 miles from London, which had become the family home in 1579, and which Evelyn's father, Richard, inherited in 1595 (illus. 5).

Wotton would be at the centre of Evelyn's life, if not physically, at least as the lodestone or compass that guided his life, until, by accident, he actually inherited it in 1699, when his brother died without any heirs. It was not the still point of the turning world, for the world was changing rapidly in many ways, and Evelyn would both encourage and lament the results. But Wotton would be – in the words of John Donne – the fixed foot of the compass that directs its other, roving path:

And though it in the centre sit,
Yet when the other far doth roam,
It leans, and hearkens after it,
And grows erect, as that comes home.

In later life, when responding to Aubrey's *Natural History of Surrey*, Evelyn noted that 'Surrey is the land of my birth, and my delight; but my education has been so little in it by reason of accident' that he was ashamed to be so ignorant of it. But he hailed Wotton for being 'environed as it is with wood (from whence it takes its denomination)'. Surrey was a territory 'capable of furnishing all the æmoneities of a villa and garden, after the Italian manner', replete with prospects, green hollies and 'sugar-loaf mountains which with the boscage upon them, and little torrents between, make such a solitude as I have never seen any place more horridly agreeable and romantick' (*MW*, pp. 687–91). He had been allowed by his

5 John Aubrey's sketch of Wotton House and its grounds.

elder brother George to augment the grounds with a study, fishpond and 'some other solitudes and retirements' (*Diary*, II.81; see illus. 8). Its landscape, above all its woodlands and gardens, would be the inspiration for and solace in his life, inclining him to establish useful and thoughtful gardens in the light of both his Continental travels and a concern for the livelihood and needs of producing English timber. Wotton was for him, in his measured but deliberate patriotism, what in his *Numismata* he apotheosized as 'our British Elysium' (p. 323): 'Few Nations that I know of under Heaven (on so short a time) consisting of so many Ingredients . . .'.

The family had been farmers since the late fifteenth century, though a great-grandfather had been attached to the court of the young Edward VI. During Elizabeth's and James I's reigns it had prospered under Evelyn's grandfather, George, as purveyors of gunpowder; thus Evelyn, writes John Bowle (p. 6), was the 'grandson of a tycoon of the armaments industry'. In 1673 Evelyn wrote to Aubrey that he recalled how 'many powder mills' had been erected by his ancestors along the stream and ponds around Wotton. Despite the collapse of the gunpowder industry, the family yet possessed land, and John's father, Richard, lived his life in the country and 'in good husbandry'. He was well-off, an esteemed local official, the supporter of a grammar school and almshouses at nearby Guildford, a Justice of the Peace, and served for a while as High Sherriff of the county. He declined, as his son would do later, any further honours or a knighthood. Wotton, then, could be held up as a model of the gentry estate, which – beyond the great aristocratic houses – was an exemplary fulcrum of the English nation.

Evelyn's education, such as it was, had a shaky start in the 'church porch at Wotton', and thereafter took place in his grandfather's home and in the household of his grand-mother's second husband near Lewes in Sussex, where in the Free School he acquired Latin and some French, and an inclin-ation for drawing, of which his father disapproved. He refused to go to Eton, though his father wished it, on account of its harsh disciplinary regime (though he later chose to send his grandson there), and in this he was supported by his grand-parents. He returned occasionally to Wotton: in September 1635 he was summoned home when his mother was ill. Her death at the end of 1635, distressed by the death in childbirth of a daughter, Elizabeth, would be a sad domestic motif in Evelyn's own lifetime.[2]

In May 1637 Evelyn went up to Oxford as a fellow com-moner at Balliol, where he matriculated on 19 May; his older brother was already at Trinity (where Aubrey would later matriculate in 1642), and his younger brother, Richard, would join him at Balliol in 1639. A few annotations that Evelyn recorded in *A New Almanack and Prognostication for the year of our Lord God 1636 and 1637*, now held in Balliol College Library,[3] do little to account for his life there, apart from recording prog-nostications on weather and some pretentious notes on human anatomy and the 'working of the heavenly spheres'; it is against these commonplaces and quaint 'verbosities' (Bacon's word) that Evelyn and members of the Royal Society would work. He made friends with a fellow undergraduate, James Thicknesse (who became a fellow of Balliol in 1641), one 'learned and [of] friendly Conversation', and with whom he would travel through Europe in the years after 1643.

He began early with an interest in new places, new ideas, new stimuli, by joining his brother in a trip to Portsmouth and the Isle of Wight, and then in May 1639 taking a 'short journey of pleasure' to Bath, Bristol, Cirencester and Malmesbury, after which he spent the summer at Wotton. After returning to Balliol at the end of the year (nobody then exactly 'kept terms' at Oxford), he left permanently in February 1640 without a degree – getting one was both expensive and unnecessary. He went first to Wotton where his father was ill and then, with George, to take up lodgings in the Middle Temple. Here he would, at his father's wish, submit himself to what he himself called 'th'impolish'd study of law'. Both brothers had been admitted earlier to the Bar (in 1636) by their father.

England was already much disturbed by the long simmering conflicts between Charles I and Parliament. Evelyn witnessed the Short or 'Addled' session of Parliament of 1614 and then the Long Parliament that the king was forced to call in November 1640, which Evelyn (in retrospect) termed 'that . . . ungrateful and fatal Parliament; the beginnings of our sorrows, for 20 years after and the ruin of the most happy Monarch'. Both city and Court presented themselves as 'often in Disorder', with Lambeth Palace 'furiously assaulted by a rude rabble from Southwark, set on doubtless and formented by the *Puritans* (as we then call'd those we now name *Presbyterians*' (*Diary*, 1.18).

If the state was in disarray, Evelyn's family also suffered, with his father's illness throughout the summer of 1640 ending with his death on Christmas Eve. Evelyn stayed at Wotton through the summer of 1641, though visited London for the trial and execution of the Earl of Strafford: 'under the cognizance of no human-Law, a new one was made, not to be a precedent, but his destruction, to such exorbitancy were things arrived' (*Diary*, II.28). With his elder brother now installed at Wotton and the state of the nation much disturbed, the nineteen-year-old John choose to flee 'this ill face of things at home' and take himself to the Low Countries. After a brief return to England later that year, he resumed his European adventures in 1643 and was away for the best part of six years. Exile would prove an apt education if the country could ever recover its stability.

'The fruit of travel': Continental Europe, 1641 and 1643–7

HILE EVELYN'S TIME in Oxford was nothing that he chose to remark upon ('of very small benefit to me'), it would be his education in Europe that served him better. 'Travel in the younger sort', wrote Bacon in his *Essays*, 'is a part of education; in the elder, a part of experience.' And Evelyn, as a younger brother and as yet unfocused in both education and experience, clearly found the list of foreign customs 'to be seen and observed' (in Bacon's phrase) an apt agenda when he left England in 1641 for a four-month visit to the United Provinces and to the Spanish (and Catholic) Netherlands – 'these two jealous States'. Even though eleven years later he admonished French culture in *The State of France*, it was still the fruitfulness of travel that he emphasized in its Preface: 'from a certain vain emulation which I had, to see the best of education, which everybody so decrying at home, made me conceive was a commodity only to be brought *from a far country*' (my italics). Travel, or exile in troubled times, was indeed a useful commodity, for persons who were 'never out of sight of their own chimneys' smoke' would much diminish their contributions to the world they lived in. As he noticed once abroad at Flushing (Vlissingen), things were 'infinitely changed'

after being absent from England. Invoking one of Evelyn's, as well as one of the seventeenth century's, frequent metaphors, God had furnished and adorned '(as I may say) . . . this terrestrial cabinet' with things to be seen that would be to 'the profit, and emolument of his own country at his return'.[1]

The motto that Evelyn devised for himself – to explore everything and retain the best: *Omnia explorate, meliora retinete* (*LB*, 1.3) – was eagerly observed in 1641. Later, in *The State of France* (*MW*, p.45) he would take note of 'things mechanically curious and useful, as altogether in the mysteries of government and polity, which indeed are more appositely termed philosophical'; thus he saw virtue in registering the equal significance of both practical ('mechanical') and philosophical matters. From courts and ambassadors to monuments, both ecclesiastical and secular, from antiquities and ruins to gardens and fortifications, from cabinets and rarities to 'whatsoever is memorable in the places where you go' – all must be recorded, and these memoranda (again Bacon) put 'into a little Room', a sort of mental cabinet of curiosities.

Curiosity was not, in the seventeenth century, what killed the cat, but whatever promoted intellectual knowledge. Evelyn would eventually own two actual cabinets, one made for him in Florence, one in Paris (illus. 6).[2] No single cabinet, inevitably, could contain the accumulated experience of Continental tours, nor even the landscape paintings and 'drolleries' that he purchased at Rotterdam, nor the books, engravings, maps and anatomical notations that he later shipped from Padua on his way home and that eventually arrived in London in 1649. These acquisitions, and what promoted them in his journey, allow us to understand what directed his thinking in

the six years abroad. His Diary, composed in retrospect, may
have invented memories and certainly reinforced his original
tourism with subsequent reading from guide-books (some references were misplaced when he wrote up his journal). But the
Diary was still a compendium of keen observations first stored
and then rescued for their importance in England. It was these
notations and observations that were his true 'cabinet'.

In 1641 Evelyn travelled with a cousin, John Caryll, in the
company of Thomas Howard, Earl of Arundel, a Surrey neigh-
bour from Albury, who was accompanying the Queen Mother,
Marie de' Medici; Evelyn would meet her again in Dort en
route to Cologne ('toss'd to and fro by the various fortunes of
her life'), together with members of the French royalty. From
Flushing, Evelyn and Caryll travelled widely throughout the
Low Countries, mainly by boat on the canals, returning sundry
times to the same town and everywhere curious about sights,

6 John Evelyn's cabinet, commissioned by him.

monuments, rarities, architecture, gardens, urban enhance-
ment and fortifications (for the wars were a constant presence,
as the Dutch were still battling Spain). Evelyn even joined a
company briefly at Gennep, and 'trail'd a pike'. But after being
'pretty well satisfied with the confusion of Armies and sieges',
and perhaps after a heavy bout of drinking in the garrison, he
thought to call it quits on a military life.

Curious about everything he saw, even indiscriminately as
when pillaging the guide-books he would read later, some
things nonetheless stuck in his mind, whether at the time or
subsequently. One was a curiosity for, indeed a tolerance of
and interest in, rival faiths. He eagerly explored the practices
and places of worship, visiting a synagogue in Amsterdam and
a variety of Protestant sects, kissing the hand of the deposed
and widowed Protestant 'Winter Queen' of Bohemia (the
elder sister of Charles I), meeting with the English who had
fled from Parliamentary censures as well as English nuns in
Brussels, visiting convents and a friary, meeting Carmelites,
and Jesuits, whose school and educational building he much
admired in Antwerp; all without wavering in his own English
Protestant faith (in Bacon's *New Atlantis* Christianity was
insisted upon, even while its inhabitants accepted the existence of other religions). So, too, was his openness to meeting
interesting foreigners ('two Polish noblemen, who were travelling out of Germany, and had been in Italy, very accomplished
persons').

He compared what he saw constantly with things back
home in England, not always to the latter's advantage; he
admired the state houses in European cities, 'all magnificently
built', and any modern, classicizing buildings. He noticed

lepers on the riverbanks as his boat went by, saw his first ele-
phant in Rotterdam, visited a hospice for lame and decrepit
soldiers in Amsterdam, admired the 'wenches [in a seminary
or charterhouse] so well brought up to house-wifery' that
suitors sought them in marriage, and a kind of Dutch bride-
well where 'lewd women are kept in discipline and labour;
but in truth all is so sweet and neat'. In Brussels he admired
paintings of the recently deceased Rubens, peered through a
keyhole to observe the latticework of book presses in a closed
library there, and marvelled again at gardens, with statues
and artificial music from manifold waterworks.

    Given Evelyn's later regard for garden-making and garden-
writing, his visits to these sites were noted, at least retrospectively, and sometimes glossed briefly – 'a fair garden
and park, curiously planted' in The Hague, or a lime tree in
the Convent of St Clares at 's-Hertogenbosch ('the like whereof for evenness & height I had not observed'). And while
always eager to inspect military installations – he found those
at 's-Hertogenbosch the 'most matchless piece of fortification in the world' (to the extent that, as a 'stranger', he was
allowed to inspect them) – nothing pleased him more than
the 'delicious shades and walks of stately trees' throughout
the city of Antwerp. Earlier, he had visited the botanical
garden at Leiden, having matriculated at the University (a
device for avoiding taxes and excise), where he acquired a
catalogue of its exotic plants. He also marvelled at the theatre
of the Anatomy School and the University's cabinet or
Repository of natural curiosities, the many contents of which
he enumerates (illus. 7). He visited the Elsevier printing house
in Leiden, bought books from Plantin's press in Antwerp and

visited the premises of the great mapmakers Blaeu and Hondius, in Amsterdam.

In October at Ghent he met up again with Arundel, now returned from taking the ailing Queen Mother to Cologne, and together they finished their journey through the Spanish Netherlands and took ship to Dover. Once in London, Evelyn took leave of his lordship at Arundel Stairs, whence he returned first to the Middle Temple and then to Wotton, where he resolved to 'possess myself in some quiet if it might be, in a time of great jealousy'.

His return to England was brief, and within two years he was once again on the Continent. The months in England were restless and perturbed, the kingdom troubled, and the king at war ideologically, and soon militarily, with Parliament, whose members determined to address their longstanding

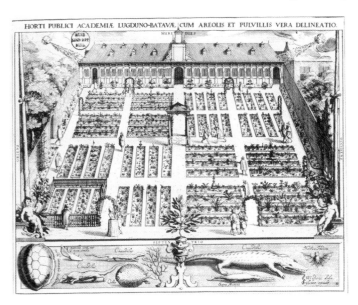

7 J. W. Swanenburgh's engraving (after J. C. Woudanus), 1610, of a view of the Botanical Garden and Ambulacrum, Leiden.

grievances and to curtail the king's authority over those who advised him. Evelyn was in 'perpetual motion' between London and Wotton, visiting family members on several occasions in Lewes, in Godstone and Long Ditton in Surrey and Hertingfordbury in Hertfordshire; Evelyn's paternal grandfather, George, had spawned a large family of 24 children from two marriages, so there were many contacts to maintain. Early on, he witnessed the king's state entry into London on his return from Scotland, 'to great acclamations and joy of the giddy people', but declined some of his duties as one of the organizers of Christmas festivities at the royalist Middle Temple (setting up only a series of bronze busts of the Caesars) and thence retreated to Wotton. He noted his regular taking of the blessed sacrament, mainly at Wotton but also at the Middle Temple.

At Wotton, with his brother's permission, he built a 'little study over a cascade', which he sketched (illus. 8), and created a pond and island, along with 'some solitudes & retirements', a needed respite in the gathering storm. He and his brothers purchased saddle horses in Northampton, when the First Civil War made such provisions urgent, and then he followed some of the king's battles – arriving at Portsmouth when it fell to the besieging Parliamentary forces in September, but still going to take his leave of the vanquished governor on his departure to France. In 1642 Queen Henrietta Maria was escorted to safety in the United Provinces in search of funds for the king's party, accompanied again by Arundel, who then settled in Padua to avoid the conflict at home; Evelyn would meet up with him there later. In November 1642 Evelyn decided to aid the king at the battle of Brentford, but arrived

too late 'with my horse and Armes', during the withdrawal of the victorious royalists; the next year he sent only his horse 'and furniture' with a friend to support the king, who had rashly retreated to royalist Oxford rather than moving upon London.

Evelyn still managed some 'journeys of pleasure' to relatives and friends, with other visits to cultivate his 'curiosity', fuelled doubtless by his recent experiences abroad and perhaps concerned at how much damage the Parliamentary forces would wreak in the land – he had witnessed the destruction of the 'stately Cross in Cheapside' by a 'furious and zealot mob' – and he returned thence to Wotton 'with no little regret for the confusion that threatened us'. He had visited Albury soon after his return from the Low Countries and learned there from Arundel of the Irish massacre of thousands of Protestants, which had fuelled Puritans' anti-Catholicism. He went with his brothers to view the monument to Sir Francis

8 Detail from a sketch of Evelyn's study and the cascade at Wotton.

Bacon at St Albans, admired Winchester Cathedral, twice visited the gardens and vineyard at Elizabeth I's Hatfield and another royal palace at Theobalds Park (largely demolished in 1651 by the Parliamentarians), and got to visit the new house at Balls Park, which must have reminded him of the Dutch classicist buildings he had seen abroad. He also viewed Parliament's new fortifications now surrounding London (incognito – not declaring his 'having been in his Majesties Army').

By late summer of 1643 he realized that what he had witnessed in his constant toing and froing around southern England made it 'impossible to evade the doing of very unhandsome things'. He refused to sign the Solemn League and Covenant, thereby implying his opposition to Presbyterianism. Parliament was granted power to gather funds, to be repaid with interest, from properties assessed within twenty miles of London; Wotton was spared at that point, yet eventually would seem threatened and was where troops would later be billeted. So Evelyn obtained the signature of the king, still at Oxford, to license his departure from England. Though his brother George urged him to remain and 'think on your own country', he decided to leave once again, realizing perhaps that his own country could benefit in the long run from time he spent abroad. In October 1643 his brothers accompanied him as far as Tower Wharf, where he took sail downriver to Gravesend and thence by post arrived at Dover. He was accompanied now by the 'very dear friend' from Balliol, James Thicknesse.

The Diary of these travels (reworked in 1660) actually addresses the mid-1640s from the vantage point of the

Restoration. By then a king was once again on the throne, Evelyn had returned a married man, with a house (courtesy of his father-in-law) that he was able to lease and where he would make a garden, and he had acquired new and learned friends and was above all eager to find ways of using what he had learned on his Continental travels. So we may read between the lines of his Diary to find some of the interests that began to absorb him when he was back finally in England.

Besides his increasingly strong garden interest, on which more later (since he seemed largely to have relied upon his own observations when writing up that part of the Diary), he clearly took cognizance (as who could not at that time) of the political wars in Europe, in particular the role that religion played in them, the various political identities and structures of different foreign states, along with an assessment of their value to a visiting Englishmen, and – above all – his search for new scientific ideas, not simply in matters of what today we would term the physical sciences, but in matters of agriculture, urban planning, arboriculture, chemistry and local history, as revealed by cultural materials and informed by questioning local observers (shepherds, for example, reporting on an attack by wolves near Rouen) and by readings in foreign texts. He purchased books, pictures and engravings and was acquiring a decent command of French and, later, Italian. In Rome, though his frugal family were concerned, he bought books on mathematics, music and languages and amassed 'no inconsiderable collection too of pictures, medals, and other trifles' (*LB*, I.330).

France, in particular Paris, gave him the opportunity to explore all 'mechanically curious and useful' interests as well as those that would be vital in less practical ways (*MW*, p. 45). Doubtless much drawn, given the situation in England, to considering the history and fortunes of the French monarchy, he observed the memorial sculptures of their monarchs at St Denis, noted the mourning for the death of Louis XIII and the regency of the young Louis XIV, and the chequered history of the Protestant faith after Henri IV had converted to Catholicism in 1593. One of his first duties was to pay a formal visit to Charles I's resident ambassador in Paris, Sir Richard Browne, a meeting that would prove particularly momentous, as Browne would eventually become his father-in-law.[3] He visited hospitals. He enjoyed listening to Jesuit disputations at the Sorbonne, and was greatly pleased with the singing at a French Protestant service, though dismayed by the lack of pews to sit on, unlike in England. Urban developments he found particularly interesting – flagstones rather than the cobbles of London, new stone bridges and 'streets, suburbs and common buildings', and the elegance of public buildings both Gothic and Baroque. Likewise, later, at the Vatican Library he found its decoration with 'Emblems, Figures, Diagrams and the like learned inventions found out by the wit & industry of famous men' was more impressive than the 'Antiques & Grotescs' at the Bodleian Library in Oxford. In Paris, he visited Pierre Morin's garden ('tulips, anemonies, ranunculus's, crocuses &c being of the most exquisite') and its adjoining cabinet with collections of shells, flowers and drawers of carefully preserved butterflies ('the like I had never seen'); this would be a garden that he would later copy back home at Sayes Court. At the Palais-Royal he also observed skills of riding, fencing, dancing, music-making '& some skill in fortification & the mathematics', and the garden in its midst. He travelled westward to Dieppe with Sir John Cotton from Cambridgeshire, and in Le Havre, where he was allowed to visit the fortifications, he observed the inscription on one cannon – *ultimata ratio regum* (the final argument of kings). Travelling southwards, he paid his respects to Queen Henrietta Maria, who had escaped from Exeter, and after some adventures of his own he arrived at Tours; here he spent almost five months to improve his knowledge of the French language.

The amount of attention given to gardens in his Diary is considerable, and much of it (as its modern editor notes frequently) original and not dependent on sources he may have consulted after his return. The list of garden visits included the botanical Jardin du Roi (illus. 9), which he visited early on during his time in Paris, noting its 'enclosure wall'd in,

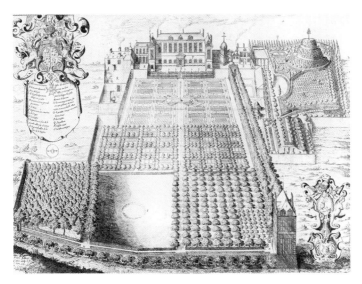

9 The Jardin du Roi 'pour la culture des Plantes', Paris, drawn and engraved by Frédéric Scalberge, 1636.

consisting of all sorts of varieties of grounds, for the planting & culture of medical simples. It is certainly for all advantages very well chosen, having within both hills, meadows, grown wood & upland, both artificial and natural' (*Diary*, II.102). He recognized the necessity in a garden of providing a variety of microclimates and topographical opportunities, similar to what was noted in Bacon's *New Atlantis* – 'variety of ground and soil, proper for diverse trees, and herbs'. In 'Elysium Britannicum' when he sketched plans for a new botanical garden he presumably copied the similar layout at Paris, notably the mount with its variety of microclimates (illus. 10). In the same manuscript he also drew a plan for an 'artificial echo' that he had observed in the Tuileries, laid out in the Italian mode by Catherine de' Medici (illus. 11). If this seems an odd observation, and even odder that he would wish to construct one in an ideal garden, it confirms

10 Sketch of a botanical garden, from Evelyn's manuscript compilation 'Elysium Britannicum'.

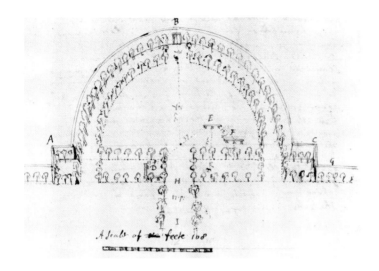

his interest in physical properties; for he also noted a similar acoustical effect on a bridge over the River Marne, 'where the renowned echo returns the voice 9 or 10 times being provoked by a good singer'.[4]

Other excursions took him to Saint-Germain-en-Laye, where he enjoyed the 'incomparable prospect' beyond the river; to Saint-Cloud, 'so rarely watered, & furnished with fountains, statues, & groves, as I had never seen anything exceeding it', to which he then adds an original and fairly detailed description; to the former garden of Cardinal Richelieu at Rueil, where the garden was far grander than the house and struck him most with its grove of evergreens; and to the Bois de Vincennes, also with its 'grove of goodly pine trees'. At the Palais du Luxembourg he admired the library, its shelves lined with green velvet, its cabinet, paintings, and the good-quality air in the gardens, noting in particular the well-trimmed box in the parterre, the hornbeam hedge, the

11 A sketch of an artificial echo, from Evelyn's 'Elysium Britannicum'.

array of vases and statues, a star-shaped wood with a fountain at the centre and, above all, the garden's visitation by
'infinite numbers of persons of quality, & citizens, &
strangers'. At Fontainebleau, where the palace 'is nothing
so stately & uniform as Hampton Court', he contrasted the
accomplished design of its landscape of pools, canals and
fountains with the 'white & horrid rocks at some distance
in the Forest [that] yield one of the most august & stupendous prospects imaginable'. He may have sketched some of
his sights there,[5] for he was notably alert to how garden
design was both dependent on reformulating the natural
world and yet how it was best appreciated by being juxta-
posed to those original materials. This dialogue seems to have
pleased him particularly in city gardens, even though such a
contrast had actually to be invented: in the rue de Seine he
admired 'an excellently painted perspective, strangely enlarged
to appearance' that intimated by its depiction a larger and
less designed prospect beyond that contrasted with the 'little
garden' (illus. 12). Such perspectives could also represent
distant, if famous, places, and at Rueil he was struck by the
utterly realistic painting of the Arch of Constantine in Rome:

> [Even] a man well skilled in painting may mistake it
> for stone, & sculpture: and indeed it is so rarely per-
> formed that it is almost impossible to believe it
> painting, but to be work of solid stone. The sky and
> the hills which seem to be between the Arches, are so
> natural that swallows and other birds, thinking to fly
> through, have dashed themselves to pieces . . . (*Diary*,
> II.109)

Thoughts of Rome must have spurred Evelyn and Thicknesse onwards and down into southern France. They had reached Marseilles in October, and then from Cannes took a boat to Genoa.

Italy would make an even greater impact on Evelyn, as it carried him into the heart of the latest works of architecture, painting, sculpture and garden-making as well as into a mosaic of authorities and governments: there were republics (Venice, Genoa), independent states like Lucca, the Duchy of Tuscany, the Spanish Kingdom of Naples and Sicily and the Spanish rulers of Milan, and the papal states of Rome (though he had already seen one of them at Avignon); Bologna, through which he returned in 1645, was also under papal control. On his return, after a troublesome passage through the Alps, he passed through the Duchy of Savoy and into the federal cantons of Switzerland. Through these different regimes and cultures he moved with an intelligent

12 A painted perspective in a French garden.

and taciturn observation, and along the way acquired a new friend and travel companion, Thomas Henshaw (later to be a friend and colleague in the Royal Society) (illus. 13).

Italy was, he wrote in a rather dreadful poem upon leaving Rome to travel north, 'the World's sole Cabinet' (*Diary*, II.402–5). Its verses surveyed the sights he had seen, but he began – via an allusion to Virgil – by noting that thoughts when 'kept house at home . . . knew no more / Than what might be survey'd from my own door'. What was at home 'circumscribed in self-Content' was in Italy a volume opened to architecture, gardens, paintings, sculptures, glorious ruins and 'speaking stones' that enlarged his understanding of the world. He was indeed a busy tourist, so much so that three times his Diary notes 'being pretty weary of my continual walkings' around Rome. There he viewed religious festivals,

13 Evelyn's etched print from a suite of *Views between Rome and Naples* dedicated to *Thomas Henshaw* of 1649.

processions, and midnight services on Christmas Eve, only
once noting outright annoyance, at a Good Friday flagellation
in St Peter's ('very horrible, & indeed heathenish pomp'). He
was drawn while in Rome (he wrote later to Thomas Keightly)
by his wish to explore the 'verity of things', confessing to an
'admiration of the Discipline of the Roman Church', but less
so of its 'Doctrine'.[6] And visiting many churches he was struck
by their 'busy devotion, great silence, and *unimaginable
Superstition*' (my italics).

On his first day in Rome he made a point of getting
acquainted with various English Jesuits, including the poet
Lucius Cary (who, he noted, 'afterwards came over to our
church'); he watched a Jewish rite of circumcision, visited
hospitals including that of S. Spirito, which he much admired,
and visited an innumerable number of cabinets and collections, like the antiquities of Cassiano dal Pozzo. He was
shown the dispensary and gardens of the German Father
Athanasius Kircher, whose experiments in optics, reflection
and 'perpetual motions' were admired by both Evelyn and
Henshaw.

Throughout, he took in and sometimes sketched what he
saw; his wide-ranging curiosity as well as his scepticism would
match what would characterize Sir Thomas Browne's
Pseudodoxia Epidemica, or Vulgar Errors, first published in 1646
(with later editions in 1650, 1659 and 1672):[7] Browne would
later become a valued correspondent. Thus Evelyn climbed
and drew the chasm of Vesuvius (illus. 14), studied the
Leaning Tower of Pisa, visited the ducal zoo in Florence,
heard a eunuch sing in a church choir and enjoyed carnivals
in both Rome and Venice, but doubted the veracity of two

thorns from Christ's crown of thorns, St Thomas's 'doubting finger', and a seven-foot unicorn's horn or the 'only talon or claw of a Griffon that I ever saw'. A deformed cat (two tails and six ears) seen in Orléans he was more disposed to accept, and his regard for the rarest of jewels and other precious stones and shells was enthusiastic.

Southwards from Rome, he encountered a succession of resonant places – Virgil's birthplace, Cicero's tomb, rich and fertile landscapes, the supposed arm of the historian Livy in a Neapolitan church, the 'exotic rarities' of Ferrante Imperato, and (after the ascent of Vesuvius) a visit to the Phlegraean Fields and the bay of Baiae. His later account of this area is more full than he could have seen on that one visit, so must have been later reinforced with other readings.[8] But in retrospect it provided an intriguing mix of historical and mythical landscapes, Roman ruins and biblical associations, 'delicious' fruits and vines, sulphurous fumes, from all of

14 Etching after a drawing of Vesuvius by John Evelyn, signed with the monogram 'J E f[ecit]', from the 1649 suite of etchings.

which he derived a cluster of memories, at once sceptical yet fascinated and duly empirical. Some, on the effects of sulphur upon humans and dogs, were explored in an experiment with two dogs, which expired in a grotto but revived (or just one of them) when dunked in an adjacent lake; other experiences, like his view of Virgil's supposed tomb, he would utilize when redesigning the terraces for Arundel's grandson at Albury in 1667 (see illus. 33–5).

After Naples, they had four more months in and around Rome, with further visits to see antiquities and hospitals, to purchase books and engravings, and further excursions to more gardens, some in unexpected places (Circus Maximus, the Mausoleum of Augustus), others at Villas Giustiniani, Farnesina, Borghesi, Ludovisi and, beyond the city, at Frascati and Tivoli. But then, a shortage of funds and a desire to return homewards meant Evelyn moved swiftly north, now accompanied by the poet Edmund Waller. In Venice he heard Monteverdi's *Coronation of Poppea* and witnessed the Doge's 'marriage' to the sea with a golden ring. He travelled several times to Padua, in which medical school he obtained a certificate of matriculation, and studied medicine, visited hospitals and purchased charts of the veins and nerves ('the first of that kind [that] had been ever seen in our country'). In Padua he visited the sick Arundel, who presented him upon leaving with a list of things to see (some of which, like Palladio's Villa Rotunda, his hurried northwards progress forced him to miss). In February 1646 he finally left Venice, and after the passage of the Alps arrived in the federal cantons of Switzerland ('half be Roman Catholics, the rest reformed, yet all mutually agree'). He fell extremely ill with smallpox in

Brig during May and June, but recovering, this granted him immunity against the subsequent incursion of the disease into the life of Sayes Court. By July, after many 'disasters and tedious peregrinations', he was in Paris, thankful to have 'gotten so near home'.

But *home*, which he had critiqued in the verses composed at Rome, was surely England, not even perhaps Wotton, which was then the only 'home' he knew. One who simply surveyed everything from the comfort of his own door was but 'circumscribed in self-content'. After his travels, he would not be so circumscribed, but what he could do back in England was uncertain, both in the conditions there and in the application of his new skills and knowledge.

FOUR

Marriage, and the Interregnum

NYONE WHO HAS been away, especially for a long time, must adjust to dealing with issues left unresolved, catch up on friends and obligations, and carefully review new experiences and ideas in the light of conditions at home. Evelyn, 'so near home' (albeit in France), confronted the same needs. During the next thirteen years before the Restoration, to which he looked forward though at times with little confidence, he attended to what was in effect a virtual résumé of both his European tour and its adaptation to the conditions of his own country and times. He addressed matters to do with family, cultivated and expanded the circle of his friends and drew into it a world of other intellectuals. And he married.

In particular, he needed to find a place where he could settle, raise a family and cultivate his own ground, where he could implement some of what he had learned from French and Italian gardens. Wotton was of course out of the question as a home, so he sought a location where, in the true spirit of a 'cabinet'-maker (that is, one who delights in collecting items for his cabinet), he could establish his own library and set out his collections of engravings, paintings, medals, even plants. He translated books that, seemingly of little import today, concerned matters that clearly affected him: books on politics, religion, science, philosophy, libraries, ancient and modern architecture, the characters of different countries, and some works on horticulture and arboriculture. At this time he also began to conceive of a major work on British gardening, the 'Elysium Britannicum', an endeavour that he would continue to augment for almost the rest of his life, but which remained unfinished.[1]

If his Diary of these years is often sparse, it may be attributed to his giving it less time during busy searches for where and how he wanted to be and to his increasing correspondence. After years of wandering he thought to settle down, but with unsettled times and his own sense of purpose constantly under review, that was not altogether easy, and his movements, though briefly noted, precluded much reflection in the Diary itself. If the Diary, which was revised or at least reviewed later, is silent, his often more private letters provide some insight into his current opinions, as do his publications that sought to domesticate new and non-English ideas.

In 1647 when he had returned to Paris, Evelyn could relax ('the only time in my whole life I spent most idly') and enjoy a round of visits and contacts, both new and established; he found the French capital lively and full of royalist and religious refugees. He read French books on liberty and on the making of libraries and, notably, on gardening, and friends urged him to address these useful topics for an English readership.

But he also was in the process of falling in love with Mary, the young daughter of the royalist ambassador, Sir Richard Browne, whom he had first met at the start of his European tour. They were married, with Church of England rites, on 27

June 1647, by a chaplain to the Prince of Wales (later Charles
II) in a chapel of the ambassador's residence. After some
celebrations and more visits in and around Paris, Evelyn
returned to England in October to reconnoitre the future.

Soon after his return he kissed the hand of Charles I at
Hampton Court Palace, where, at the end of the First Civil
War, the king was being held by 'those execrable villains who
not long after murdered him'; the king's chaplain there was
Jeremy Taylor. At Wotton he 'refresh'd' himself with family
and friends. While abroad, he had learned of the death of
George's wife and his remarriage two years later in 1647, so
there was much on which to catch up, not least the state of
affairs at Wotton. George was now an MP and continued as
a sitting member for Reigate until Pride's Purge (December
1648) and the Rump Parliament, carefully playing both sides
as both a passive royalist and commissioner for sequestra-
tions. John also went to see his younger brother, Richard, who
would also be married within a year, and his sister, who had
married a barrister.

But he wanted a house, if not a home, of his own. In this
political climate, land could be purchased reasonably, so
Evelyn bought, sold or resold properties, but nonetheless for
security he chose to ship some pictures and other portable
objects to France. He visited the estate of Sayes Court in
Deptford, occupied by an uncle of Lady Browne and looked
after by a steward, William Peters. There his father-in-law
allowed him to stay during this visit, and he re-ordered and
catalogued Browne's books.[2] In the end it would be Sayes
Court – though by no means an ideal home and one for
which he continued to have issues with the lease – that Evelyn

settled on as his choice. In 1652 he wrote to his wife (*LB*, 1.128) that he was purchasing some land around it 'not for any great inclination I have to the place', but because it would allow him to develop its 'other conveniences, and interest annexed to it' (that is, the chance to make a garden). Eventually purchasing the lease and title to it allowed him later to send much-needed money to Sir Richard, who was short of funds and sometimes besieged in Paris during the disturbances of the Fronde. But otherwise his time in and around London was a whirl of visits, making some new friends, such as the botanist and bibliophile Jasper Needham and persons met briefly in Italy, like the physician George Joyliffe. The political and religious scene he viewed with much distrust, observing the many factions at work in the land and listening carefully to rumours, all the time reporting under a pseudonym ('Aplanos', that is, steadfast) to Sir Richard in France, writing to 'safe' addresses and telling him that he was 'altogether confused and sad for the misery that is upon us' (*Correspondence*, pp. 4 and 35).

Church services were proscribed or were conducted in secret. The Levellers were spreading like 'a distemper', and in May 1649 the 'Parliament Act' abolished the monarchy, and the king's statues were 'thrown down at St Paul's portico and Exchange'. Later Evelyn inspected pictures seized from the royal collections by the rebels who sought to dissipate 'a world of rare paintings of the King's and his Loyal Subjects'. There were times when he wondered whether he should leave England altogether, but the pull of family, the link to Wotton, and his concern to write about matters that he thought important to his country made him loath to opt for a permanent break. Even as early as 1651 he wrote to his sister that 'I might have one day hoped to have been considerable in my country,' but now would settle for 'A friend, a book, and a garden [that] shall for the future perfectly circumscribe my utmost designs'.[3] This phrase about his future ambitions is one used on several other occasions; it suggests that being 'considerable' or useful in England had been, or might have to be, exchanged for that triad of very local pleasures.

He found time to sit for his portrait (a melancholy figure holding a skull) by Robert Walker (illus. 15), which was to be sent to his wife along with the beautiful little book of *Instructions Oeconomiques*, transcribed by his secretary and decorated with a frontispiece of a seated woman with a cornucopia, to which were added poems and recipes, and allusions to ancient scenery, like Seneca's fishponds and the Garden of Eden – hope for their future, surely. He also got involved in a project to develop and patent a perpetual motion engine, a mechanical scheme that lured many to become involved.[4] But he wished to return to France, so he obtained, with difficulty, a permit to leave from the regicide John Bradshaw, the President of the Council of State, and, after being 'merry' with his brothers at Guildford, left for France in July 1649.[5] He was accompanied by his amanuensis, Richard Hoare.

Six months earlier, on 30 January, King Charles had been beheaded in Whitehall, outside Inigo Jones's Banqueting Hall. While his brother George witnessed the execution, Evelyn stayed away and kept 'his *Martyrdom* a fast'. A week before, Evelyn had risked being 'severely threatened' for publishing his translation of François de La Mothe Le Vayer's 1643 pamphlet *On Liberty and Servitude*, 'translated out of the

15 Robert Walker, portrait of *John Evelyn*, sent to his wife. Besides the skull, there are some stoical words of Seneca on a paper on the table, and a Greek inscription proclaiming that 'Repentance is the beginning of wisdom.'

French into the English tongue'. He later noted on his own copy that 'I was like to be called in question by the rebels for this book being published a few days before his Majesty's decollation' (that is, beheading).[6] He had found the tract in Paris, ostensibly a defence of the young Louis XIV, but its general thrust impinged much on the conflicts in England. His translation was dedicated to his brother George 'of Wotton in the county of Surrey' and signed only 'Phileleutheros' (that is, friend of freedom), though a dedicatory poem mentioned the translator by name. Evelyn told his brother that this publication was 'the first time of my approach upon the theatre'.[7] In 'To Him that Reads' he wrote that in these 'licentious times', with 'impious offerings to the people', Liberty was not an illusion, was no 'Platonic *chimera* of a state, nowhere existent save in Utopia', and that the reader must reject 'verily [that] there is no such thing in *rerum natura* as absolute perfection'. Yet liberty *can* be realized, and he argued that for the last five thousand years there had been no 'more equal and excellent form of government than that under which we have lived during the reign of our Gracious Sovereign'. No wonder the rebels might have censured him; but they were probably too preoccupied to notice a writer, as yet, unknown.

Back in Paris he was warmly greeted by friends, took communion with Mary – from whom he had been absent nearly two years – and went to kiss the hand of Charles II (as he now was) at Saint-Germain, before the king left to continue battles in Scotland. Evelyn travelled to meet the king in a coach with the Earl of Rochester and one of the king's mistresses. He also paid his respects to the young Louis XIV. He needed to repudiate the rumour that he had been knighted ('a dignity I often declined'). He visited more gardens and heard a good lecture at the royal physic garden. He met royalists like Abraham Cowley and John Denham, both attached to the now widowed Queen Henrietta Maria in Paris, and a cousin of Mary's, Samuel Tuke, with whom he sought out gardens in the Île de France; Edmund Waller often came from Rouen to meet and talk with him in Paris.

He was also working on his essay on *The State of France*, spurred by 'conversations' with a friend.[8] This contained remarks upon the virtues of travel and gave a rather dry account of French society and its monarchy, court, army and constitution, yet found that France does 'rather totter than stand' and was much subject to favouritism, with a slavish populace uninterested in trade or mechanical arts, and its children, 'angels in the cradle' were 'devils in the saddle' (MW, p. 78). Though he had got to know and like France, he was still quick to make comparisons with England, so that the River Seine was not 'comparable to our Royal river of Thames'; he liked Paris's streetscapes, but not its muddy thoroughfares, and found its air better that our 'putrified climate, and accidentally suffocated city' of London (by accidentally, he meant that its climate was sullied by the accidents or occurrences of burning sea coal, which he would write about in *Fumifugium*). *The State of France* was published in London in 1652 (although its concluding epistle is dated Paris, 15 February); on the title page of some copies was an engraved author's monogram, where the initials JE lurk behind oak and bay leaves, a prophetic emblem for his later fame as the author of *Sylva*, or even perhaps for his sometimes reclusive self (illus. 16).[9]

He returned briefly to England between June and August to settle 'some of my concerns'; to observe how the now officially named 'Commonwealth' or 'Free State' was faring; to visit George, Richard and his sister Jane, who now had a son; and to witness soldiers around Wotton confiscating gentlemen's horses 'for the service of the state'. In late August 1650, after visiting Sayes Court, he was back in Paris mixing with royalists and exiles ('a Little Britain and a kind of Sanctuary'[10]) and took his wife to revisit the mansion designed by François Mansart for the Marquis de Maisons; here he again admired the river prospect, the 'incomparable' forests, woods, the

16 Engraved monogram from Evelyn's pamphlet *The State of France* (1652).

'extraordinary long walks set with elms', and its 'citronario' (a term Evelyn invented) – the whole estate ('all together') not exceeded by any things he had seen in Italy.[11] He talked with Thomas Hobbes, who had known Francis Bacon and whose English text of *De Cive* (*Philosophical Rudiments concerning Government and Society*) he was now reading. He heard sermons in Browne's chapel, as well as a Jesuit preacher and 'excellent music' in their church on the rue St Antoine, discussed chemistry with both Nicholas Blanchot and Sir Kenelm Digby (the latter an 'errant mountebank', he decided at that point), took his wife to visit more gardens, and revisited the gardens and cabinets of Pierre Morin. He was also writing to his brother with suggestions for his 'Garden at Wotton & fountains'. He was busy with visits, meetings with expatriate English, attending services, and even bathing with his wife in the river at Conflans. It was in fact a very exciting time and place, with expatriates coming and going and much intellectual exchange and opportunities for experimentation (Evelyn was pursuing chemistry and anatomy, and buying books). Some English converted to Catholicism, for the current circumstances in religion in England offered no immediate or even pleasing resolution; but others found themselves pulled towards England, even if the practice of religion there was threatened.

It was a troubled time even in Paris, with more, if different, political chaos than in England. But that made opting to return to England, to bury oneself in private, unostentatious and patient retirement, like Richard Fanshaw or Thomas Henshaw in the village of Kensington, not an easy decision for Evelyn to make; some friends urged him to stay put in

France. Hearing on 22 September 1651 of Charles II's defeat at the battle of Worcester (though Charles escaped and later got back to Paris), Evelyn decided that there was no hope for a restoration at home. Yet Evelyn himself was being lured to return by members of his family and by the steward at Sayes Court; in his Diary (III.59) he 'was persuaded to settle henceforth in England, having now run about the world' for almost ten years, and this he did (albeit with reservations) in January 1652. He would never again cross the Channel. By March that year he was arranging for his wife, now pregnant, to be brought over to England with Lady Browne, and he welcomed them at the port of Rye in Sussex.

They used Mary's new coach to show her some of the Kent countryside while waiting a month in Tunbridge Wells for Sayes Court to be readied. The house needed much refurbishment, having been confiscated in 1649 by the Commonwealth, then sold, and Evelyn was seeking to buy the lease back, which he finally did on 22 February 1653. Sayes Court was now his own place, and in mid-July they finally moved in and enjoyed a warm reunion with John's two brothers, their families and coachloads of friends. In August his son Richard was born there. But a month later Lady Browne died, after which, to distract her, he took a mourning Mary to visit Wotton for the visit time.

In the remaining seven years of the Commonwealth, cautiously preserving his own integrity without parading it, he settled to enjoy himself and survive under the 'rebel' Cromwell. He cultivated his family in its happiness and disappointments and helped with the education of his brother's son, also called George, finding him a tutor in Christopher Wase, a relation of Mary's. He worked on his house and gardens, increased his wide circle of friends and colleagues, attended carefully to understanding the character of his own country and continued to write and translate books or pamphlets that he found important and some whose publication was a particular and personal pleasure. He worked at translating the first book of Lucretius, which he had probably started in France when the task was urged upon him by friends there. It appeared in 1656. Two years later came his English version of Nicolas de Bonnefons' *Le Jardinier françois*, dedicated to his fellow tourist Henshaw and where he first introduced the term 'olitorie' to refer to a kitchen garden, a garden space that he now possessed for himself.

He travelled the country with Mary in 1654 to visit some of her relations and to show her a country that she barely knew, having been brought up in France, but it was none-theless a tour to satisfy 'my own curiosity and information' about England. And for the first time he also visited more 'northern parts'. While alert to the ruinations perpetrated on the country, the 'fatal' sieges of towns like Gloucester and the cathedral at Worcester 'extremely ruined by the late wars', he was always curious about gardens, parks, woodlands, lib-raries and 'monuments of great antiquity'. The cathedral at Gloucester was a 'noble fabric', the acoustics of its 'whisper-ing passage', mentioned by Bacon in his *Sylva Sylvarum*, 'very rare'. He was gladdened that York Minster alone among the great cathedrals of England had been 'preserved from the fury of the sacrilegious by composition with the rebels', a refrain he took up on several occasions, as when writing to Jeremy Taylor of 'this sad catalysis and declension of piety to which

we are now reduced' (*LB*, 1.160). He saw sugar refined for
the first time at Bristol and admired the cliffs of the Clifton
Gorge there, 'equal to any of that nature I have seen in the
most confragose [broken] cataracts of the alps' (an oddly patri-
otic remark, since the cliffs there are hardly 'confragose'). At
Salisbury the canals were 'negligently kept' (by comparison
with the Low Countries), and he found it difficult to number
the stones at Stonehenge,[12] a structure that he first thought was
the representation of 'a cloister', but then saw as a 'heathen &
more natural temple'. Returning from the north via Cambridge,
he admired the university town's buildings and libraries, but
found it 'a low dirty unpleasant place, the streets ill paved,
the air thick, as infested by the fens'. After a four-month
journey of over 700 miles, they returned to Sayes Court.

One of the highlights of his English tour with Mary was
a visit to Oxford. He heard speeches, disputations, sermons,
dined at Exeter College, All Souls and Wadham, saw Arch-
bishop Laud's new quadrangle at St John's, the chapel of New
College 'in its ancient garb, not withstanding the scrupulous
of the times', and the libraries at Christ Church and
Magdalen, where the double organ in its chapel (anathema
for Puritans) was played for them by Christopher Gibbons.
Bodley's librarian showed Mary and him old books and 'curiosities', and they went to the Physic Garden, where the ladies
tasted 'very good fruit'. Evelyn also visited 'that miracle of a
youth, Mr Christopher Wren'.

But among the particular pleasures of this Oxford
return for Evelyn was his meeting with John Wilkins, the
Warden of Wadham, who would show him a transparent
beehive, an example of which he would proudly display later

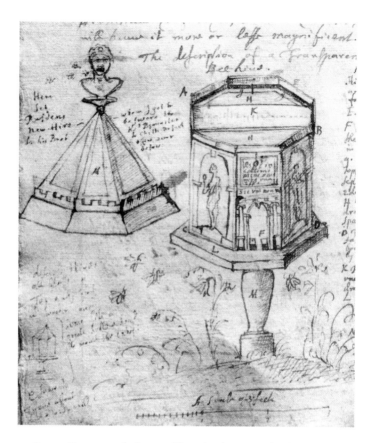

at Sayes Court and show off to the king, and which he discussed and illustrated (illus. 17) in Chapter XIII of the 'Elysium
Britannicum'; over a dozen pages were devoted there to bees
and beekeeping (*EB*, pp. 273ff.), and in this he was sharing his
enthusiasm with Samuel Hartlib, whose *The Reform'd Commonwealth of Bees* (1655) he cites. Wilkins also showed him the
'gallery' above his lodgings, where there were 'Shadows, dials,
perspectives . . . & many other artificial, mathematical, magical
curiosities'. This was a time when virtuosi were exploring and

17 A transparent beehive, from Evelyn's 'Elysium Britannicum'.

experimenting with various instruments that would gauge rain and wind, thermometers and barometers, a pneumatic engine that performed sundry experiments, and a device for measuring a distance travelled (what Evelyn's Diary called a 'way-wiser'), an example of which would be presented by Wilkins to the Royal Society in 1666; some of these instruments and experiments were gathered in Wilkins's laboratory.

The 'way-wiser' had already appeared among the '20 Ingenuities' in *Samuel Hartlib, his Legacy* (1651), a copy of which Hartlib gave to Evelyn when they first met in 1655. Hartlib was briefly and importantly at the centre of intellectual inquiries in England, and Evelyn learned more about him during that Oxford visit. Though within a generation of his death in 1662 Hartlib was 'more or less forgotten', his role in sharing, communicating and reforming ideas through what he termed his 'Office of Address' was considerable, and in many ways it animated numerous members of what would become the Royal Society. Yet it seems also certain that it took the various and collected members of the Royal Society, given its royal charter the very year of Hartlib's death, to move ahead on more scientific and intellectual fronts than a single, though enterprising, man could promote singlehandedly, even with his connections.[13] Nonetheless, the first governor of Connecticut, John Winthrop Jr, thought Hartlib the 'great Intelligencer of Europe', and John Dury, Hartlib's great collaborator, emphasized his role as a facilitator, calling him 'the hub of the axletree of knowledge'.

Born of German and English parents in Elbing, the Prussian first came to London in the 1620s, where after his permanent return in 1628 he seemed to be in contact with everyone of importance. He knew of Evelyn, for example, before they met in November 1655 and had noted down Evelyn's interest in 'husbandry and planting', beekeeping and etching. When Hartlib eventually visited Deptford, he noted in his 'Ephemerides', the logbook of visits to English virtuosi, that Evelyn was 'a chemist [who] hath studied and collected a great Work of all Trades', and found that he spoke French, Italian and Latin, and had 'many furnaces a-going and hath a wife that can in a manner perform miracles, so curious and exquisite she is in painting or limming and other mechanical knacks'. Evelyn did indeed establish a laboratory and maintain chemical notebooks, and had worked on and studied chemistry while in France;[14] he was also planning a book on the secrets and mechanical recipes of various trades, on which he reported to the Royal Society in 1661, though it was eventually left unfinished; and his wife was undoubtedly skilful, receiving help in her painting from a visiting Frenchman, M. du Guernier. Evelyn, like Boyle, would call Hartlib a 'good friend',[15] a 'Master of Innumerable Curiosities, & very communicative', but also, less warmly and much later, would say that Hartlib was though 'not unlearned', yet 'zealous and religious; with so much latitude as easily recommended him to the godly party then governing'.[16] Hartlib did, however, appeal to John Milton, who saw him as sent 'hither by some good providence from a far country to be the occasion and the incitement of great good to this island' and dedicated to him his book *Of Education* in 1644, which Hartlib had himself commissioned.

While Evelyn appreciated much of what Hartlib communicated about horticulture and gardening, he distanced himself from his evident and more radical commitment to a political reformation of England. But they were 'an interesting duo',[17] seeing what was (in Milton's phrase) 'good to this island', but in different ways and at different times: while Hartlib was a dominant and involved guide to gardening and horticulture during the Interregnum, his 'closeness to the Cromwellian regime made him persona non grata at the Restoration', where Evelyn's concern was directed to making these matters both 'royal' and above sectarian ideology. The distance between their attitudes towards 'God's husbandry' (1 Corinthians 3:9) was also an issue that came to preoccupy Evelyn, though in a slightly different way, when he came to confront the impact of Epicurus' atomism on his faith.

Among Evelyn's more arduous tasks during the early 1650s was a translation of Lucretius' *De rerum natura* (On the Nature of Things). He had started on translating the Latin verses into rhymed couplets while still in France, where a French version in prose had appeared in 1650; its frontispiece was the model for Evelyn's own, engraved by Wenceslaus Hollar after a design by Mary Evelyn (whose name is noted on the rim of a vase pouring forth waters, which 'source' does not appear in the French image). Evelyn's Diary in 1656, when the translation appeared, noted that 'Little of the Epicurean philosophy was then known among us'; that was not entirely true, as Howard Jones makes clear: Lucy Hutchinson had undertaken a translation in the early 1650s, though it remained unpublished at the time; Thomas Creech also published a full English version of this important text in 1682, to be revised later by Dryden.[18] Evelyn's translation was, in Jones's phrase, 'entirely forgettable', but it is significant on two important counts: it enmeshed Evelyn in reconciling his faith with his scientific empiricism (specifically Epicurus' physical theories of atomism), and this in turn had some direct impact upon his inability to bring 'Elysium Britannicum' to any conclusion (this second point is taken up in Chapter Ten).

Epicurus enjoyed (at least for some) the reputation of prioritizing sense impressions (the Greek for which translates as 'fantasia') – the atomic succession of images upon our senses, particularly that of sight, which was Aristotle's prime organ of reception. But he also had the reputation of celebrating the 'luxurious and carnal appetites of the sensual and lower man', or, as one opponent of Epicurus put it, 'the whole sum . . . of his Ethicks . . . is . . . that pleasure was the alpha and omega of all happiness' (quoted Jones, p. 200). This was therefore, if not plain atheism and impiety, of dubious appeal to Christians like Evelyn. But on the other hand, what was advanced in support of Epicurus was his evident empiricism, that the house of nature that he explored was primarily founded upon atomism ('small atoms of themselves a world may make'[19]). Moreover, Bacon, to whom Evelyn was always indebted, had himself explored atomism, at first sympathetically, in *Cogitationes de natura rerum*, where the 'doctrine . . . concerning atoms is either true or useful for demonstration', because it is through material things rather than thought that we grasp the 'genuine subtlety of nature'. In his 'On Atheism' in the *Essays*, Bacon also argued that the school of Epicurus 'is a thousand times more credible, [in that] that four mutable elements, and one immutable fifth sense, duly and eternally placed, need no God: then that an army of infinite small portions of seed unplaced [that is, atoms] should have produced this order, and beauty, without a divine marshal'.

Bacon came to modify those ideas by the *Novum organum* of 1620, where a 'doctrine of atoms' will hypothesize 'a vacuum and . . . the unchangefulness of matter (both *false* assumptions)' (Jones, pp. 183–4). Bacon's *Cogitationes de natura rerum* saw publication only posthumously in 1653, while Evelyn was at work translating the first book of Lucretius.

Yet that very year (1653) Evelyn sent a manuscript of his translation to a cousin, Richard Fanshawe, who praised his work, significantly, because its 'exactness' would happily prevent Lucretius from eluding those who accused him of irreligion – 'no running away now, no denying the fact for which he is accused'.[20] Yet in April 1656, when Evelyn's translation was in press, Jeremy Taylor regretted his embarking on the work and hoped it would meet with his own 'sufficient antidote'. Evelyn attempted to assuage his 'ghostly confessor' by hoping that his own 'animadversions upon it will I hope provide against all ill consequences', promised 'caution' and thanked Taylor for his 'counsel'. In that year, though, was also published Walter Charleton's *Epicurus' Morals*, where its author – physician, royalist, true believer in English Protestantism – gave support for Epicurian philosophy as a basis for human happiness.

So even as Evelyn let his translation of the first book of Lucretius proceed through the press, he was confronted both by others' scepticism and by his own hope that somehow he could reconcile his faith with Lucretius' empirical responses; the Epicurian emphasis clashed with the approaches of both Bacon and Evelyn's future colleagues in the Royal Society. Yet the appearance of his book was heralded with pages of support and encouragement – a usual habit in those days; but they seem, at least in retrospect, to have been a response to a nervous need to obtain endorsements – from his father-in-law, from Edward Waller, from Christopherus Wase (in Latin) and the letter in support from Richard Fanshawe. To some of these Evelyn himself responded both in his introduction ('The Interpreter to Him that Reads') by insisting that Lucretius nonetheless 'persuades to a life the most exact and moral', and by printing marginal comments to affirm 'not that the Interpreter [that is, translator] doth justify this irreligion of the poet, whose arguments he afterwards refutes'. But that was more easily stated than argued. Yet at least it was a plausible attitude to adopt, and one year later Charleton's dialogues on *The Immortality of the Human Soul* cast Evelyn in the person of 'Lucretius', who was to make the argument that 'atomism' was a proof of God's existence.[21]

Epicurus, in Evelyn's own version, did indeed penetrate with courage and wit the 'remotest doors' of the natural world, to the extent that the Englishman had to confess that he could not manage adequately to render the 'Greek's obscure conceptions' into English (maybe the rhymed couplets cramped his usually fastidious style).[22] Between the unique world of God's Creation and a scientific probing of its complexities and the material atoms of the natural world, Evelyn wavered. In this, he was unlike Robert Boyle, whom he first met at Sayes Court in April 1656, for Boyle was both an ardent Christian and a keen scientist; but more akin to Jeremy Taylor, who preferred Evelyn's religion to his scientific scrutiny (in part because Taylor did not share the latter). When Evelyn used the epitaph for Pierre Gassendi at the end of the first book, it must have seemed suitably affirmative, since the late scholar and Christian was also an 'Assurer of Epicurus's Institution'.[23]

At least one of the encouraging remarks appended to his translation would seem ambiguous, maybe even double-edged, and Evelyn was alert enough to register the difficult waters into which he was wading; enough to question his commitment to publishing the remainder of the original. The commendatory lines lent by Waller to grace Evelyn's translation made much of Epicurus' determination to expand his inquiry, to throw down ('dispark') the fences ('pale') of a traditional garden world:

> For his immortal boundless wit
> To nature does no bounds permit;
> But boldly has removed the bars
> Of Heaven, and Earth, and Seas and Stars,
> By which they were before suppos'd
> By narrow wits to be inclos'd,
> 'Till his free Muse threw down the Pale,
> And did at once dispark them all.

But this decorous compliment concealed a more disturbing idea: that Epicurus had breached conventional boundaries, thrown open the world of the 'park', previously enclosed and circumscribed by 'narrow wits', and so removed all the constraints that heaven and earth imposed upon an inquiry into the realm of nature:

> Lucretius with a stork-like fate,
> Born and translated in a state,

Comes to proclaim in English verse
No monarch rules the Universe;
But chance and atoms make this all,
In order democratical,
Where bodies freely run their course,
Without design, or Fate, or Force.

In those opening lines Waller touched upon a disturbing new vision of the world – with no monarchy, all chance,
democracy. So we have 'as antipathetic a conclusion as it is
possible to imagine for a man of Evelyn's stamp';[24] Evelyn
himself wrote 'that out of nothing, nothing ever came'. That
he could not bring himself to publish the rest of his translation
of Lucretius was in itself important, not least because he was
frustrated in bringing into English a book of extreme scientific
relevance at the time. But it was also, arguably and indirectly, a
roadblock to his work on finishing the 'Elysium Britannicum',
especially when it was subtitled 'or the Royal Gardens': for an
appeal to royalty implies an appeal to English religion. While
he finished his translation of most of Lucretius and was publishing its first book, he wavered endlessly about committing
the rest to the press: he blamed his printer in several letters
for its mistakes, sometimes pondered the issue of a second and
'more careful edition', and at other times 'determined to proceed no further on that difficult author' and 'rude poet', whose
fourth book disturbed him with its explicit sexual matter and
animadversions on the soul, which he could not accept.[25]

It might have been better to have concentrated his energies on his 'History of all the Mechanical Arts', which people
like Hartlib and Boyle urged. This was an elaborate index of

'secrets and receipts mechanical' that he collected himself
and for which he sought help from others to provide him
with further materials. These were categorized under trades
(artisans, engineers, architects, shipwrights, stonemasons and
so on) and status or occupation (midwifery, laundry-making,
sewing, women). That enterprise too was left incomplete,
though for reasons unconnected with his faith, and more
likely with his unwillingness to take on the sheer bulk and
intricacy of collecting sufficient evidence, when his 'Elysium'
needed the same attention and correspondence. Indeed, it
seems possible that Evelyn's gardening and horticultural writings, always at the very centre of his intellectual and domestic
life, were simply his preferred focus upon what was, after all,
one element of the greater history of trades.[26]

Indeed, by the end of the 1650s he was engaged in another
and more congenial translation, of Bonnefons' *Jardinier françois*
into *The French Gardiner* (1658), in which he thanks his good
friend Thomas Henshaw ('as a lover of gardens') for urging
him to do it; those personal touches of the dedicatory epistle
were eliminated in the next edition, part of his sense that the
book was important and should move beyond merely personal
regard. It was, he wrote, published 'for the benefit and divertissement of our country'. The first three issues of the first
edition announce the French author only by repeating his
initials backwards, and in the editions thereafter that was
omitted entirely and the book became, so to speak, Evelyn's
own; he affects a pseudonym ('Philocepos') in the first edition, but still signs the dedication with his initials; his full
name appears on the title page of the second and subsequent
editions. The dedicatory epistle explains that the French text

dealt well with 'the soil, the situation, and the planting', but that what he himself was moved to do was to use his own first-hand experience to introduce what he termed 'the least known (though not the least delicious) *appendices* to gardens':

> such as are not the names only, but the descriptions, plots, materials, and ways of contriving the ground for parterres, grots, fountains; the proportions of walks, perspectives, rocks, aviaries, vivaries, apiaries, pots, con-servatories, piscinas, groves, cryptas, cabinets, echoes, statues, and other ornaments of a *vigna*, &c. without which the best garden is without life, and very defective . . . (MW, pp. 97–100)

That treatise would indeed make him the 'first propagator in England' of 'flowers and evergreens', 'palisades and con-tr[a]-espaliers of Alaternus', and the 'right culture of [incom-parable verdure] for beauty and sense'. And he glosses such terms as 'espalier' (palisades), then in a margin note explains this as 'pole-hedges set up against a wall, much used in France'. He omitted sections of the French text that discussed cook-ing, averring that he had little experience of the 'shambles', and he also protested that he has probably mistaken or had chosen to omit English names for French fruits. So *The French Gardiner* was, thus, Evelyn's first publication on gardening matters, at once a distraction from the problems in Lucretius and a new commitment to focusing on the hortulan world. Its second edition in 1669 appended *The English Vineyard Vindicated*, to which Evelyn himself added some pages on the 'making and ordering of wines'.

Despite his immersion and inquiring into matters scientific, Evelyn was, all the while, chafing at the repression of Anglicanism, convening services in his own house, and constantly preoccupied with bad sermons elsewhere and what he termed 'extempore prayers after the *Presbyterian* way'. His Diary constantly listed the topics and emphases of sermons and advised that he should consult the notes he had taken after hearing them.[27] In 1657, despite an ordinance that proscribed Christmas celebrations in London and Westminster, Evelyn and his wife went there to celebrate the festival; at a congregation for the Anglican service and sermon in a private chapel at Exeter House they were challenged by soldiers and held prisoner, whereupon two officers loyal to the new regime demanded of Evelyn why he dared to observe 'the superstitious time of the Nativity'; Evelyn got off by saying that, far from praying for Charles I, he was actually praying for all 'Christian Kings, Princes & Governors' and pretended not to know that the Spanish king was a papist!

Meanwhile, Evelyn was working on *A Character of England*,[28] a wonderfully self-critical and yet ironic attack on some of his cherished beliefs. It also suggests how much Evelyn could enjoy himself even in his writings as well as (at least by his own report) being funny and 'merry' in company. The supposed French author whom Evelyn 'translates' finds most of England appalling and distasteful, and Evelyn writes that on his first finding this 'severe Piece, and [reading] it in the language it was sent me', he thought it would honor our country most if it were suppressed, 'as conceiving it an act of great inhumanity'. But 'upon second and more impartial thoughts[!], I have been tempted to make it speak English, and give it liberty, not

reproach, but to instruct our Nation.' It seems that much of
what the 'French' writer impugns in the English are things that
Evelyn himself might find distasteful. While the Frenchman
admits (as would Evelyn) that Inigo Jones's Banqueting Hall
and (the old) St Paul's are admirable, that is as far as 'he'
will go: 'he' finds that Hyde Park lacks 'order, equipage and
splendor' and in Spring Gardens they 'walk too fast'.[29] The
English are rowdy and unpleasant (Evelyn may have agreed),
they drink too much ale, and are constantly toasting. But the
thrust of the 'Frenchman's' attack is on the Presbyterians'
theology and behaviour in church, manners introduced by the
Scots and, beyond that, to all other 'pretenders to the Spirit'
– the 'madness of Anabaptists, Quakers, Fifth Monarchy Men
and a cento of unheard of heresies besides'.

It is great fun to read, and one rhetorical strategy antic-
ipates – and the comparison is not unfounded – Jonathan
Swift's *A Modest Proposal*. In 1729, advocating the economical
and dietary usefulness of eating young children, Swift would
support his arguments with an assurance of 'a very knowing
American of my acquaintance' that juvenile cannibalism had
sound social and economic merits. Evelyn similarly defends
the French attack (which he himself has concocted) not only
by relying on the precedent of satires by Juvenal and Persius,
but by noting that he had been 'reliably informed [on this
matter] by a person of quality, and much integrity', namely
a lady who was herself an 'auditor' in a congregation when
the preacher of a 'serious sermon' advanced the same
'French' strictures against the English! Evelyn tells his female
reader to whom he presents his translation that some others
(that is, Evelyn himself in what follows) might better access

England's character than this 'whiffling capon-maker' or 'Gallus Castratus'.

The wit and humour of this *Character* are in sharp contrast to another book, in this case an actual translation, that Evelyn published in the same year, 1659. Evelyn must himself have sent both books to Jeremy Taylor in June, for Taylor thanks him for 'his two little books', the second of which was Evelyn's own translation of the Greek text of St John Chrysostom's *Golden Book Concerning the Education of Children*, a recently discovered manuscript which had just been printed in Paris in 1656. It was by translating this text that Evelyn solaced himself after the death of his young son Richard, aged five, in January 1658. Taylor wrote to him that it 'made a pretty monument for your dearest, strangest miracle of a boy . . . an emanation of an ingenuous spirit; & there are in it observations, the like of which are seldom made by young travelers' (*Correspondence*, p. 112).

Infant mortality and death of the mother in giving birth were sad and too-familiar incidents in seventeenth-century England,[30] and Evelyn and his family were not spared them. His sister would die in childbirth, as did the child. His wife had already had a miscarriage in France before the safe arrival of her son, Richard, in Surrey. And three weeks after Richard's death, another infant son also died. Evelyn's and Mary's distress was intense, and many friends shared the sorrow of their loss. His praise of Richard and his unfulfilled hopes for him were vividly penned in one of the lengthiest passages in his Diary (III.206–9). Much of that Diary entry was then echoed in his translation of the Greek text, where he addressed how a child might be educated.

In dedicating the *Golden Book* to his brothers, Evelyn recalled Plato's remark that 'those who are well and rightly instructed, do easily become good men'. But it was a terrible irony for Evelyn that the education of his son, to which he had devoted himself, was hardly 'complete' by the time of his death. Indeed, while recalling that both his brothers had lost infants, he had himself engaged with and taught what he called a 'hopeful child'. He dilated upon Richard's 'early piety, and how ripe he was for God', his skill with languages, learning to read both books and manuscripts, his delight in music and pictures, how he listened attentively to sermons and learned verses by heart. Evelyn recalled a young boy who seemed a better emanation of himself; yet his father-in-law had worried that the father was 'over charging' the young boy, whose 'tabula rasa [was] easily confounded'.[31] The work of translation may have consoled him, but at the end of his dedication to his brothers he broke down: 'my tears mingle so fast with my ink, that I must break off and be silent.' The young Richard was buried at Wotton.[32]

Excitement, confusion, rumours and countermoves about the Restoration were reaching a climax in 1659. Richard Cromwell, son of Oliver, had abdicated as Protector in May, and, fearing that there was 'no Magistrate [that is, supreme ruler] either own'd or pretended', Evelyn called for God's mercy to 'settle us'. He took lodgings in London's Covent Garden for the winter and relied heavily on the comfort that sermons provided – those that advised that 'reaping was not to be here, but at [postponed to] the end of the world', or on 'the Superiority of the Spiritual part' (*Diary*, III.234).

In November 1659 Evelyn published *An Apology for the Royal Party*.[33] Noting in his Diary that 'it was capital [offence] to speak or write in favour' of Charles II, he used a supposed letter 'To a person of the late Council of State' written 'by a Lover of Peace and of his Country' (as the title page announced) to make an impassioned and eloquent attack against the parliamentary party; it was also a rebuke to a pamphlet that was circulating in late October – *The Army's Plea for their Present Practice: tendered to the consideration of all ingenuous and impartial men*, and Evelyn's response was signalled on his title page as 'A Touch [that is, stab, as in fencing] at the Pretended Plea'; his Diary recorded that the *Apology* was 'twice printed, so universally it took'.

In January 1660 Evelyn tried to persuade an old school-friend, Colonel Morley, the Lieutenant of the Tower of London, to side with the king, presenting him with a copy of his *Apology*. Morley declined his approach, but later in May, when Charles II was proclaimed, came belatedly to seek Evelyn's help in procuring a pardon for 'his horrible error and neglect of the counsel I gave him'.

Later from February until April Evelyn was exceedingly ill, and doctors feared for his life. But he revived himself sufficiently to write a lively and tough response to the journalist Marchmont Needham, whose purported news in letters from Brussels defamed the king and worked against his restoration; the restoration was (Evelyn wrote) the 'hope and expectation of the General [Monck] and Parliament recalling him, and establishing the government on its ancient and right basis'. Evelyn's *Late News from Brussels Unmasked* was published in April 1660,[34] after which he retired to the 'the sweet and native air of Wotton'. *Late News* is lively and witty journalism ('a rat is found out by his squeaking'), while rebutting 'your forged calumnies' and the invented letters with agility and confidence. The so-called *News*

> will freight his soul down to that place of horror prepared for him and his fellow regicides, his pin, crust, and dog, dam and kittlings, and the concealed nuntio and all that sort of enigmatical and ribald (yet very significant and malicious) drollery . . . The filthy foam of a black and hellish mouth, arising from a viperous and venomous hearts, industriously and maliciously set upon doing what cursed mischief lies in the sphere of his cashiered power . . .

After this, more level-headedly, Evelyn responds with praise of the king, effectively identifying his good birth and extraction and that he is 'obliging in his friendships', a man like ourselves, not to be chased from 'an ample and splendid patrimony'. Its affirmation of the state's supremacy subtly mirrors the virtues of family: a 'loyal Protestant Christian' nation hopes for a 'right Pilot [to] come at the head and stern' of the new ship of state, as a father does his household.

In May 'came the most happy tidings of his Majesty's gracious *Declaration [of Breda]*, & applications [that is, Charles's letters] to the Parliament, General, & people &c and their dutiful acceptance & acknowledgement, after a most bloody & unreasonable rebellion of near 20 years'. Evelyn was still too weak to accept the invitation to travel to Breda to accompany the king back to England, but by May he was well enough to stand in the street to see the triumphant return to London on 29 May, 'after a sad, & long exile, and calamitous suffering both of the King and the Church'. The roads were covered with flowers, the bells were rung, tapestries hung from windows and a fountain ran with wine. Evelyn grossly exaggerated the number of soldiers in the king's procession, but like the *Panegyric to Charles II* that Evelyn presented to his majesty in April the next year, exaggerations might have been in order. Yet the *Panegyric*, extravagant in its ascription of wisdom and every conceivable virtue to Charles, must (writes Keynes in *Bibliophily*) have 'caused Evelyn some distress if he ever read it again it later years', not least when he came to realize that Charles had converted to Roman Catholicism on his deathbed. But now Evelyn was happy enough to organize a semi-private meeting with the king, who received him graciously, after which he returned home to meet his father-in-law, also returned after nineteen years of exile as Ambassador to France.

FIVE

Sayes Court

I have observed so many particularities [in Continental gardens]
as, happily, others descend not to.

A gardener's work is never at an end.[1]

VELYN'S SEARCH FOR a place to live with his new
wife (and soon thereafter a son) found him staying
at his wife's ancestral home in 1652. It was an Elizabethan gabled house of three storeys that Evelyn would later
declare as 'ruined' and in need of endless refurbishment,
which turned out to be costly.[2] He acquired the lease first
from the Commonwealth in 1653, and in 1663 again from the
Crown, following its return. While staying at Sayes Court,
he made offers on one property, then also bought and sold
another, and, disappointedly, also failed to purchase Albury,
of which he had good memories because of his visits and
acquaintanceship with the Earl of Arundel (see Chapter
Seven). In the end it was Sayes Court that became his home
and where he would make his garden; the latter, in his wife's
words, would be 'his business and delight'.[3] He would tell
Cowley in 1666 that gardening was 'the mistress I serve and
cultivate' (LB, II.436). Yet it was also, in his more morbid

moments, but his 'poor villa and possessions', a phrase often
used in letters to his brother or to Benjamin Maddox in 1656
(*LB*, I.157 and 174). He confessed to Jeremy Taylor that they
were 'indeed gay things' and he apologized to him for living
in a 'worldly manner near a great city' (*LB*, I.170). As he frequently consulted with Taylor on 'spiritual matters, using him
. . . as my Ghostly Father' and who occasionally reprimanded
his worldly life, this response reveals one side of Evelyn's per-
sonality, a melancholic manner that could be muted or even
overcome when his gardening interests took over; and to
be in thrall to a 'great city' as opposed to a country estate in
Surrey, for example, did not wholly suit him. It suggests, too,
how much Taylor, in his concern that Evelyn was translating
Lucretius, would contribute later on to his unwillingness to
finish the ambitious manuscript of 'Elysium Britannicum'; as
Frances Harris argues, his pride and enthusiasm for his house
and garden would 'become a matter for confession and self-
castigation' in the 1680s.[4]

The site at Sayes Court was not promising – simply fields,
a few elms, small orchards, in the furthest northwest corner
'an extravagant place mangled by digging gravel', and an awkward juxtaposition to Deptford dockyard (illus. 18); but, as he
wrote to Mary, he would take it on and make it tolerable by
putting in order its 'conveniences, and interests annexed to it'.
Work began on bringing the house and some essential service
buildings into better shape, and its southern entry was given a
classical porch. By 1653 Evelyn's laboratory was acquiring the
necessary apparatus of furnaces and other equipment. But the
garden was clearly his main hope and objective. A plan of this
'villa and possessions' from 1653 suggests what arrangements

Evelyn took over, but also what refurbishments of the house itself and the gardens were either made or envisaged. The plan – the handwriting and draughtsmanship of which are uncertain – is numbered throughout, and a long, itemized list down the left-hand side of the sheet annotates its 'particulars', to which some references will be made (illus. 19).[5]

An approach road across fields from the south crosses a walled courtyard to a paved porch with Doric columns. Inside was a typical and not always coherent Elizabethan house, but now evidently reorganized: a 'hovel' has become a 'buttery', a 'clockhouse' becomes a withdrawing room for the parlour, a storehouse turns into a bedroom, and a cheese house into a 'pastry'. There are 'new cellars, much enlarged, formerly an hovel', more 'lights' and windows throughout, a kitchen sink 'elevated and altered'. Mary Evelyn's 'Closet of Collections' is established above the porch, while Evelyn's

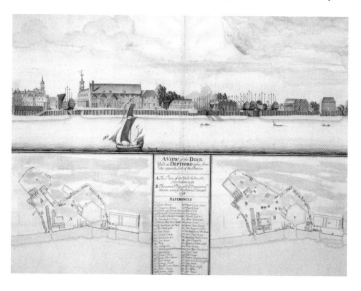

18 Two plans and 'A VIEW of the [Royal] DOCK Yard at DEPTFORD taken from the opposite Side of the Thames', 1698, probably by the then Surveyor of the Royal Navy, Edmund Dummer.

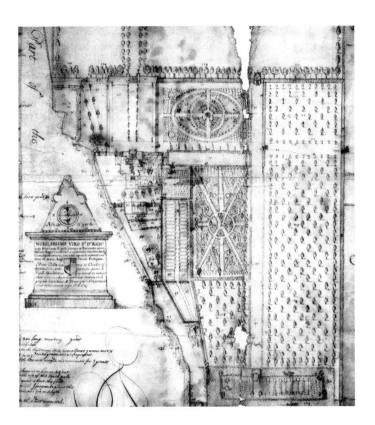

new study is explained as 'This I have built from the ground, so that my Study is 23 foot long, & 11 broad besides a little Study within it near half as big.'

The exterior, too, was a medley of small spaces, some walled courtyards with walks and arbours, as well as utilitarian functions: a pump and cistern, a pigeon house over 'my [new] elaboratorie' with its portico 'towards the private garden', an aviary, a beehive 'in the private garden', a wood yard, milking close, a brew house that replaced stables, a freshly dug carp pond that was replenished at high tide through a culvert

19 Plan of Sayes Court (then in Kent). Evelyn's home from 1652 to 1699, showing the Oval (top) and Grove (centre). A detail, not showing the list of 'particulars' at the left of the plan.

from the Thames, and so on. The whole site (illus. 20) lay between the Deptford dockyards, with, just beyond, the Thames, which also fed the horse pond. From a banqueting house, above where the new oval garden would be established, a long walk ('526 foot long, 21 broad') would lead to an island with a moat, and from there a passageway and then stairs led to the Thames along the mast dock. Beyond these necessary domestic and working spaces were those parts of Sayes Court that constituted Evelyn's garden of pleasure.

Despite the fact that Sayes Court no longer exists (and indeed its site is barely registered these days, though there are some vague plans to recreate part of it[6]), Evelyn's large commitment to garden writing and garden-making has meant that Sayes Court has attracted considerable attention, and rightly so. Over the forty years in which Evelyn made, tended and revised his garden, he encountered excitement, expense, disappointments and certainly the need to understand how to domesticate what he had witnessed in his European travels, as well as his readings about them, to local conditions of place, location and society. No garden is ever 'finished', whether it is just one site or an attempt to establish a national typology, such as he embarked upon in his 'Elysium Britannicum' as he was beginning his gardening at Sayes Court; every garden is different, even though we may try to generalize about them. Gardens also suffer from weather and climate changes, and however much we force them to respond to our wishes and desires, they cleave to local conditions. Sayes Court was no exception.

Given Evelyn's own foreign experience and his wide reading in Continental treatises, he could hardly settle in

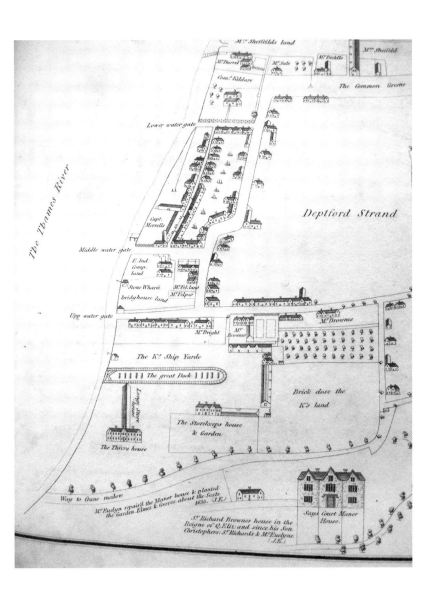

The Thames River

Mrs Sheffields land

Mr Thorrel   Mr Sale   Mr Diddle   Mrs Sheffeild

Comr Kildare

The Common Greene

Lower water gate

Deptford Strand

Capt. Merrells

Middle water gate

E. Ind. Comp. land

Stone Wharre
bridghouse land

Mr Fel. land
Mr Filpes

Upp water gate

Mr Bright

Mr Brownes

Mr Brownes

The Ks Ship Yarde

The great Dock

Longe store house

Brick close the Ks land

The Storekeeps house & Garden

The Thore house

Way to Crane medow

Mr Euelyn repaird the Manor house & planted the garden Elmes & Groves about the Scite 1650. J.E.

Sr Richard Brownes house in the Reigne of Q. Eliz: and since his Son Christophers: Sr Richards & Mr Euelyns. J.E.

Says Court Manor House

20 Plan of house and Docklands from Evelyn's *Miscellaneous Writings* (1825).
This is a redrawn map after a sketch by Evelyn (BL Add MSS 78629A) from
about 1698, showing the adjacency of Sayes Court to the dockyard, which
increasingly came to disturb him.

mid-seventeenth-century England for recollections of an Elizabethan gardenist past, even if the house itself and its larger relationship to its surroundings remained somewhat old-fashioned. There were, indeed, some telltale gestures to that past, like the carved mottoes that he placed over doorways in the house or hung from trees in the garden, for in 'Elysium Britannicum' he noted the incidence of '*Impresses, Mottos, Dials, Escutchions, Cyphers* and innumerable other devices' (*EB*, p. 75). Yet to bring *hortulan* culture into the early modern world required attention to a host of often competing concerns: foreign forms and ideal devices jibing with local and native circumstance; personal taste with a sense of national imperatives; enthusiasm for a new gardening with a recollection of the pleasures of melancholy in garden traditions; keen, careful and modern observation of plants and animals requiring, nonetheless, some respect for ancient lore on both planting and husbandry; plants from abroad that needed to tolerate the local climate and plants from English nurseries or acquired from acquaintances. It also required a dialogue between a respect for celestial bodies, acknowledging 'prognostications' and 'astrological niceties' (though Evelyn was 'no friend' of them, notes Mark Laird), and whatever intervenes in an actual garden on the banks of the Thames – prodigies of weather, animals (like moles, frogs, mice, snails, noxious caterpillars, yet also the glorious butterfly) and bad air that 'kills our Bees and Flowers abroad', as Evelyn noted in *Fumifugium* (see Chapter Six). He seemed particularly eager to distance himself from the 'nice and hypercritical punctillos' that astrologers imposed upon gardening matters.

It is useful to situate Evelyn's garden work, particularly
his garden vocabulary, in a larger context of European practice and publications.[7] His range of reference was considerable: beyond his visits to many gardens in the Low Countries,
France and Italy, he drew on books by Nicolas de Bonnefons
(which he translated), Charles Estienne and Jean Liébault,
Olivier de Serres, Claude Mollet and Jacques Boyceau, as well
as native writers like Thomas Mill, John Parkinson, Stephen
Blake, Thomas Hanmer and Gervase Markham. But this considerable learning raises a question: how do those formal
devices and foreign terms *translate* into an English garden
practice and vocabulary of the mid-seventeenth century?[8]
These terms can be, as Mark Laird showed well, 'diverse and
rather elusive' when Evelyn uses them (Evelyn DO, p. 175).

Though Evelyn was undoubtedly composing the 'Elysium
[or 'Royal'] Britannicum' during the 1650s, since he published a synopsis of it, which he communicated to Sir Thomas
Browne and others, in 1659, it seems that what he was doing
at Sayes Court was his primary focus and was his own personal project for a gentry (and not a royal) garden. And while
the making of Sayes Court's gardens obviously contributed
to modelling his 'Noble, princely, and universal Elysium' in
the unfinished book, it was, as he well knew, only in spe-
cifics and hands-on practice that a gardener and designer
could see what he was doing.[9] While he was constantly alert
to what ancient authorities such as Columella or Virgil in his
Georgics could teach him, it was the actual work at Sayes Court
that directed his ideas, and it was the wisdom and aphorisms
about his own work there that sustained both his *Kalendarium
Hortense*, published with *Sylva* in 1664, and the 'Directions

for the Gardener at Sayes Court' that he wrote 22 years later (1686) for an apprentice.

On what once had been an orchard and 'one entire field of 100 acres', Evelyn saw the beginning of 'our Elysium' in 'gardens, walks, groves, enclosures & plantations'. Two major interventions were an oval grove at the south of the garden and another grove towards the north; between them was an elevated terrace walk, edged by a holly hedge on one side and with a hedge of berberis towards the grove. Evelyn began these designs with both very specific memories of Morin's garden in Paris, which he had visited in 1644 and again in 1651, and a more generalized recollection of the many groves, *bosquets, boschetti*, flower displays and cabinets in France and Italy.

So when in January 1653 he started to set out his Oval Garden in imitation of Morin's garden (see illus. 23), he wrote to his father-in-law that 'we are at present pretty well entered in our gardening'. Mark Laird's reconstruction shows two ovals within a rectangle, marked with sentinel cypresses,[10] the inner oval set as a parterre, the outer one in grass, with a raised mound and 'dial' at the very centre[11] surrounded by eight cypresses; walks surround the two ovals and also cross it from north to south and from east to west. Outside the larger oval are 'wildernesses' or groves, with on one side an 'evergreen thicket, for birds[,] private walks, shades and cabinets' and, on the other, another walk also ending with a small cabinet at both ends. By May, Evelyn was also telling his father-in-law that his own Oval would 'far exceed [Morin's] both for design & other accommodations'. 'Exceeding' allows several meanings – better or later in time, because we improve upon what went before; but also more apt, more suited, or more accommodating, to what that particular garden needed. Laird notes that a 'hierarchy of elements' is introduced: a miniature version of what pertains in larger spaces, where small and low-level planting gradually gives way to bigger and taller items behind, or (in this case) where the large forms are established at its edges, appropriate to the oval.

The Grove, to the north, echoed those Evelyn had seen in France and above all in Italy. It has the overall aspect of a Baroque *bosquet*, but experience of the interior must have been a pleasing meander of surprises and planting. Rectangular, 40 by 80 yards, it was divided into eight, with walks from each corner and side that converged upon a central mount at the centre, ringed with laurel. But inside, beneath the canopy of over five hundred standard trees, with an under-storey of 'thorn, wild fruits, greens, etc', its shape was less apparent, the richness of leaf and form much more various; some of the walks even morphed into what Evelyn called 'spider's claws' – dead-end alleys that twisted into little cabinets with a 'great French walnut tree' at the centre of each. After five seasons, Evelyn would think it 'infinitely sweet and beautiful'.

But 'accommodations', noted in the letter to Sir Richard Browne, involved other things. Sayes Court was, Evelyn wrote in 1664 (if not before), his 'villa';[12] yet in each move of that useful Latin term, translated without alteration into the Italian 'villa' and then directly into the English villa, it acquired fresh significance, not least that in Evelyn's case it was only leased. While the word remains the same, the culture and use of a 'villa' on a bank of the Thames would have a different feel, a new attention to different circumstances in the life of a seventeenth-century Englishman, even if the

Latin or the Italian term brought its owner some appreciable and rich associations with cultures elsewhere. Even the measurement of a foot of ground was slightly different in France and in England. But situation, scale, climate, plants, animals, birds and vermin were also different. The soil at Sayes Court needed enrichment with hefty mixes of lime, loam and cow dung.[13] Evelyn gathered plants from many sources; some locally in east Greenwich, but many from the Continent, some of which needed careful tending in Surrey. From his earliest days at Sayes Court he was sending his father-in-law requests for cypress seeds, for what he had 'did not prove according to my expectation', or soliciting 'half a dozen bearing trees from Paris', along with a list of plants 'all unknown to me'. He urged Sir Richard to consult *La Jardinier françois* with its catalogue 'of all sorts of fruit in France, out of which you will be easily able to collect what kind are best'.[14] As late as the 1690s he was still obtaining, from Flanders, '50 roots of the Royal Parot Tulips' and '100 roots of Ranunculoes' (*Diary*, IV.648 and V.59).

Different machines were also needed in an English garden. This was a time when various virtuosi were devising ways of measuring rainfall or wind speed, and using thermometers and barometers. The 'Elysium Britannicum' devotes pages and drawings to these necessary accommodations to English gardening: not only the tools required but instruments for watering (see illus. 32, where no. 43 is a water truck), or to measure and predict weather conditions, like the hygroscope, or the 'thermoscope or weather-glass' that would ascertain the degree of wet or dry in an English garden (*EB*, p. 151). In his manuscript 'Directions' of 1686 he listed a 'Hot-bed', while a new edition of the *Kalendarium Hortense* in 1691 added remarks and diagrams for heating systems and a greenhouse, so that tropical plants, like the banana tree, could thrive in England. Evelyn is credited in the OED with first using the word 'conservatory', in the 1664 edition of the *Kalendarium*, but he had seen one in 1644 at Cardinal Richelieu's garden at Rueil (*Diary*, II.109, though that reference might well be a subsequent addition when he wrote up his notes). He continued to be interested in systems to maintain plants inside; he admired the conservatory and (somewhat confusingly) also a greenhouse at Euston Hall in 1677, and had visited in 1685 John Watts's subterranean stoves in Chelsea (*Diary*, IV.462). He was convinced now that, rather than utilizing stoves to create heat, experimenting with solar heat would inaugurate an English paradise of perpetual fruiting, since it may not be too 'late for me to begin new paradises'.[15]

Evelyn was eager to note how his plants, improvements or accommodations made good sense of their translation onto English ground. Of his evergreens, Evelyn wrote that 'an English garden, even in the midst of winter, shall appear *little inferior* to the Italian'. His 'glorious nursery of 800 trees' transplanted in 1653 was 'Two foot high', and 'as fair as I ever saw in France'. Again, writing of palisade-hedges, espaliers and close-walks, he saw that we have brought aliterus [*Rhamnus alaternus*] into '*use* and *reputation* for those works in England' (my italics).

The *Kalendarium Hortense* that Evelyn appended to the first edition of *Sylva* in 1664 set out 'An almanac directing what [the gardener] is to do monthly throughout the year', for an earthly paradise needs attention and weeding. He encouraged 'an extraordinary inclination to cherish so innocent

& laudable a diversion [gardening], and to incite an affection in the nobles *of this nation* towards it' (my italics). Each month are noted the fruits and flowers that are 'in prime', or 'yet lasting' so that they can be used early in the next year. In both the orchard and 'olitory' (Evelyn's coinage for the vegetable garden) and in the parterre and flower gardens, the tasks were listed – dealings with wasps, tending bees (in April, 'open up hives for now they hatch'), feeding birds in the aviary before they breed, sweeping and cleaning paths of leaves in October and again in November, lest worms pull them into holes. Once December is reached, the year starts all over again: 'As in January, continue your hostility against vermin.'

But if some accommodations for English garden-making were necessary or even welcomed, others were not. Vermin might be controlled, but storms could not be avoided. If gardening was the result of planning and careful maintenance, then what Laird terms 'an environment of chaos as much as stasis' (*Milieu*, p. 116) at Sayes Court was 'troubling' and unforeseen both for plants and indeed people. Deadly disease felled Evelyn's daughter Mary and his servant Humphrey Prideaux, both dying of smallpox. Storms had certainly to be accepted and (unlike humans) their consequences could be repaired in some measure: 'Extraordinary storm of hail and rain. Cold season as winter and wind northerly near 6 months', Evelyn wrote in his Diary in June 1658; it felled 'my greatest trees' and destroyed winter fruit. The next day he reported the grounding and slaughter of a whale in the Thames.

Evelyn was gardening in what we would now call the 'end of the Little Ice Age'.[16] He chronicled the bad winter of

1685–6 in a report to the secretaries of the Royal Society (*LB*, II.732–5, later published in *Philosophical Transactions,* no. 158; see *MW*, pp. 692–6). While elms and young forest trees were unscathed, exotics like the cork tree would hardly recover, cedars were lost, pines, rosemary and laurel were dead or discoloured; he lost a few fish and his long-lived tortoise. But nightingales were 'as brisk and frolic as ever'; by 14 April 1684 he was welcoming their arrival from Africa, and noting that this migration deserved proper study by ornithologists (*MW*, p. 696).

It was that devastating winter of 1685–6, when the Thames was frozen, that impelled Evelyn to rethink his garden layout. A new plan from February (illus. 21) shows what he envisaged, and that plan is supported by two surveys of the late 1690s that show what was implemented (illus. 22). Essentially, he eliminated the Oval Garden entirely, and modified and extended the Grove.

The new half-moon of grass or 'bowling-green', surrounded by plantations, was twice the size of the previous Oval; at its centre and head was still the banqueting hall, which faced across the grass and down the original walk to the moated island. What is interesting about this enlarged hemicycle is that it may also have recalled two Continental designs, though in both cases they are substantially revised for Sayes Court. One model was the *demi-lune* that Evelyn had observed at the Château de Richelieu in September 1644; but now it was cleared of the elaborate parterre work, and what in France had been a ring of statues is replaced with holly and fruit trees, with gooseberries and currant bushes, strawberries and violets that fill out the corners or 'triangles' of the half-circle. But

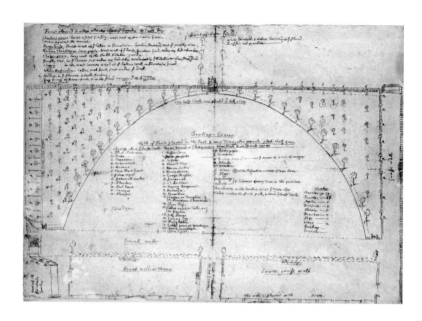

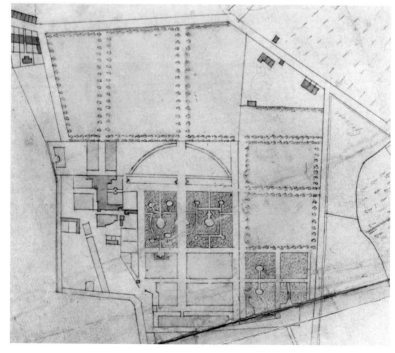

this new bowling-green also recalls the shape of the artificial echo that he saw in the Tuileries and sketched for his 'Elysium Britannicum' (see illus. 11), though the French space was greater than at Sayes Court and its half-circle was graced with two lines of trees; nor did it enable an artificial echo. Such hemicycles or *demi-lunes* are nothing unusual in seventeenth-century European garden design, but Evelyn accommodates those foreign recollections into a grass lawn and a celebration of fruit trees, many recommended by John Parkinson in 1629, that produced fruit during an English summer and some that lasted through the winter (the 1684–5 plan contains lists of what he was planting[17]). And his 'Directions' for the apprentice gardener, composed soon afterwards in 1686, now contained careful advice on how to deal with the grass of the bowling-green – 'rolled and cut once a fortnight, with ease'.

The enlarged area of the former oval is now answered by a pair of groves either side of the walkway that leads from the banqueting hall; the original one stays the same size, but loses some of its regular grid of *allées*, though retaining the 'spider's claws'; the new and matching one to the west is larger, and has a square of walks with a central cabinet and one at each corner of the square. Both groves continued to be filled with varieties of trees.

Whatever the motivation for Evelyn's far less intricate layout – a need to reduce maintenance, loss of funds, an inclination to simplify, compensation for either the bad weather or his own age (he was by then 64) – Sayes Court was still an acknowledgement, if more distant, of Continental garden design. It had been from the first an 'invented' garden, playing with elements of Italian and French design, but now it

21 New plan of the southern part of Sayes Court, dated February 1685.

22 Detail of map from *c.* 1690 by John Grove (?) of the later layout of Sayes Court, showing the new oval and the matching pair of groves.

was even more so, yet the invention more his own. However, whatever it was, it was *not* proleptic, no anticipation of the landscape ideas that, twenty or thirty years later, would either in format or usage begin to shape the design and thinking of English garden-making.

In his introduction to *Kalendarium Hortense* Evelyn notes that dressing and keeping an Eden necessarily required that it be kept 'continually cultivated'; yet it was also 'a labour full of tranquility'. In 1686 Evelyn took on an apprentice gardener, Jonathan Mosse, for whom he wrote 'Directions', including what exotics would be able to thrive in England. These instructions were an agenda of everything he had learned on the ground of Sayes Court, listing fruit trees suitable for different sectors of the garden (Fountain Court, Greenhouse Garden, the 'Island' and so on), forest trees and 'trees for the Grove', the necessary tools to be kept and used, 'measures which a Gardiner should understand', and noting everything from 'dunging and compost' to preparing salads for the table 'according to the seasons'. Also included was a careful list of 'Terms of art used by learned gardeners': some were straightforward, but presumably useful for an apprentice gardener – 'Estival, Autumnal, Hyemal, the same as Brumal' to designate what could flourish in which season, or 'Botanist, One who has knowledge of plants'. Others were more unusual, like 'Aspect' ('the quarter of the heaven, East, West, North & South'), 'digest' ('to rot and consume like dung'), or 'mucilage' ('clammy stuff, such as in yew-berries'). In notes on 'garden and physical plants necessary to be known and had' for the physic garden, the plants should be 'set in alphabetical order, for the better retaining them in memory'.

Frustrated by his inability or unwillingness to publish his 'Elysium Britannicum', he pulled a section headed 'Of Sallets' and published it separately in 1699, as *Acetaria, a Discourse of Sallets*.[18] This clearly drew upon his work at Sayes Court, and now he enlarged upon the 'Directions' he had penned for its new gardener by discoursing on the ingredients of a salad, the herbs and vegetables to be used therein. But now he moves from Baconian, practical matters into 'a glorious disquisition on primitive innocence and the early state of the world': Adam and Eve lived on salads, and Milton is summoned in support of the 'wholesomeness of the herb-diet' – 'vegetarian as by God's will' (writes Graham Parry). Evelyn was clearly something of a connoisseur on the preparation of salads, though (as Keynes notices in *Bibliophily*, p. 237) his dedication of *Acetaria* to the Lord Chancellor and President of the Royal Society is marked by nothing if not 'his usual long-winded solemnity' – what the writer himself describes as 'to usher in a trifle, with so much Magnificence'. To the Duchess of Beaufort, however, he explained that it was 'but of an handful of herbs'; they were, he added, 'yet the products of the same great Author', by which we presume he meant God, not himself, 'and have their peculiar virtues and uses too'.

The house and garden at Sayes Court has long since disappeared, while the Evelyn family home at Wotton survives. If Evelyn had read Ben Jonson's poem 'To Penshurst', for he certainly knew Penshurst Place in Kent,[19] he would have appreciated much of the poem's praise of the estate. In July 1652, the year he himself settled at Sayes Court, his Diary records a visit to Penshurst with his wife, newly arrived from France: it was 'finely water'd', once famous 'for its gardens &

excellent fruit' and was marked by the 'conversation' of those who frequented it. Jonson praises the Sidney estate for its modesty, for boasting neither marble nor 'polish'd pillars, or a roof gold'; there were walks for pleasure and sport, and it was peopled with dryads on its mount, Pan and Bacchus, and all the Muses; praise is notably bestowed on its woods ('the broad beech, and the chestnut shade'), which Evelyn would have appreciated. Altogether, it shows itself as an antique and sacred place that echoes much of Evelyn's own visions of a paradisal garden sustained by ancient virtues and modern skills.

Jonson ends his celebration by comparing Penshurst with 'other edifices', 'proud, ambitious heaps, and nothing else' that aristocrats had built. Their 'lords have built, but thy lord dwells'. That is a supreme compliment. Yet one might wonder whether Evelyn would have agreed – whether he would have found it hard to say he *dwelt*, in the full richness of that word, at Sayes Court. It was certainly similar in that it did not pretend to aristocratic or royal power, but it was, when all was said and built, not the home that Evelyn wanted or could in fact preserve. When in the 1690s Evelyn finally repossessed his true family home in Wotton, Sayes Court was let, first to Vice-Admiral Benbow and then to the young Tsar of Muscovy, Peter the Great, who wrecked the place – smashing the windows, ruining Mary's best sheets, damaging pictures and driving his wheelbarrow through the hedges.

SIX

The Restoration

HE RESTORATION WAS both a relief for Evelyn and something of a challenge. After unsettled times, where little if anything (at least for Evelyn) seemed to have been gained during the Interregnum, he was happy that the monarchy had been restored with no bloodshed and by an army that had once rebelled against it. Finances for country and monarch were precarious, but a new parliament was convened in May 1661, regicides met their deaths, and Cromwell's body was removed from the 'superb tomb' in Westminster, displayed at Tyburn and buried in a 'deep pit'. The Church of England reasserted its authority, with bishops being reinstated or appointed.

Evelyn continued to wait upon the king, who 'was pleased to own me more particularly, by calling me his old acquaintance [they had met in Paris in the 1650s], & speaking very generously to me'. After the coronation he presented Charles, along with the Lord Chancellor, with copies of his *Panegyric*, and later in September with his discourse on air pollution, *Fumifugium*. He hunted with the king and sailed with him on the royal yacht in a race against one of the Duke of York's, during which they discussed how to promote remedies against air pollution and 'the improvement of gardens & buildings (now ever rare in England, comparatively to other countries)'. He was also requested to draft an account of a contretemps or 'bloody encounter' between rival ambassadors over precedence, a task he performed but reluctantly and with some interference from the king to revise its text.[1] But he had further private conversations with Charles about the (later to be named) Royal Society, and held the candle for the painter Samuel Cooper – who preferred to work by candle-light – when he was drawing the king's head for the new, minted money. He also obviously enjoyed the renewed pageantry, notably the visits by foreign embassies that everywhere attended the king's movements, including his coronation in April 1661 and the river pageant in August 1662 to bring the new queen from Hampton Court to Whitehall. Whether or not he approved of Charles's resumption ('according to custom') of touching for the King's Evil in July 1661, as it may have challenged his scientific instincts, he noted that Charles did not shrink from stroking the faces of the sick with his hands.

The newly established world of the Restoration court gave Evelyn opportunities, personal and professional, and allowed him occasions to serve the nation in ways that pleased him – with horticulture, arboriculture, scientific investigations and experiments, architecture and urban planning. Hence, no doubt, his determination to subtitle his ongoing garden manuscript 'or, Of Royal Gardens', for as he told the king on the royal yacht, good garden-making in England lagged behind foreign countries, and a royal imprimatur or invocation was useful. And he resumed contacts with those who had stayed out of England during the Interregnum.

But the new regime also irked him by the 'concourse of people' thronging about the king, and his distaste for grand and expensive banquets ('cheer not to be imagined for the plenty and rarity – an infinity of persons'), from which he chose to slip away 'in the crowd and come home late'. Indeed, he was best suited to small encounters rather than crowds, which explains his careful and thoughtful letter-writing to individuals, whereby he might 'open up excellent conversation[s]' (*LB*, 1.247); he also resented the similar throngs of visitors that his brother gathered at Wotton. Neither did he like court intrigue, nor the gaiety and fashions of dress and social behaviour, which he tackled in his 1661 *Tyrannus; or, the Mode; in a discourse of sumptuary laws*, nor stage appearances of actresses, since for the first time, they performed in public theatres ('inflaming some noblemen and gallants [and] became their whores and to some their wives'). He continued to refuse honours. Evelyn's aloofness, fastidiousness and even piety nevertheless consorted with a need to deploy himself in a new social world of visiting and being visited in his gardens at Sayes Court – Charles II and his queen paid a visit to his 'poor cottage, and [took] a view of my little villa' (*LB*, 1.309). His Diary records his busy toing and froing between London and family, either in Deptford or Surrey. He constantly listened to sermons, noted their topics and texts in his Diary, and made summaries of their contents.

Two activities in particular gave him personal pleasure and a sense of working for his country: the work at Gresham College that preceded the formation and establishment of the Royal Society in 1661, which is discussed here and in the next chapter, and his work for what today we would call the civil service (see Chapter Eight).

The first edition of *History of the Royal Society* by Thomas
Sprat of 1667 had an allegorical frontispiece (illus. 23)
designed by Evelyn and engraved by Wenceslaus Hollar. It
shows Charles II about to be crowned with a laurel wreath,
and to his right the seated figure of Francis Bacon. The setting
maybe (says Keynes) reflected the tiled piazzas on the side of
the Garden Court at Gresham College; scientific instruments
are displayed on the wall, and books in a case at the left; in the

23 Wenceslaus Hollar, frontispiece from Thomas Sprat's *History of the Royal
Society . . .* (1667), designed by Evelyn with John Beale's help. (Many copies do
not include this frontispiece, which suggests either that it has been removed
or that it was not bound in to every copy.)

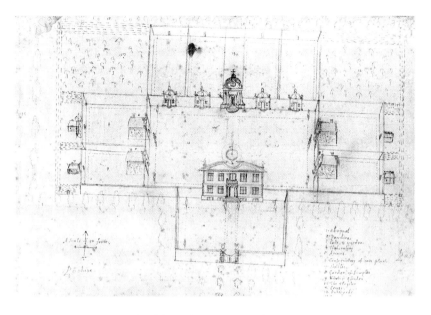

far right distance is a building that Keynes also suggests may
be a representation of Solomon's House in Bacon's *New
Atlantis*. In 1660 Evelyn had also sketched alternative coats of
arms for the Royal Society, depicting ships, telescopes, a
plumb line held by a hand in the clouds (an interesting gesture to a divine sense of measurement), cannons, a sun or
terrestrial globes, along with mottoes like *Omnia probate* (Try
all things), or *Quantum nescimus* (How much we do not know).[2]

   In 1659, before the formal establishment of the Royal
Society, Evelyn had proposed a plan and prospectus for
a new house dedicated to enquiries similar to those that
Bacon had espoused in Solomon's House; this would seem
to have been an alternate, more elitist 'college' than the public
Society looked to become. Perhaps it suited his own preferred
sense of intimacy in an age that 'not only robs men of their

24 Evelyn's sketch for a 'new college'.

time, but extremely of their virtue and best advantages'. He
sketched a layout of the residential college to be erected on
30 or 40 acres of land 'in some healthy place' (illus. 24), and
he described its academic purpose and scope in a letter to
Robert Boyle in September 1659 (*LB*, 1.253–6). The annotated perspective or 'Ichnography' shows a central, classical
pavilion, a 'pretty small chapel' on the far side of its courtyard, living quarters for students, each with their own garden
('after the manner of the Carthusians'), a laboratory, a library,
a 'Conservancy of rare plants', stables, and a 'wood', with
'uplands or downs'. Writing to Boyle, he envisaged that it
would consist of a small group who would 'live profitably, and
sweetly together', eat modest meals, with 'bowling, walking,
or other recreation' on the central lawn; he would himself
live there with his wife; it was a 'sort of domesticity'.[3] The
Society would engage a 'chaplain well qualified', as well as
an artist, and the members could either sell to colleagues or
quit if their circumstances changed. Evelyn also estimated the
cost and upkeep of its foundation. The letter concluded with
the 'Orders' that would guide the community. Presumably
the return of the king and the subsequent elaboration of a
much bigger and more open society, and perhaps the fact
that his scheme smacked too much of retreat (apt for him
in the Commonwealth, but not for a royalist nation), would
have made Evelyn's plan less plausible, as were several other
schemes hatched during the Interregnum, like Cowley's
Proposition for the Advancement of Learning (published in 1661) of
a college with courtyards, gardens and experimental cellars.
Other schemes had also been proposed – Thomas Bushell
of Enstone, who had worked with Bacon, thought of a

Baconian New Atlantis, Hartlib envisaged similar schemes, Henry Hammond envisaged a college of 'godly men' as early as 1654, and even earlier Thomas Henshaw, Evelyn's friend, came back from France in 1650 with the notions of a 'Model of Christian Learned Society' at his retreat in Kensington.

The Royal Society that followed and resumed some of these ideas has been extremely well researched and described, and there is no need here to repeat that narrative.[4] It effectively formalized the early meetings held at Gresham College (with a splinter group in Oxford gathered around John Wilkins and Robert Boyle), where its discussions were deeply indebted to extending the work and example of Francis Bacon, an inspiration that was frequently celebrated by its members (see illus. 29). Bacon's vision was that all this could be achieved by the *collaborative* endeavours of its various members, and it was this institutional character of the Royal Society, with regular meetings and committees, that carried further the ideas that had circulated through Hartlib's Office of Address during the 1650s. If during that decade Evelyn had been, as Michael Hunter argued, 'a virtuoso in search of a role' (cf. Aubrey's 'One of our first virtuosi'), the creation of the Royal Society allowed him a more clarified 'role' or (as he himself explained much later) 'some calling or other' in English intellectual life.

Given that the Royal Society's attention today is specifically on the physical sciences, it is important to note that at its inception it gathered humanists as well as scientists, what Evelyn tended to refer to generally as 'natural philosophers', or virtuosi, like Samuel Pepys, John Aubrey, Henry Oldenburg, Thomas Henshaw, Robert Plot or William Aglionby. It was a truly astonishing mix of landed gentry, aristocrats, astronomers, antiquarians, clergy, poets, architects and surveyors, mathematicians, courtiers and diplomats, military, and self-styled virtuosi, not all of whom were active participants.[5] It was a public, not private, society. Its members were elected (Evelyn was himself nominated by Charles II) and dedicated themselves to the advancement of useful knowledge at home and abroad. Evelyn himself certainly was involved in scientific experiments: his Diary records attending experiments on snakes in Boyle's pneumatic engine, and on cures for viper bites; but he also was fascinated with mechanical instruments like the machine for weaving silk stockings, with architectural projects and urban street improvements, histories of different trades, and old paintings – taking his relations to see his Majesty's Cabinet at Whitehall ('rare miniatures' and other curiosities). In the Society he was a member of the Mechanical Committee and the 'Georgical' or Agricultural Committee (see Chapter Seven), and another that was established to discuss ways of preventing famine. And in the years after the Restoration, while Evelyn certainly expanded the scope of his involvements and his publications that attested to the range of these philosophical interests (including trades and science), I would argue that both *Sylva* and his 'Georgical' work did constitute a sufficient 'role' and, moreover, one that would give him a significant position in the landscaping affairs of his country during his own life, and thereafter. Even when he was ostensibly discussing air pollution in London, one of his proposals focused on establishing gardens and woodland.

He continued to write and publish in the years after 1660, producing not only the book with which he would be forever associated, *Sylva, or A Discourse of Forest-trees*, but books on fruit trees (*Pomona*), air pollution, libraries, fashion and engraving, and his *Mysteries of Jesuitism*. These were all dedicated, directly or indirectly, to his concern for promoting English ideas and practices at home and comparing them with those from foreign parts; many of these works pertained to his (again unfulfilled) history of 'Trades. Secrete & receipts mechanical', which was his own somewhat eccentric addition to Bacon's 'Catalogue of Particular Histories' that formed part of *Novum Organum*.[6]

His *Fumifugium* was provoked while walking in the palace at Whitehall, as he recounted in his 'Dedication' of it to the king. There he registered that 'a presumptuous smoke issuing from one or two tunnels near Northumberland House and not far from Scotland Yard, did so invade the Court, that all the rooms, galleries and places about it were filled and infested with it.' It was not the first time he had been made aware of this pollution, since in 1652 he had compared London's air unfavourably with the air of Paris. But in 1661 he saw it as a nuisance and hazard to Charles's own health, though his address 'To the Reader' of *Fumifugium* also insisted upon the 'universal benefit' to 'this Nation', especially after the late 'sad confusions' and the Restoration of 'a Prince of so magnanimous and public a spirit'. So he proposed what could be done for 'meliorating and refining the air of London'.

Most of *Fumifugium* addresses the 'hellish and dismal cloud of sea-coal' that hangs over wharfs and warehouses. If, as he argues, London has rendered wood into brick ('like another Rome') and brick has been made into glorious stone and marble, why should it wrap 'its stately head in Clouds of Smoke and Sulphur, so full of stink and darkness'? The vapours of smoke and smut will insinuate themselves into 'our very secret cabinets, and most precious repositories', yellow mould will infect pictures and tapestries, and bees and flowers will be spoilt in London's gardens.

After an expansive disquisition in Part One upon architects, similar putrefactions with a scattering of ancient wisdom, contemporary science and foreign examples, he makes two proposals: in Part Two, to banish several miles from London those responsible for the bad air – brewers, dyers, lime-burners, soap and salt boilers (but not fires associated with cooking); in Part Three, to make extensive plantings of trees, shrubs and flowers, whence scents and odours would waft over London from low-lying grounds from the east and southwest. It is essentially an extensive garden enterprise, modelled, as he notes himself, upon the Old Spring Garden in St James's Park and the new Spring Garden at Lambeth, which his Diary of 2 July 1661 called 'a pretty contriv'd plantation'. Fields of varying size are interspersed with 'shrubs, as yield the most fragrant and odiferous flowers, and are aptest to tinge the air upon every gentle emission at a great distance'. There follow lists of suitable plants, like jasmine, roses, rosemary; between the fences or palisades that enclose the plantations should be 'beds and borders' of pinks, carnations, cloves, stock-gilly-flower, primroses, auriculas, violets, not forgetting the white, which are in flower twice a year . . . cowslips, lilies, narcissus, strawberries, whose 'every leaves as well as fruit emit a cardique and mist refreshing halitus' (that is, vapour). These fields and crofts with the enclosures or 'environing gardens' can also be planted with crops (not cabbages, which smell unpleasantly), be used for recreation, provide nurseries 'for Ornament, Profit and Security', and afford better pasture for sheep and cattle. Tenements and 'nasty cottages', eyesores near the city, will also be prohibited.

But though Charles encouraged Evelyn to present a bill to Parliament, and one was drafted by the Queen's Attorney, which included a further prohibition of all 'several trades which are the cause of [London's smoke]', nothing came of it and the bill died. Evelyn's indignation and rhetoric continue to resonate to this day; a half-dozen re-editions of his text, including those by the National Smoke Abatement Society in 1933, the National Society for Clean Air in 1961, and an edition prefaced by a scientist at the National Center for Atmospheric Research in Colorado in 1969, make *Fumifugium* sound a lively note in a world still relying upon fossil fuel.[7]

A far less resonant topic today concerns Evelyn's satire on Frenchified clothing, brought in on the heels of Restoration courtiers, that he published in 1661 as *Tyrannus; or, the Mode* (it was, though, republished in 1951). He asked how can the English 'submit themselves' to French modes, when they dislike the nation so much? In Westminster Hall, Evelyn observed

> A fine silken thing . . . had so much ribbon on him as would have plundered six shops and set up twenty country pedlars. All the body was dressed like a May Pole or Tom a Bedlam's cap. A frigate newly rigged kept not half such a clatter in a storm as this puppet's streamers did . . .

Why indeed do we need 'such foreign butterflies'? Surely every nation has identified with its own fashion – the Swiss would not be a nation if they had abandoned their 'prodigious breeches', and when Romans gave up the toga, they declined. The king should resume the practice of making Sumptuary Laws – prescribing rational clothes in plain materials for the English. Evelyn was somewhat flummoxed the following year, too, by the 'monstrous fardingals' of the ladies with the new Portuguese queen, but he would have perhaps appreciated, during the wars with France, that Charles II gave up 'the French mode, which had hitherto obtained to our great expense and reproach' and took up 'solemnly' what Evelyn assumed were Persian fashions; not that this would, as Evelyn argued, have helped home industries to prosper. Today's sartorial wear and culture are random, bizarre and unpredictable, so his recommendations for specific wear for specific social occasions have lost their force, though that does not prevent fashion houses these days from promoting what Alexander Pope would explain as 'diff'rent styles with diff'rent subjects sort, / As several garbs with country, town and court'; maybe 'Persian' garb for Near Eastern vacations?

Publications during the 1660s all stemmed from his contacts with the Royal Society. In 1661 he published a translation ('interpretation', says its title page) of Gabriel Naudé's *Advis pour dresser une bibliothèque* (1627), on forming and building a library. Naudé had been librarian to both Richelieu and Mazarin and was a member of an erudite and freethinking society in France that included Pierre Gassendi, whom Evelyn had invoked for the epitaph to his Lucretius translation. Evelyn's own love of books and his continuing need to bring European ideas into England, including the need for libraries to be open and available, made him think that an English version of this text was needed. He had started a catalogue of his own library in 1653, substantially increased during the 1650s, fragments of which document survive, and he was constantly attentive to other libraries, including those of Oxbridge colleges and especially the Bodleian; he made notes on book classifications suitable for the Royal Society (BL, Add. MS 78344). The dedication to the Lord Chancellor was fulsome and much appreciated by Pepys ('a very fine piece'), even as he found the work itself 'beyond my reach'. Evelyn himself was not pleased with its printing mistakes, where he was 'at the mercy of sots & drunkards that can neither print sense nor English', and even tried to suppress it, though he distributed copies with his own *corrigenda* (Keynes, *Bibliophily*, p. 106). But the translation does contain the first mention of the term or title Royal Society, for Evelyn had envisaged its name and its function in his dedication to *Instruction Concerning Erecting of a Library*, where he twice used 'the name of the Royal Society' to refer to the new 'philosophic assembly', about which he was unashamedly pleased (see *Diary*, III.305).

The next year saw the publication of *Sculptura: or The History and Art of Chalcography and Engraving in Copper*, dedicated to Robert Boyle, which arose out of discussions and demonstrations at the 'Philosophic Club' at Gresham College. Evelyn's Diary credits Prince Rupert with introducing him to mezzotint, a method announced on its title page: he 'showed me with his own hand the new way of graving called *mezzo tinto*, which afterwards by his permission I published in my history of chalcography; this set so many artists on work that they soon arrived to that perfection it is since come, emulating the tenderest miniature' (*Diary*, III.274).

Evelyn wrote a further account of the laborious process, apparently to submit to the Royal Society, but it remained in manuscript until added to a modern edition.[8] The technique was indeed a useful advance, since it added a tonal process to the image that introduced patches of light in various shades of grey. A mezzotint by Rupert of the head of the executioner from a painting of John the Baptist, now in Munich, has made this a much sought-after work. But Evelyn's text is useful for its place in the historiography of print culture, its relation to an emerging antiquarianism, and his awareness of his sources: unsurprisingly, he searches far and wide in antiquity, but draws also on modern sources, like Abraham Bosse, Vasari's *Lives* and Johann Amos Comenius for his interest in pedagogy, which Evelyn takes up in his emphasis on children's education. It also includes the account by Sorbière of the life and virtuosity of Giacomo Favi, who announced his intention to publish a 'Complete Cycle and History of Trades', which obviously paralleled Evelyn's own interests; that life was added as 'an encouragement and example to the gentlemen of our nation, who, for the most part wander, and spend their time abroad, in the pursuit of pleasures, fruitless, and altogether intolerable'. But it is strange, in an age much given to the use of engraved illustrations, that *Sculptura* should contain only two other engravings, including a clumsy one drawn by Evelyn himself, engraved by Abraham Hertochs; Beale urged him in 1668 to issue another edition with more engravings, a proposal that came to nothing. But Darley conjectures (pp. 185–6) that it was advice from Evelyn about engravers that ensured another Royal Society book, Robert Hooke's *Micrographia* (1665), would have marvellous engravings of what scientists could now see through the microscope.

In 1664 he published two books. *The Mystery of Jesuitism*, dedicated to the scientist Sir Robert Moray, one of the founders of the Royal Society, being another translation from the French, was published without his name, 'so little credit there is in these days', he wrote to Boyle, 'in doing anything for the interest of religion' (partly reprinted in MW, p. 499). The other, infinitely more important, book, which gained him contemporary fame and a place in the narratives of English landscaping, was *Sylva*. Bray in 1852 notes that 'he [Evelyn] has often been known by the name of "Sylva Evelyn"', and the 1689 portrait of him, painted by Sir Godfrey Kneller at the request of Samuel Pepys, shows him holding a copy of *Sylva*, his 'bony fingers' (writes Mark Laird) grasping the volume 'emblematically' (*Celebration*, 103). What is emblematical is his contemporary fame as its author, and that this is the book and topic by which he is best known today.

A 'Discourse, concerning Forest-trees' was first delivered to members of the Royal Society on 15 October 1662. It was approved and commanded to be published by the Society's official printers, and thus *Sylva* became the first formal publication of the Royal Society. Other members of the Society contributed material from Germany, France and New England, and Beale provided material on fruit trees for the section on *Pomona* – so once again, the hand of Hartlib's 'office of address' was steering these collaborative efforts. Keynes notes that *Sylva* is a 'book nobody in recent times has read', which seems a bit unfair (Keynes, *Bibliophily*, p. 130);[9] but on the next page he adds that perhaps more 'scientific' writings have diminished what is still 'a wealth of interesting information and practical instruction'. To which we might add the light that Evelyn's knowledge of trees and tree planting throws upon the narrative of the forms of English landscaping that emerged in the later seventeenth century.[10]

Evelyn told his grandson in 1704, in anticipation that he would inherit Wotton, that the 'planting of timber-trees [is] in truth the only best and proper husbandry the estate is capable of' (*Memories*, p. 7). So he advised Jack to pursue 'those laudable diversions and improvements of your estate in Surrey, especially in an early and continual storing it with timber trees, oak, ash and elm, frequent copses, which in few years will prove no incredible emolument and restore the name of Wotton'.

He himself had known from his youth the arboreal riches of Surrey, and he always celebrated the woods at Wotton and praised them at every opportunity, as he did in writing to thank John Aubrey for sending observations on Surrey; for Wotton, he told Aubrey, is 'environed as it is with wood from whence it takes its denomination' (*MW*, pp. 687–91). During his travels on the Continent he constantly noted interesting and extraordinary trees, most of which were recorded without recourse to guidebooks: thus his enthusiasm for the street trees in Antwerp, the 'evenness & height' of a lime tree in a Dutch convent, and the citrus trees and groves of evergreens through Italy. And in subsequent excursions throughout England his central concern was always with woodland: he found a 'pretty finely wooded and watered estate' at his cousin's in Westerham, was pleased with the trees at Penshurst, was saddened at the overgrown trees at Beddington, though praised it for having the 'first Orange garden of England', and in Tunbridge Wells, where his wife was taking the 'medicinal' waters, he admired 'the extravagant turnings, insinuations, and growth of certain birch trees among the rocks' (*Diary*, III.294–5). In the introduction to *Sylva* itself, he comments frequently on specific trees and plantations ('a cloister of French elms in a little garden at Somerset House'), but also notes importations and their success – the 'vulgar Italian myrtle . . . supports all weathers', or the Alaternus, lately received from the hottest parts of Languedoc, 'thrives with us in England and is good for hedges'. At Sayes Court it was trees that he most relished and cared for, and for which he sought seeds and cuttings to replenish them. It was, as many visitors noticed, 'most Boscaresque', and an unnamed visitor commented that 'part of his garden is very woody and shady for walking'.[11]

So it is no surprise that *Sylva* would be infused with this enthusiasm for trees, but also with the need to advocate timber for England. The Royal Navy was the 'bulwarks of this nation' (*LB*, I.279), and timber was vital to furnish its 'wooden walls' for both military and commercial activity in the second half of the seventeenth century. Beyond the nation's need to produce the necessary timber for ship-building, his argument ensures that a landscape depleted during the Interregnum would flourish again with groves and forests. 'How goodly a sight were it', he wrote, 'if most of the desmesnes of our country gentlemen were crowned and encircled with such stately rows of limes, firs, elms and other ample and venerable trees as adorn New Hall in Essex . . . and our [own] neighbouring pastures'. Later editions praise the estates of Cassiobury (the Earl of Essex's, whose gardener was Moses Cook), Euston

(Lord Arlington's), Wimbledon, and Cornbury Park (Lord Clarendon's). These days 'stately' may largely mean lofty and perhaps regal, but for Evelyn it could also mean the state itself, and it was vital that private estates furnish timber for the Navy; yet beyond these necessary and national requirements, the amenities of 'walks and avenues' or 'venerable and stately arbour-walks' should be valued.[12]

Upon publication in 1664, copies of *Sylva* were presented to the Society, the king, the Lord Treasurer and the Lord Chancellor (illus. 25). On 26 February 1664 and again on 27 October in the Privy Garden, Evelyn received Charles's 'great thanks' and a 'long discourse with him of divers particulars' (*Diary*, III.369, 386–7). It must have pleased both Charles and Evelyn that one of the pageants that greeted the king's return to the City of London in 1660 had 'represented a great wood, with the royal oak, & history of his Majesty's miraculous escape in 1651 at Boscobel', when Charles hid himself in an oak tree after the battle of Worcester.

Sylva had a second edition in 1670, where Evelyn was proud to affirm that the book had been 'the sole occasion of furnishing your [Charles's] almost exhausted dominions with more than two millions of timber-trees; besides infinite others, which have been propagated within the three nations, at the instigation and by the direction of this work'. There was a third edition in 1679, and a fourth in 1706, the year of his death, with the spelling of the title now changed to *Silva*. A fifth appeared in 1729, an abridged edition in 1827 and a 'new edition' in 1908. But in 1776 an extended and heavily annotated text was published by Dr Alexander Hunter of York, noting how corrupt had been editions after the author's

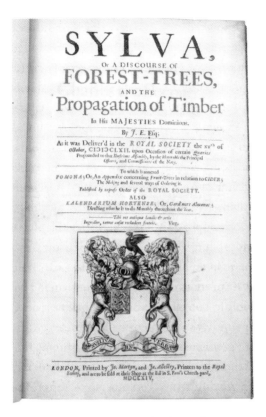

death; he prints his own notes at the foot of every page below Evelyn's original text; among its large subscribers' list was the name of Lancelot Brown. *Hunter's Silva* had four more editions, now in two volumes, the last of which appeared in 1825.

Evelyn's most famous book had something of a fresh afterlife in 2014: with support of the Sylva Foundation, *The New Sylva: A Discourse of Forest and Orchard Trees for the Twenty-first Century* by Gabriel Hemery and Sarah Simblet appeared; this elegant publication, with modern woodcuts by Simblet, is annotated in red in such a way as to give an effect of

25 John Evelyn, title page of *Sylva; or, A Discourse of Forest-trees and the Propagation of Timber . . .* (London, 1664).

seventeenth-century printing. Its text lists the trees of
Evelyn's volume with a single quotation from him at the head
of each chapter and occasional citations in their own modern
and up-to-date 'scientific' descriptions. So, while *Sylva* has now
a new audience, it is still not Evelyn's book, though it might
send people back to one of his editions. Its continued publication addresses our own modern concern with and need to
understand and enrich our forests and environments.

The first edition of *Sylva* also contained not only his *Kalendarium Hortense,* but *Pomona: or, an Appendix concerning fruit-trees
in relation to cider.*[13] To the second edition he added chapters on
the 'Poplar, Aspen, Abele' and on 'Alder', and expanded other
chapters on individual trees; further, 'An historical account of
the sacredness and the use of standing groves', which Keynes
thought (somewhat unfairly) a 'tedious discourse in the
manner, though unfortunately not in the spirit of, Sir Thomas
Browne. The erudition is there, but the music and the art-
istry are lacking' (*Bibliophily,* p. 132. This appeared as chapter
35 in the second edition, but reached its final form as Book
IV in the 1706 edition.) Yet it is ultimately on modern groves
that Evelyn's wide-ranging approach is focused, and his translation of ancient sources (Virgil, Horace, Petrarch) is designed
to bring a tradition of groves into contemporary culture: not
everything has to be novel and new, 'as if novelty only should
be of more force to engage our enquiry into the causes of
things, than the worth and magnitude of the things themselves'. He is 'inclined to believe' ancient perspectives because
they still teach us to observe the natural world afresh. More
importantly, Virgil, who saw groves as the final dwelling of
the blessed, can find a modern appreciation in the notion

that groves were still 'a kind of heaven on earth' (thus Thomas Traherne in his poem 'Ease', from the 1670s[14]). We have often lost this significance, as William Blake put it later in *The Marriage of Heaven and Hell*: 'Thus, men forgot that all deities reside in the human breasts.' But well before moderns decided they would like to hug trees, an affection for groves, woodlands and forests is a resonant, appreciated inclination; we may not care whether Moses's burning bush was in fact a grove, but if (as Evelyn argues) 'Paradise itself was but a kind of . . . temple, or sacred grove, planted by God himself and given to man' as the first priest, then we must still care that woodlands survive, in the Amazonian forests or anywhere, as we are their custodians, if not their priests. Nor is it irrelevant, in the light of Evelyn's struggles with Lucretius, that Traherne found that atoms expressed 'another glory of the soul'.

The third edition was augmented with three further pieces – Abraham Cowley's poem 'The Garden', a translation by his son of Rapin's *Nemus* (that is, grove, or wood with glades and pasture), and Evelyn's essay on *Terra, a Philosophical Discourse of Earth*; both *Terra* and Cowley's poem had been published earlier. To the fourth edition of 1706 Evelyn added *Acetaria, a Discourse of Sallets*, which had also appeared seven years before. This last edition in his lifetime added an engraved portrait of himself, aged thirty, taken in Paris by Natteuil, to suggest perhaps his longstanding and youthful absorption with trees; in January 1696/7 he recalled that he had been 'foolishly fond of these and other rustications' of his youth, 'which had been my sweet diversions during the days of destruction and dev-astation both of woods and buildings, whilst the Rebellion lasted so long' (Keynes, *Bibliophily*, p. 135).

Other augmentations to later editions of *Sylva/Silva* involved engravings, which increased considerably after his death. While the first contained simply a diagram of how to store logs, the second, now 'much enlarged and improved', had engravings for a machine to grub up tree roots, one for drawing sap from a tree, and other machines for sawing timber and boring tree trunks for pipes. Posthumous editions branched out (the pun is contagious, as Evelyn himself, in 'To the Reader', plays with laborious metaphors pulled from timber talk, like the reader encouraged to pull sap from the 'dry sticks' of his book) with more illustrations. In Hunter's 1776 *Silva* there are forty plates, which visually document Evelyn's 'living gallery of aged trees': these include four engravings of the Green Dale Oak at Welbeck, the Cawthorpe Oak, near Wetherby (illus. 26, 27), and descriptions of others like the Great Oak in Salcey Forest (Northamptonshire).

Two chapters of *Sylva* can usefully suggest the range and the quality of Evelyn's writing: one on elm trees, and (now citing the expanded third edition) Chapter XXX, 'Of the Age, Stature, and Felling of Trees'. That his work was admired for its 'elegancy and eloquence' but equally criticized for its 'embellishments & flourishes'[15] suggest one reason why it has not, as Keynes argues, seen much modern readership. Yet its range, its combination of enthusiasm with observation and (as Bowle notes) 'recondite and curious learning' (drawing often on his commonplace books), make *Sylva* a continuing model for any who wish to elevate discussions of gardening and arboriculture.

Evelyn had already praised elms in various parts of Paris; now, he says (and this heads the relevant chapter in *The New*

26, 27 Two engravings from Alexander Hunter's 1776 edition of Evelyn's *Silva*.

Sylva, p. 176) it is a tree that 'does not thrive so well in the forest, as where it may enjoy scope for the roots to dilate and spread at the sides, as in hedge-rows and avenues, where they have the air likewise free'. It has many uses: being able to survive both wet and dry, it is therefore 'proper for water-works, mills, the ladles, and soles of the wheel pumps, aqua-ducts, pales, ship-planks beneath the water-line'; even buried in bogs, they survive 'like the most polished and hardest ebony'. It is also tolerant of how it is planted, for while it 'delights in a sound, sweet, and fertile land', more inclined to 'loamy moisture, and where good pasture is produced', it can prosper equally in gravels, as long as there is a depth of mould and it is 'refreshed with springs'. Evelyn planted them in his home and west fields at Sayes Court in 1664, just as Charles II had ordered to be done in Greenwich Park. An illustration of its leaves and seeds was published in Hunter's 1776 *Silva*, opposite page 119.

The other chapter is wide-ranging, a compendium of what Evelyn terms 'instances' of tree age, stature, girth and felling. It depends upon his own observation and first-hand experience ('measured by myself'). He fondly allows memories of a huge tree that his grandfather felled, a large plank of which was made into a pastry-board and was kept at Wotton. But for the most part he draws upon other readings, other authorities both ancient and modern, and even upon the much vaguer 'I am told' or 'I am informed' – as with a letter from Sir Thomas Browne in Norwich – describing a lime tree in Depeham. He has learned, maybe from Hartlib, the virtues of useful collaboration in such inquiries: he had written to John Wilkins in 1661 that he hoped for many occasions on which he could share correspondence with members of the Royal Society.

Both here and throughout the book there are frequent appeals to, and occasional dissents from, Theophrastus, Cicero, Pliny, Strabo, Varro, Virgil, Eusebius and Petrarch, and to what ancient writers like Xerxes had written of trees and timber. But he needs also to rely on 'our modern authors', since his emphasis on 'all the liberal and useful arts' means that for recent English expertise he must call upon those 'who love the solid honour and ornament of their country'. Hence the invocation of Bacon, Nehemiah Grew, Beale, Plot, Thomas Tusser, Markham and William Lawson, to which he adds 'foreigners'. Some older and recent verses are printed in black type, and a Latin poem by Beale at the start of *Sylva* is extracted and quoted throughout.

The geographical range of sites where trees are noted and recorded is extensive: from Lorraine, Flanders, Moravia, Mt Aventine in Rome, Barbados and New England (good for producing firs for ship masts), and Persia for cypresses, to pear trees in Herefordshire, important specimens in Gloucestershire and Oxfordshire, ending with some extensive notes on trees at Sheffield Park and Worksop Park. Yet in respect of all his sources and references, he warns that the reader must only abstract 'things practical, of solid use, and material, from the ostentation and impertinence of writers, who . . . swell their monstrous volumes . . . upon the credulous world'. And again, it is 'far easier to make than to find a good husbandman; I have often proved it so in gardens'. An empirical insistence on the making of place, or at least searching for what good husbandry and garden-making could be discovered in England, serves him also in his 'Georgical' work, which forms, besides *Sylva*, the other major contribution to his landscaping legacy.

SEVEN

The 'Georgical' Committee

YLVA WAS ONE of several, and the most important, of the published works that Evelyn devoted to an understanding and description of England landscape, especially the materials of its trees, forests and gardens. It was published two years after the formation, in 1662, of what was called the 'Georgical' Committee of the Royal Society, named after Virgil's agricultural poem the *Georgics*.[1] This committee included Evelyn, John Beale, John Ogilby, Robert Plot, John Aubrey and Henry Oldenburg, among others, and it attracted correspondents, if not active members, like the poet Henry Vaughan. Aubrey noted his own election to the committee, which has 'thirty-two members and will collect information on the history of gardening and agriculture in England, Scotland and Ireland. We will draft a set of questions and send them out to knowledgeable people in different regions'.[2]

The committee's homage to Virgil was particularly contemporary and apt, the poet a valued predecessor and model. Virgil had first taken up agriculture in the *Georgics*, where he promised, but did not fulfil his wish, to write also a poem about gardens; at the very start of Cowley's essay 'Of Agriculture', he says that 'the first wish of Virgil . . . was to be a

good philosopher; the second, a good husbandman', and at
the end he appended his translation of part of *Georgics*, Book
2. Translations of Virgil's works by Ogilby and by Dryden, in
1654 and 1697 respectively, included engravings of English-
looking landscapes and agriculture (illus. 28). These were used
to illustrate not only the *Georgics*, but Virgil's epic poem, the

28 Illustration from John Ogilby's translation of Virgil.

Aeneid, which narrated the founding of Rome. Since England was, as *Fumifugium* noted, the 'new Rome', English landscapes could not only be properly used to illustrate Virgil's poetry, but could equally testify to the agriculture of that 'new Rome'.

Evelyn finds his place in this English landscape inquiry with several works: *Sylva* has been discussed in the previous chapter; its fourth book or 'Dendrologia' of 1706, 'An Historical Account of the Sacredness and Use of Standing Groves', drew attention to their use in modern parklands. *Sylva's* third edition in 1679 added two pieces: the *Kalendarium Hortense*, and a topic that had been separately published three years before, a *Discourse of Earth*, which by the third edition was subtitled *Terra*. This makes sense: earth or soil is the groundwork of gardening, husbandry and the cultivation of timber, and the textual Imprimatur of *Earth* notes that it 'concerned agriculture'. Aubrey, too, was fascinated by soils and the different clays to be found in Wiltshire. Jonson's 'Penshurst' specifically celebrates soil as well as air, wood and water.

Discourse of Earth proceeds in great detail through a considerable agenda, but at a general remove from specific mention of site or place, though it is abundantly clear that the remarks were based on observations and experience. *Earth* clearly sprang from Evelyn's own gardening concerns, as well as from what the Society's correspondents contributed on all aspects of the landscape that form and sustain its natural materials, including the earth; as a member of the 'Georgical' Committee Evelyn would have had access to replies to its queries and questionnaires. The *Discourse* was first delivered at a meeting of the Society in June 1675, the week after Sir Robert Southwell had spoken on the topic of water, and it was first printed in *Philosophical Transactions* 10, probably longer than its original *viva voce* presentation. It acknowledges, among others, Hesiod, Theophrastus, Platt, Digby (now approvingly), Laurenbergis, Bacon, Boyle and especially Beale, 'from whom I have long since received the choicest documents upon this and many more curious subjects'. Yet he is not above passing the comment 'and if that be true' about a remark of Boyle's, and even more strenuously, having cited Bacon's notion on the effect on the soil where the rainbow ends, suggests that is 'may be very fallacious', not least because there are two ends to a rainbow!

In dedicating the *Discourse of Earth* to the President of the Royal Society, Evelyn played down its importance by noting that a 'thousand things of infinite more value' would better add to members' collections; but his own preamble then seems pleased to have 'once again pitch'd upon a subject of somewhat a more brisk and lively nature; for what is there in Nature so sluggish and dull as Earth? What more spiritual and active than vegetation, and what the earth produces?' A detailed discussion then follows of earth's components, forms, amendments and uses and how it is relevant 'to the use of the husbandman, the forester, and the gardener'. He accordingly explores in great detail many kinds of soil: what earth best suits, for example, the coronary garden, or which soil suits fruit trees; how the senses respond to and identify different soils, how different types of rain affect different soils, how compost may be created and treated, and the ways in which dung can improve earth: the dung of asses is best, because they 'chew more', but as there are few asses 'in this country', he passes to other more available resources.

What Evelyn's text called his 'dull discourse' on earth, mould and soil was eminently typical of the Society's mixture of first-hand observations, instinct for curiosity and even wonder, and citation of ancient and modern authorities, yet marked by scepticism. The conclusions of this general and theoretical treatise are grounded on innumerable particularities. The following passage, chosen in part because he had been alert to the different microclimates found in the physic garden in Paris, suggests his habitual mode of discourse (it is quoted from the third edition of *Sylva* of 1670, where *Terra* was included):

> Whatever then it be in which the earth contribute, or whether it contain universally a seminal virtue, so specified by the air, influences, and genius of the clime, as to make that a cinnamon tree in Ceilon [Ceylon], which is but a bay in England, is past my skill to determine; but 'tis to be observed with no little wonder, what Monsieur Bernier in his History of the Empire of the Mogol [sic] affirms to us of a mountain there, which produces on one side of it intolerably hot, Indian plants, and on the other, as intemperately cold, European and vulgar.

Evelyn's early interest in understanding landscape was fuelled by his youth around Wotton, and by his attention in Europe to landscapes, its culture of buildings, gardens and their related history and even by the legends that were provoked during his travels. Later when revising his diaries he used his readings of Pflaumern's *Mercurius Italicus*, Totti's *Ritratto di*

Roma moderna, Sandys's *Relation of a Journey*, Raymond's *Itinerary* and Lassels's *Voyage of Italy*, all of which reminded him of how landscape was the foundation of the Roman land that Virgil celebrated.[3] Once returned to England and finding that he was exploring more of his own country (as on his northward journey with his wife in 1654), it became of paramount importance to provide similar, yet more authoritative, descriptions of the particularities and curiosities of England. And his frequent excursions after the Restoration, if primarily urged by his inquiry into woodlands and country estates, were a major contribution that he would make to the 'Georgical' Committee.

English interest in the culture and history of its landscape was not new: William Camden's *Britannia* (1586, with a sixth, enlarged edition in 1607) was written in Latin, but translated in 1610; Michael Drayton's *Poly-olbion* (1622) was still being cited in the early eighteenth century by William Kent, who annotated his *capriccio* of Hampton Court and Esher with some lines from it concerning English rivers.[4] But the Royal Society's dedication to inquire into English landscapes, topography and their use in both the past and present required empirical observation. An insistence on 'history' or 'histories', rather than on fable, myth or other superstitions, was a central theme of the early English Enlightenment: 'Natural Philosophy, next to God's Word,' wrote Joshua Childrey in 1661, 'is the most Sovereign Antidote to expel the poison of Superstition'.[5] Superstition was by the second half of the seventeenth century a dominant topic for probing and discounting: Aubrey, like Sir Thomas Browne, was constantly preoccupied with recording and sometimes questioning the actions of witches, accounts of people turned into stones, or

Britannia Baconica:

Or, The Natural

RARITIES

O F

England, Scotland,& Wales.

According as they are to be found in every
S H I R E.

Hiſtorically related, according to the Precepts of the Lord *Bacon*; Methodically dige-
ſted; and the Cauſes of many of them
Philoſophically attempted.

omens conveyed by weather.[6] Evelyn, as noted earlier, noted
'Superstitions still remaining among us' in a notebook of
'Adversaria'.

Childrey's *Britannia Baconia, or, The Natural Rarities of England,
Scotland and Wales* was written 'according to the Precepts of the
Lord Bacon' (illus. 23). In this, Childrey was one of many
contemporaries following and exemplifying the 'agenda' set
out in Bacon's work, in particular Bacon's 'Catalogue of
Particular Histories by Titles', or *Sylva Silvarum*.[7] Not unlike
Sir Thomas Browne's similar approach to vulgar errors in his
*Pseudodoxia Epidemica, or, Enquiries into Very Many Received Tenents,
and Commonly Presumed Truths*, first published in 1646 and with
five revised editions until 1672, Childrey negotiated his way

29 Detail of the title page of Joshua Childrey's *Britannia Baconica; or, The
Natural Rarities of England, Scotland and Wales* (1661).

past dubious concepts, based on his own empirical study of British topography, geology and sometimes fauna; he argued that people must 'attend to observation' (B5r). Otherwise, he relied either on citing early 'authorities' like Camden, on his own sceptical instinct, or by falling back on phrases like 'as it is reported' or 'They say' (p. 158). But his concern was with mirroring British landscape, and – unlike some later writers in the seventeenth century – he refused to 'meddle with matter of Antiquity, Pedigrees, or the like' (B2r). His preface did what many Englishmen did, making boastful comparisons, sometimes laughable, between their own country and Italy: thus England, says Childrey, has its equivalents – Italy had Virgil's Grotto and the Sybil's Cave, but Somerset has Wookey Hole (B1r)! Similarly, while the manuscript of Robert Plot's *Oxfordshire* records that Sir Timothy Tyrrels's seat enjoyed 'the bella vista of Italy [that] is pretty well imitated', when the book was published in 1677 the Italian reference is dropped, and he simply applauds the 'pleasant vista' of the Chilterns scenery.

The 'Georgical' Committee promoted an interest in local history, in part by promoting mapping, chorography and archaeological discovery. John Ogilby's *Britannia Depicta; or, The Traveller's Guide; or, A Most Exact Description of the Roads of England* (1675) utilized ribbon maps to document routes for both walkers and riders, noting items of local meaning and explanations of what was to be seen, an instructive way of viewing the English landscape. Each route delineates a stretch of road, for example from London to Bagshot, Surrey, in a map and an image ('scenographically, or in Prospect', Ogilby writes), then notes mileage and whatever the traveller should notice to left or to right of his route. Cartographic portrayal of Britain could not be accomplished without a careful and detailed accumulation of empirical evidence on sites, which could then be registered in maps; this required recovering the meaning and association of places, listing and identifying monuments, ruins and other archaeological remains and records of antiquity. Childrey had tackled some of these items – like Stonehenge in his discussion of Wiltshire. Aubrey in particular, as well as stressing the importance of an English chorography, had visited and sketched both Stonehenge and Avebury Circle with far more attention and care, long before he joined the 'Georgical' Committee.[8] But its members wished to extend such inquiries, by printing and circulating questionnaires, entitled 'Enquiries' or 'Queries', that asked for information on a whole agenda of these topographical matters.[9]

The questionnaires asked for what were termed 'observables', that is, what could be seen or observed while walking the land. One member, Oldenburg, drew up a document on which to base 'inquiries for all Counties' in England, asking about such items as water and earth – the topics discussed by the Royal Society in 1675 – but also about 'air, plants, animals, minerals, and famous inhabitants of particular locales'.[10] These enquiries would be sent to parish clergy and other literate landowners. In a request by Ogilby, dated 1673 (illus. 30), designed to support his 'Description of Britannia', he sought information on urban centres, houses and their topography – 'mountains, valleys . . . rivers, brooks, [and] springs'. A manuscript annotation on this Query notes that this was discussed ('considered') by Christopher Wren and John Aubrey, among others.[11] Robert Plot printed his 'Enquiries' in 1674,[12]

QUERIES

In Order to the Description of

BRITANNIA.

WHEREAS *John Ogilby* Esq; His Majesties *Cosmographer*, being Authoriz'd by His Majesty to make an *Actual Survey* of His Majesties Kingdom of *England* and Dominion of *Wales*, in order to the Compiling *An Historical and Geographical Description* thereof, more Accurate than whatever has been heretofore done, in a fair large Volume, still d *BRITANNIA*: accompanied with another Volume of all the Principal ROADS of *England*, Ichnographically describ d in Copper Sculptures. And being sensible that the Well-performance hereof will render it a Work highly grateful to the Publick, his Request is, That the Nobility and Gentry, and all other Ingenious Persons, would be pleas'd to return him, to his House in *White-Fryers, London*, such Remarques of the Country or Places of their Residence, or what other they may be acquainted with, as shall happen within the Verge of these following *Queries*.

1. *Cities*, their Antiquity, Government, Privileges, Commerce, &c.
2. *Towns Corporate, Market-Towns, Fair Towns, Villages, and Hamlets, &c.*
3. *Houses of Nobility* and *Gentry*, with the ancient as well as present Possessors.
4. *Castles, Churches, Chappels, Schools, Colleges, Hospitals*, and other *Publick Buildings, &c.*
5. *Mills, Beacons, Bridges, Crosses, Towers, Pyramids.*
6. *Chaces, Forests, Woods, Groves, Parks, Warrens, Commons, Heaths, &c.*
7. *Mountains, Valleys, Dikes, Rivers, Brooks, Water-works, Sluces, Ponds, Meres, &c.*
8. *Springs, Wells, Baths*, Cold and Hot Waters, Medicinal, Aluminous, Bituminous, Nitrous, Petrifying, &c.
9. *Works* and *Mines* of Gold, Silver, Copper, Lead, Black-lead, Tin, Iron, Salt, Salt-petre, Allom, Coperas, *Gems, Precious Stones, Glass, Crystal, Marble, Alabaster, Plaister, Fullers-Earth, Ochre, Tobacco-pipe Clay, Potters Clay, Lime, Chalk, Marl, Freestone, Millstone, Grindstone, Whetstone.*
10. *Precincts* of *Dioceses, Bounds* and Limits of Counties, Hundreds, and Parishes, Peculiars, and Privileg'd Places.
11. *Roman Ways* and *Stations, Coins* and *Monuments*, and other Antiquities.
12. *Extraordinary Accidents, Calamities*, and *Casualties.*
13. *Peculiar Customs* and *Manners.*
14. *Decay'd Places*, whether Cities, Towns, Castles, Monasteries, Abbies, or other Houses of Note.
15. *Vaults, Caves, Caverns, Holes, Hollows, Subterraneous Passages*, or other Rarities.
16. *Places* of Birth, Education, Habitation, and Sepulture of *Eminent Persons.*
17. *Improvements* in Husbandry, Mechanicks, Manufactures, &c.
18. *Extraordinary Productions* of Cattel, Fowl, Fruit, Plants, Herbs, or other Animals or Vegetables.
19. What Part of the Country is *Arable, Pasture, Meadow, Woods*, and *Champain.*
20. On the Sea-coasts, *Ports, Harbors, Havens, Creeks, Peels, Peers, Watch-Towers, Land-marks, Light-houses, Sands, Sholes, Islands, Eits*, &c.
21. *Productions* of the Sea-coasts, of *Fish, Shell-fish, Amber, Jet, Coral, Herbs, &c.*
22. *Extraordinary* or Irregular *Ebbings* or *Flowings* of the Sea, &c.

To such Ingenious Persons as shall be more Eminently Instrumental herein, either by themselves or others, the Author will make Honorable Returns of Books, and carefully discharge whatever necessary Expences shall appear to have been laid out in this Concern.
And to whom Money shall be more acceptable, the Author promises such Wages and Allowances as may handsomly correspond their Pains; Always presuming, That nothing will be impos d upon him, without sufficient Authority for its Assertion; Truth being the main of his Design in all his Collections.

From the Office in White-Fryers, London Anno 1673.

These Queries were considered of at severall meetings by F. a.

Christopher Wren. U.D.
John Hoskyns Esq R.S.S.
Robert Huck R.S.S.
Mr Jo. Ogilby
m Jo. Aubrey
m Gregory King

asking observers travelling through England and Wales to
supply materials on climate, 'waters', 'Earths and Minerals'
and 'stones'; he also sought information on vineyards and
'curious Gardens for rare plants'. Others, like Thomas Machell
in 1676–7, requested that his enquiries be answered by indict-
ing the exact topic, marked with a T, R or E (that is, tradition,
record or personal 'experience'); Machell would also ask
whether churches be 'elegant or mean'.[13] These requests for
information were destined for volumes or histories somewhat
different from Childrey's book, which he designed for the use
of the 'vulgar' (A8r) and the 'gentry' (B1r), and published as
a small volume suitable to carry in the pocket while travelling.
His was a rudimentary guide, covering all the English counties
often very skimpily, whereas the Committee wanted a far
more systematic and extensive inventory.

Yet with so much varied and miscellaneous information
circulating and arriving for consideration by the Committee,
not much found its way into publication. Among the interesting manuscripts focused on 'Georgical' matters that either
remained unpublished or waited some time before appearing
were Aubrey's 'Designation de Easton-Piers in Co: Wilts',
'The Natural History of Wiltshire' and 'A Perambulation of
Surrey' (all now held in the Bodleian Library), John Beale's
letters on garden matters (in the Hartlib papers at Sheffield),
Aubrey's 'Monumenta Britannica',[14] and Evelyn's own 'Elysium
Britannicum'. Some of these Enquiries and Queries did result
in publication: Aubrey published his *Natural History of Surrey* in
1718, but Evelyn had already corresponded with him about
this in 1673. Robert Plot's Enquiries bore fruit in his books
on *Oxfordshire* in 1677 and *Staffordshire* in 1686–8; Evelyn owned

a copy of Plot's *Oxfordshire* and subscribed to the *Staffordshire* volume. The 'Georgical' Committee's endeavours continued to draw in both Society members and others whose works were in the same vein: *The Ancient and Present State of Gloucestershire* (1712) by Robert Atkins, elected a fellow of the Royal Society in 1664, John Morton's *Natural History of Northamptonshire* (1712), and *The History of Kent* (1718) by John Harris, elected a fellow of the Society in 1696.[15] On Ireland came work by William Molyneux and Sir Robert Sibbald, on Wales by Lewis Morris and Thomas Pennant, and Martin Martin's *Description of the Western Islands of Scotland* in 1703.

On the title page of his *Staffordshire*, Plot, Keeper of the Ashmolean Museum in Oxford, placed a biblical motto: 'Ye shall describe the land, and bring the descriptions hither to me' (Joshua 18:6), but now the recipient of this injunction was not so much Joshua or God as natural philosophers in the land of England with sufficient curiosity to seek out and describe the land themselves. One of the dedicatory verses to *Staffordshire* applauds the fruit that can now be plucked from a modern 'inlightened tree', as opposed to the forbidden tree in the Garden of Eden.

Plot's volumes consisted of chapters on heavens and air (what we would call climate), earth, stones both found and shaped, plants, beasts, men and women, arts and antiquities. But their indexes are more revealing: *Oxfordshire* lists buildings of eminent and minor nobility (that is, local gentry), and both volumes annex armorial shields as evidence of inhabitants and their families (matters that Childrey had excluded). Indexes also note old or unusual trees 'of vast Bigness', walks and 'other curiosities in trees' of the sort that

Sylva addressed; but also barrows, burials, ley lines, waterworks, quarries, prospects, mills 'of a rare contrivance', fishponds and different soils for husbandry. The plates for *Oxfordshire* largely depict, not prospects or buildings, but plants native to that county. It is significantly in the Staffordshire volume – only ten years after that on Oxfordshire – that we see a huge increase in engravings of places, prospects and agriculture; images of houses suggest the land and estates that lay around them. *Staffordshire's* index focused on industry (coal and coal-pits), but also on 'Gardens, some curious hedgerows', walks of pleasure, and vistas or pleasant lawns in parks and woodland. Some engravings of buildings do little more than depict the fabric of the facade, but other images show gardens, the larger landscape of woods and fields, topography and the lie of the land, with cattle sometimes and always with humans, those who worked the land, their owners, or passers-by.

These 'Georgical' endeavours therefore drew upon many responses, one example of which provided by John Beale is discussed below. But their work arguably also fuelled later landscaping ideas of picturesque explorations of England, and that topic too needs to be explored.

Before Evelyn's membership of the 'Georgical' Committee, he had received a variety of observations from John Beale on landscape and gardening, examples of those choice 'documents upon many curious subjects' that clearly helped to shape *Sylva* and parts of 'Elysium Britannicum' as well as his understanding of how land was to be understood and shaped. In 1659 these included draft plans for both a 'Physic Garden' and 'A Garden of Pleasure', and a long letter on a specific landscape, Backbury Hill in Herefordshire, where Beale envisaged how it might be landscaped into an ideal garden. While the letter has been construed by several commentators as a plea for natural or even 'Picturesque' gardening (that is, eighteenth-century landscape aesthetics *avant la lettre*), it is far more important to situate it in the period when it was written and how it spoke to current perceptions of English landscape.[16]

Beale's two plans address 'soils' and manure for botanical gardens, and a necessarily varied topography for different types of plants, including a note on how ladies may find out 'unforbidden fruit'. For pleasure gardens, he specifies a more detailed agenda, but notes, as a preliminary, that it is not necessary to enforce a site in 'any particular phantasy'; thus he would devise 'an insinuating paradox', whereby the mysteries of art would be selected that are fittest for a specific design, for 'the productions of nature' would be superior to 'the charge [that is, expense] and cumber of art'. Gardens should find room for 'novel experiments' yet accommodate wild plants and work for the benefit of mankind. Both schemes invoke Pliny, Virgil and Columella as well as Bacon, Sir Henry Wotton and other contemporaries like Benjamin Worsley.

The letter admitted that 'hortulan affairs do require varieties of novel & conceited amenities', and Beale wrote that he intended to put them into chapters of a book, though now they were 'only shuffled together as a loose preface'. He proceeds to address one specific landscape and a possible reformulation of it, in the light of having seen Evelyn's outline of 'Elysium Britannicum', to which Beale now recommends adding chapters on scenic entertainments, breeding or 'transmutation' of flowers as regards beauty, taste and scent, and another on 'mounts, prospects, precipices & caves'. These suggestions conformed to current experimental ideas and were taken up in 'Elysium'.

The proposal Beale advances for Backbury Hill (along the lines of that 'insinuating paradox') is both attentive to the natural site, which he describes carefully, and the wish to understand it as an 'antique Garden . . . [that] shall as much excel most of the rest of those gardens'. This is premised on his confidence that 'God's own handiwork [in Eden, or maybe the creation of the world] did far exceed our modern gardens,' where he sees only costly work in a 'narrow, mimical way'. The 'enchanted walks, pyrhian vaults, legislative mountains, the hills of blessings, of cursings; the Muses fountain' that he will rediscover in Backbury Hill consist of a large green garden ('a perfect resemblance of an ancient flower garden'), thickets of oaks, a precipice, prospects, a natural echo, pastures, a spring and a river; all these will make of this Herefordshire site a perfect example of England, for 'how little some narrow hearted people do understand their own happiness.' (A similar appeal to shape a better England had also been made in his 1657 book on *Herefordshire Orchards, a Pattern for All England*.) In the letter he takes up ideas that seem to find their way later into Evelyn's *Fumifugium* – such as perfuming the adjacent countryside with 'hedge rows of our old English friend the sweet eglantine, or of the later lilacs', a lesson that London could learn in order to end the 'corrosive smoke of their sea coal'. Without assessing costs for this ideal garden (for he excludes – that is, does not include in his calculations – expenses for buildings, walls, statues, cisterns and horticultural 'workmanship'), he will form the indigenous materials and establish 'banks, walks, squares, or other figures for flowers, vineyards . . . hedges of all sorts'. He addresses 'what sort of trees . . . may be allowed for the ornament of the flowery regions, & to determine, whether _viridaria_, _vireta_, walks, mounds, groves & prospects be the principal, or ought to be so, & the flowery area but the trimmings (as spires, pilasters, & carved works in solid architecture'. While Backbury Hill had not been (as Hartlib liked to think) a Roman site, Evelyn certainly agreed that it was a worthy landscape 'in our own country'.

The letter is not entirely free of muddles – as he says himself, it was shuffled into a preface, and he finds it difficult to explain a phrase, 'indicative plants', that he had used in the pleasure garden; his self-confessed enthusiasm and inclination to dabble with matters that would infuriate Puritans carries him away.[17] But Evelyn, with Beale's permission, inserted the letter into his manuscript of 'Elysium Britannicum', where its themes consorted with classical writers on husbandry and with the work of modern 'terraculturists' who use 'natural philosophy' to explore an understanding of the world as they found it in England; Evelyn's own contribution is a strongly biblical emphasis that takes further Beale's gestures to 'God's own handiwork'.

Beale said also that his design was to 'rectify and purify' landscape; so Evelyn also must have glimpsed in Beale's proposed garden the sense that an art of gardens refined, epitomized, the unmediated wilder world and even the agricultural landscape. For beyond his sense that natural effects needed to be made more palpable or visible when used in gardens, Beale implied that there were hierarchies of design, whereby a layout would diminish in artifice as it moved further from the house or a fixed point in the landscape. Evelyn had seen that sequence or dialogue of forms at both Fontainebleau and in Italian villas around Rome; Hartlib, too, in Figure 112b of *A Discourse for Division or Setting Out of Land* (1653) set out a diagram for topographical layouts that established a hierarchy of control or geometry across the land, sometimes realized on an estate, or sometimes merely proposed. At least for Evelyn the purpose of this hierarchy was to educate humans in an appreciation of the ideal perfection of God's handiwork in the larger world of nature: within a garden, the eye and mind were trained to see perfect forms that needed to be intuited and apprehended when the visitor moved outside the garden.[18]

A second and related theme was Evelyn's focus on how the land should be worked or 'traded' (evidence, that is, of his unfulfilled history of all the trades). His communications with Beale, Hartlib and Aubrey suggest some ways in which their ideas would *eventually* bear fruit in eighteenth-century landscape ideas and aesthetics. This is not a question of tracking a growing 'naturalism' in landscape design, for that is clearly not what Beale writes about. But what is striking in some of their exchanges is how 'ancient' horticulture could be seen as sufficiently modern. Yet it is clear that the seeds of what would come to be acclaimed in the Picturesque movement in the eighteenth century were sown in the work of the 'Georgical' Committee and its associates; but the focus in each case was different. This can be explained briefly by comparing late seventeenth-century attitudes to topography, accidents and aspects of culture and land with the writings of someone like William Gilpin a century later; Gilpin's publications, significantly entitled *Observations* on different parts of Britain, had an enormous effect on its inhabitants' understanding and appreciation of their own landscape, but these books did not spring fully formed from his excursions into the British landscape.

To take one example, from the opening section of Gilpin's *Observations on the River Wye*, the first of his tours in 1770, though only published in 1782: his title recalls the Royal Society's pre-mium on observation, and he writes that 'We travel for various purposes – to explore the culture of soils – to view the curi-osities of art – to survey the beauties of nature – and to learn the manners of men; their different politics, and modes of life.' Such a remark echoes Evelyn's remarks on his European and his English travels, on soil or *terra*, and on the inquiries by the Royal Society that sought to ascertain the details of land-scape and topography, and precisely on what publications like Plot's and Aubury's contributed. What begins to differentiate Gilpin from writers in the late seventeenth century is how and why he narrates his travels. Evelyn certainly sketched and drew on his travels (see illus. 14) and fleshed them out with further research, and so did Aubrey, among others. But Gilpin's tours in different parts of the countryside are concerned to instruct others in sketching, while Evelyn was more focused on detail-ing his own observations. Gilpin's later *Observations*, such as those *Relative chiefly to Picturesque Beauty . . . on several parts of England, particularly the Mountains and Lakes of Cumberland and Westmoreland*, are much more focused on this pedagogic education than the *Observations* made when visiting the River Wye; by contrast, Evelyn's concern was directed to making his own country more comprehensible, less on how an individual draughtsman would see it. Yet there is some fascinating interplay in this historical sequence: Evelyn was sceptical of too much generalizing and relied on his own empirical regard as the proper basis for scientific inquiry; in Picturesque viewing, however, observation is both more generalized and the interest in science has been succeeded by an emphasis on the aesthetic aspects of landscape, such as would promote sketching or even (some argued) the making of landscape gardens.

Evelyn's commitment to empirical inquiry left him careful of theorizing, hence his passion for lists, hence his reliance on the particulars elicited by enquiries sent out from the 'Georgical' Committee. At one point in the 'Elysium' he notes that he descends 'now to the particulars' from 'rules [that] may suffice for the general [reader]', just as his *Sylva* opposed 'particulars' to 'fantasms and fruitless speculations' and his *Sculptura* praised Favi, who 'neglected nothing, but went on collecting'. Evelyn's whole life enacted this balancing act between the pursuit of detailed collections and theory (or concept, or even speculation), or between the atoms of experience (in Lucretian terms) and God's larger purpose. Though he writes at the start of 'Elysium' that a garden is a '*type* of Heaven' (*EB*, p. 2), he also knew that in this sublunary world he must find umpteen actual examples to consolidate the type, of which Backbury Hill was but one.

Evelyn was constantly in search of garden examples, some of which he found on his travels around southern England and his discussions with Aubrey about his own Surrey and Aubrey's Wiltshire. But he also found opportunities to propose designs for actual, provisional, examples of a heavenly type, and sometimes enabled others to contrive *typical* examples on other sites, besides his own Sayes Court. He helped to 'project the garden' for Lord Clarendon and his son, Henry

Hyde, at Cornbury Park, Oxfordshire, and at Euston Hall (see illus. 37). He offered advice, and advice was sought from him for other sites. Through his cousin Sir Samuel Tuke he advised Henry Howard on making a public garden in Norwich, which matured by the 1680s into 'many fine walks' and a bowling-green, reached by 'handsome stairs' from the River Wensum.[19] He advised John Shaw on gardens for Hugh May's design of Eltham Lodge, near Deptford, and later on the garden layout for May's Moreton Hall in Chiswick for Sir Stephen Fox.[20]

But perhaps the most famous of Evelyn's moves into land-scape practice came in his design of the terraces at Albury for Arundel's grandson in 1667. The first Earl had confessed to Evelyn in 1646 that he would 'have sold any estate he had in England . . . before he would have parted with this darling villa'.[21] In self-imposed exile in Italy he had commissioned Wenceslaus Hollar, well known also to Evelyn, to make engrav-ings of Albury; these were done in Antwerp in 1645. They show a wooded and peaceful landscape; in one, on a hillside, with what are maybe vineyards, is an astonishing Italianate grotto overlooking water. Evelyn even tried in the 1650s, after the Earl's death, to obtain Albury for himself before he was forced to settle on Sayes Court. Arundel had been a compan-ion and friend to Evelyn in his European travels, a mentor and guide to things to see in Italy (illus. 31).[22] More generally, Arundel's approach was an example of how the ancient world should be construed and emulated. His sculpture garden beside the Thames was one of the first attempts to make a garden after the Italian fashion (illus. 32), and in 1667 Evelyn had successfully obtained the Arundel Marbles from Henry Howard as a gift to the University of Oxford.

On visiting Albury in 1670 to see how his work was progressing, Evelyn noted that he 'found [it] exactly done according to the design & plot I had made . . . the canals are now digging, & vineyards planted' (*Diary*, III.561–2). His design (illus. 33) clearly responds to the actual site, as Beale had argued about Backbury Hill; but now, with distinct recollections of Italy and of Arundel, it was transformed into an ideal paradise. A modern aerial view (illus. 34) shows what

31 Peter Paul Rubens, *Thomas Howard, 21st Earl of Arundel*, c. 1630, oil on canvas.

still remains – an extremely long series of terraces, with slopes linking them at either end, and in the centre a hemicycle that incorporated perhaps some of the Italianate grotto depicted by Hollar, or maybe a later version of it; at the rear, pushed into the hillside is an exedra hidden now by a clump of trees.

Evelyn's elaborate plan described a complex repertory of water (pools and canals), trees and vines planted in different layouts (circular, random, quincunx), vegetable gardens or maybe orchards of fruit trees (at the ends of the long vineyards); there were little sculptures on plinths above the vineyard, while the two higher terraces have ten little exedras carved into the hillside, with two larger bays at the centre of each level. The higher exedra shows a dark opening into the hill, the slope of which is drawn as a large grassy enclosure.

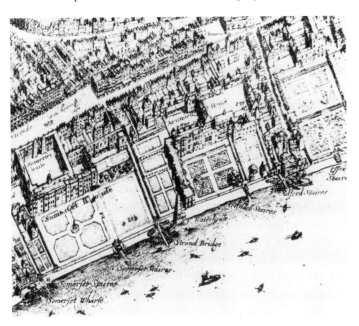

32 Lord Arundel's house on the Thames, in a detail from Wenceslaus Hollar's map of London, 1646.

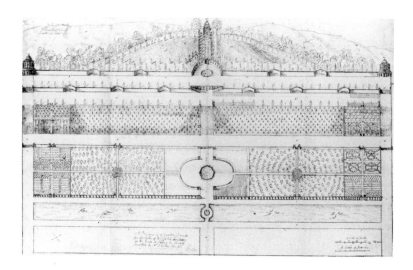

The opening was the feature that expressly pleased Evelyn in his 'new' garden – a 'crypta through the mountain in the park, which is 30 pearches in length, such a *Pausilippe* is nowhere in England besides' (*Diary*, III.561–2).

This tunnel is shown on his plan as an opening under the hillside, on top of which there seems to be a *catena d'acqua*, or water channel, leading downwards from a pavilion on the crest. The *catena d'acqua* was a feature Evelyn might have seen in Italy at the Villa Lante or Caprarola, but the 'Pausilippe' he had certainly witnessed when visiting Naples. For what he saw in Italy was a tunnel that cut through the promontory between Pozzuoli and Naples, and above it was the supposed tomb of Virgil, whose magical powers were assumed locally to have created the tunnel. In February 1645 Evelyn saw and noted the 'mountain Pausilipo, at the left hand of which they shewed us the poet Virgil's sepulcher, erected on a very steep rock, in the form of a small rotunda'; he could probably have seen the

33 Evelyn's plan for the garden of Henry Howard at Albury Park, Surrey, from the extra-illustrated copy of *The Miscellaneous Writings . . .*.

site drawn by John Raymond in *Il Mercurio Italico* of 1648 (illus. 35). It was, it must be said, an unnecessary practical invention in Surrey, for although the tunnel still exists (in the 1980s I was allowed to penetrate only a few yards into it), the need for it seems simply to be a memorial and nostalgic gesture, a studied attempt to introduce into an English site something that was 'nowhere in England' – a gesture, albeit fictitious, to Virgil and his magical powers to transform a landscape.

The reformation of the earlier terraces responded to and better articulated the lengthy site, and they may well allude to the Roman terraces at the Temple of Fortune at Praeneste (the modern Palestrina) that were explored and drawn by Pirro Ligorio, and perhaps to Ligorio's reconstructed plan of ancient Rome, where lengthy terraces above the Forum con-tained, as at Praeneste, an exedral platform; but such exedras were frequently invoked in Roman designs and taken up in Italian gardens like the Villa Aldobrandini. Whether the two

34 Modern aerial view of the terraces at Albury Park, Evelyn's Surrey estate, with the entry into the crypta hidden now by trees in the exedra at the top above the 'Roman baths'.

lateral temples at either end of the Albury terrace or the hill-top pavilion in Evelyn's drawing were constructed is unclear; the latter may correspond to part of Aubrey's account: 'In the park is a spring called Shirburn Spring, which breaks out at the side of a hill, over which is built a handsome banqueting house, which is surrounded (almost) with trees, which yield a pleasant solemn shade.'

If Beale had espoused an ideal garden where the eye and the mind could encounter the perfect forms not to be

35 Virgil's Tomb, drawn by John Raymond, from his *Il Mercurio Italico . . .* (1648).

matched in the less mediated world outside, Evelyn at Albury wished visitors' imagination to grasp how ideas and indeed forms of a classical garden past had come home to England. It was a memory theatre, its shape almost literally an amphitheatre, a conspectus of Italian garden ingredients that were 'nowhere in England besides'.

Vineyards – they clothed one of Albury's terraces – were not entirely unknown in England. The year before he visited Albury to see his design, Evelyn published *The English Vineyard Vindicated*; the text was his, though its title page attributed it to John Rose, the royal gardener in St James's Park, from whom he derived his ideas. The 'vindication' consisted in proposing that vineyards, not much encountered in England, and 'not altogether from the defect of climate', could now be introduced again into England's horticulture as an allusion to ancient Rome and Greece. In the Preface, signed with the pseudonym 'Philocepos' (friend of gardens, *cepos* or *kypos* being the Greek for garden or plantation), he mocked French gardenists 'new come over, who think we are as much oblig'd to follow their mode [that is, design] of gardening as we do of their gardening', that is, horticulture. Yet though he may have wanted to vindicate English vineyards as authentic rather than French, Evelyn eventually included this in four later editions of *The French Gardiner*. So he worked to establish a bridge between ancient horticulture and a modern English method, which was confirmed in Sir Robert Southwell dividing his time and energies, when out of office, between reading Virgil's *Georgics* and Evelyn's *Sylva*.[23]

But Evelyn's 'Georgical' work was not exclusively focused on English material. The Council for Trade and Foreign

Plantations also devised questionnaires to circulate 'to all his Majesty's plantations & territories in the West Indies & islands thereof', but equally to understand how much, for instance, New England was independent of 'old England'. Much of their discussions also centred, during the Dutch wars, on shipping as well as on horticultural matters: 'enquiries about improving his Majesty's American dominions by silk, galls, flax, senna &c & considered how nutmegs & cinamon might be obtained, & brought to Jamaica, that soils & climate promising success'. And in a letter to Christopher Wren of 1681, then President of the Royal Society, he urged the composition of a 'Natural History of our American Plantations' (*LB*, 11.665). Evelyn's 'Georgical' work, then, encompassed a wide range of activity, from landscape analysis to landscape design, from foreign or ancient lore and importations of materials to celebration of native topography, fauna and flora. It was also, in an informal fashion, one of his main contributions to his role as a civil servant.

EIGHT

Work as a Civil Servant

VELYN'S FIRST INCURSION into what today might be called the civil service was his little-appreciated job in 1661 of writing a 'Narrative of the Encounter Between the French and Spanish Ambassadors', a task 'commanded' by the king, who also then 'instructed' him in its writing. A manuscript account of this dispute about precedence is held in the National Archives, but it was probably not issued in print. Yet his eagerness to bear witness to the restored monarchy led him to engage in other activities that were for him more agreeable and profitable to his country; in many of these new activities he was driven in part by what he had learned in Europe about urban design, architecture and, in particular, hospitals, like the one he saw in Amsterdam for 'lame and decrepit soldiers'. Yet he was increasingly distressed by court intrigues, gambling ('an horrid vice, & unsuitable to a Christian Court') and generally the 'licentious times', and later still by the increasing dominance of Catholicism in and around the monarchy.

He assumed a variety of posts on different royal commissions that discussed hackney coaches, highways and regulations of the Mint, and in 1664 he was appointed a commissioner for the sick and wounded seamen and prisoners of war during the second and third Dutch wars. Later, in 1671, he was named a member of Charles II's new Council for Foreign Plantations, renamed a year later as the Council for Trade and Foreign Plantations, with an annual salary of £500; some of that business touched upon the 'Georgical' Committee's work and was referred to in the previous chapter. Evelyn's Diary also notes an appointment in 1666 to a commission to regulate the farming and making of saltpetre, which may well have reflected the Evelyn family's former business in gunpowder production. He much wanted to succeed his father-in-law as clerk to the Council, as Charles II had promised, but it was passed to William Williamson. Under James II he would be appointed a Commissioner of the Privy Seal.

This chapter will explore some of these official governmental roles, and we will return to other writings and activities in later chapters. By his own account in the Diary, Evelyn was an exceptionally busy man, listing multiple tasks, both administrative and personal: in 1675 he wrote to Beale that he was 'engaged in a sea of affairs' (*LB*, 1.566). He continued to view experiments at the Royal Society (examining poisons sent from India, examining a pelican in St James's Park, or visiting a Jesuit's very varied collection of Japanese and Chinese rarities, including garden landscapes); he visited and dined, often in the company of fellow commissioners or colleagues on Royal Society committees; he went to theatres and court masques. At Sayes Court he welcomed and dined many visitors, as well as planting elms in the Home and West fields and establishing a grove 'next the Pond'. He was a constant and concerned listener to sermons, the texts and arguments of which he noted; he attended with equal care to various commitments in the family – its births, miscarriages, christenings, confirmations, illnesses, marriages and deaths, including that of his brother Richard. He arranged for his twelve-year-old son John to be tutored at New College, where he matriculated in 1668, and in 1674 John was admitted at the Middle Temple and called to the Bar nine years later. Evelyn also began a friendship with one of the maids of honour to the Duchess of York, Margaret Blagge, 'one for whom for her many & extraordinary virtues, I did infinitely esteem' (see Chapter Eleven).

All of this, while attending to multiple obligations and journeying through the counties designated for him by the Commission for sick and wounded seamen and prisoners of war, deciding on billeting, organizing supplies and providing medical aid for Dutch prisoners and his own wounded, and above all, endlessly pleading for funds. Simply the time spent travelling, the journeys between Sayes Court and London, between Sayes Court and the southeast seaports, and responding to his obligations, would have been demanding for a modern bureaucrat, and his journeys were taken on boats, naval yachts, and carriages that sometimes overturned. He was often accompanied by armed guards when he was delivering money.

So it was not a complete surprise when in 1667 he responded to a pamphlet by George Mackenzie, a Scottish advocate, entitled *A Moral Essay preferring Solitude to Publick Employment*, published two years earlier in Edinburgh. Evelyn's reply, dedicated to his father-in-law, who had himself been active in public employment, was announced as *Publick Employment and an Active Life preferred to Solitude and all its Appanages* – these included 'fame, command, riches, conversation, &c' (*MW*, pp. 501–52).

Keynes notes that the young Mackenzie was known as a 'bigot', which probably led Evelyn to make his riposte, involving as it did another opportunity for broad satire; Keynes also says the piece 'is but a half-hearted affair', which seems a level way of assessing Evelyn's involvements in a public realm that lay *outside* his dedicated work on horticulture and his specific services to the Royal Society. Indeed 'conversation', unsurprisingly, seems to have been his main concern, for it meant living and communing with others *in society*, though these days the word has lost that larger emphasis: 'Not to *read* men, converse with *living libraries*, is to deprive ourselves of the most useful and profitable of studies.' Evelyn defends Boyle, whom Mackenzie praised for his solitude, for being in fact visible and experienced in public employment, which for Evelyn was essentially work for the Royal Society, a public not a private body. An appeal to classical ethics on the virtues of solitude was both a tribute to ancient practice and a concern, acknowledging that in its translation it acquired, as well as lost, a fresh demeanour. Evelyn's piece ends with a facetious comparison of two 'land-skips': one of a king and a working country, the other of a 'country gentleman', sleeping, gluttonous, book-reading while his family starves, sunbathing and poaching.

Mackenzie actually liked Evelyn's response, though Pepys could not find 'much excess of good matter though it be pretty for a bye discourse', something from a man not wholly convinced of what his role could be in the Restoration. Yet later writers have praised the treatise, that it 'sums up much of the Humanist doctrine concerning the active life, and is perhaps the fullest and best written discussion of it in English'.[1]

Evelyn himself tells the reader that the treatise was 'but the effects of a very few hours, a cursory pen, and almost but of a sitting'. He enjoyed 'this way of velitation' (that is, quarrelling or disputing with words, as opposed, presumably, to warfare), and it gave him the chance 'to improve the English style' of writing and rescue it from the discourse of 'the pulpits and the theatre'; the court equally was 'a stage of continual masquerade'. In terms of public service, God himself is the model for humans, being 'always so full of employment . . . [an] eternal and incomprehensible activity, creating, preserving, and governing'; but Evelyn also calls upon the ancients, like Cicero, to confirm that a philosophic life does indeed relate to knowledge ('Science') and not merely to solitude. Ambition is not only manifest in 'public places, and pompous circumstances, but at home, and in the interior life'.

There were offers of public service that Evelyn declined: to serve as a magistrate, to serve as Latin Secretary to the king, to fulfil Charles's repeated invitation to write a full history of the Dutch wars. Indeed, in 1659 he had written a lively letter to the second wife of Edmund Waller to expound the virtues for her of being a gardener's wife (like 'Eve herself'): his advice balanced a Virgilian retreat, citing the *Georgics* on a 'most serene and harmless life', with a life of 'labour, and small wealth'; this was followed by an enumeration of many ancient gardeners who had been 'Captains in war, and . . . arbiters of affairs in peace' (*LB*, 1.238–9). His own more serious, accomplished tasks were subsequently directed towards the Royal Society, about which he confessed to Lady Sunderland that he inclined towards 'employment upon a *public* account', as with his *Sylva*, adding that the task there was 'suitable to my rural genius, born as I was at Wotton, among the woods' (*Correspondence*, p. 689, my italics). He also served on a Royal Society committee for 'the Improvement of our English tongue'. During the Dutch wars he excused himself from re-election to its Council, but was elected again in 1670.

Yet *Sylva*'s plea for trees jibed with his role for his Navy work (serving those in its 'wooden walls') and with his service on foreign trade and commerce: not exactly a captain in war, but something of a maker of peace. Working and caring for the sick and wounded seamen and prisoners throughout the Dutch wars was no sinecure, and not particularly well remunerated either at £300 per year. His commission involved much travel through Kent and Sussex (the districts assigned to him), with powers of appointing surgeons, physicians, provost marshals, commanding and designing hospital space, and the endless need to procure funds to serve prisoners and wounded; these had to be begged or pried from senior colleagues, who were working for a government not yet equipped, as later governments could be, with adequate budgeting. Unsurprisingly, Evelyn also designed the seal for the Commission, showing a Good Samaritan, with the motto *fac similiter* (do likewise).

We can chart his work on the Commission both through his Diary and, more usefully, through his frequent letters on his work for the Commission, which filled many pages of his letterbooks and feature considerably in correspondence with Pepys, now collected in *Particular Friends*.[2] Pepys, a clerk of the Acts for the Naval Board, had begun his own work in government administration under Cromwell in 1654; he had also attended meetings at Gresham College, and his early admiration for Evelyn's learning changed into something like

affection. The two corresponded before their first meeting
in 1665, though Pepys had visited Sayes Court during the
Plague that year when Evelyn was absent in Kent. In a letter
of October 1665 Evelyn hoped they would become better
acquainted, and Pepys confided to his Diary that the more he
got to know Evelyn, 'the more I love him'.[3] In Evelyn's letters,
of which more survive than do those from Pepys, he 'emerges
as a far more rounded human being' than in the diaries
(*Particular Friends*, p. 13). If their main business was focused
initially on naval matters, their relationship grew, as Evelyn
advised Pepys in 1669 on a visit to France, giving detailed
advice on where to go and what to see and enclosing letters
to present to persons there (*Particular Friends*, pp. 68–75). He
commiserated with Pepys on the death of his wife, who had
fallen ill while travelling in Europe, and he visited him in the
Tower when in 1673 Pepys was committed on suspicion of
abetting popery (he was loyal to the Duke of York).

Evelyn clearly enjoyed some of his work for the Commission: a lengthy trip in January 1665, he reported, was 'not [an]
unpleasant journey'. He was efficient, punctilious, curious
(he witnessed the launch of a new double-hulled ship called
Experiment), while also caring about the tragedies of this 'terrible war'. He met with the burned sailors who survived an
accidental ship explosion, witnessed horrible amputations
('several their legs & arms off'), and had 'to consider of the
poor orphans and widows made by this bloody beginning'
as well as endlessly providing doctors and medical supplies.
Yet his anxious and importunate letters to Pepys, sometimes
enclosing copies of letters to other officials, were endless pleas
for more assistance – financial, medical, and simply support

for his work; he laments that what he was supposed to do in cooperation with other members of the Commission and their appointed officers in Kent and Sussex was thwarted by cheating, misuse of funds and excessive expenditures by apothecaries, by sailors faking their discharge papers from hospital and by the lack of a hospital ship. A letter to Pepys in early October 1665 is typical:

> finding divers Chirurgeons and sick-persons at my doors who had come from several places with sad complaints that they could not procure quarters for them. I was forced to dispatch warrants to the constables and other officers to be aiding and assistant to my deputies . . . I have had earnest entreaties from several of the commanders [in the fleet] to dispose of their sick and wounded men on shore, but the clerk . . . obstructs the effect of the warrant I sent to the constable . . . I have peopled all the intermedial villages [between Chatham and Gravesend], what I shall do with these miserable creatures, who are not able to move? . . . without money I could not feed two thousand prisoners . . . I dare not show my face, 'till I can bring them some refreshment [that is, money]. (*Particular Friends*, pp. 38–40, 56)

Travel, billeting and supplies for food and medicine were costly, and funds were slow to appear; he reported constantly to the king in person or in council, where he told him that the Commission cost £1,000 a week to function. He had to request funds from Lord Albemarle, the Commission's secretary, for guarding prisoners and himself when carrying cash to various Kent ports; together with Admiral Lord Sandwich he made 'peremptory' demands for monies to prevent prisoners from starving.

Of the more pleasant chores, he clearly enjoyed meeting with senior admiralty, lords and other commissioners ('a world . . . of earls & lords') and the various accommodations he accepted while travelling – he was 'splendidly treated' at Dover Castle. He even enjoyed some hilarious moments at a dinner in Greenwich, which Pepys described: Evelyn ad-libbed 'some verses made up of nothing but the various adaptations of *may* and *can*'. He had to visit the major ports along the south coast – Dover, Deal, Sandwich – check on fortifications at Deal and Sandown, establish officers in various towns and occasionally review their work; on one occasion he took his young son John to Dover, where he went to sea but was not sick. A royal party visited the Nore at the mouth of the Medway in July 1665 and saw the *Prince*, a vessel that Evelyn noted as being in 'good order, decency and plenty . . . in a vessel full of men'; it was captured and burned by the Dutch a year later. On other occasions he visited the fleet at the mouth of the Medway, and on 1 June 1666, hearing cannon fire while in his garden at Sayes Court, he took horse and rode through the night to Rochester, but saw no battle off the coast and returned to London, where first reassuring and then calamitous messages were received from the four-day battle: his Diary (III.439–41) recounts the loss of ships, 660 dead, 1,100 wounded and 2,000 taken prisoner.

He oversaw the requisition of a portion of St Thomas's Hospital in Southwark in preparation to receive wounded sailors from the English fleet, and alerted commanders to be ready to receive the wounded and prisoners when the fleet engaged the Dutch; later he asked for the use of the Savoy Hospital near Somerset House in the Strand, and later still hired Leeds Castle, to which he marched five hundred prisoners, and where he later flooded the moat, built a new drawbridge, brought spring water into the courtyard and did some conservation of the fabric. He reviewed prisoners at the old Chelsea College, where the Dutch complained of the insipid English white bread. He also had to request of the king how to proceed with assisting some important Dutch commanders whose ship had been lost at sea and were captured; Charles recalled the kindnesses he had received from the Dutch in the Interregnum and wished to help (such were the civilities in wars at that time). As the Dutch ambassador was still in London, Evelyn took up the matter with him. Yet on some occasions he could take himself to the Royal Society to 'refresh among the Philosophers'.

Meanwhile, in 1665 the Plague struck in London, borne largely by the black rats who swarmed in the crowded and filthy slums; deaths came in the thousands. Evelyn claimed that over four hundred had died in his Deptford parish alone. The king retreated to Hampton Court, then to Salisbury and finally to Oxford, and Evelyn took his wife and family to Wotton, 'trusting to the providence and goodness of God' (*Diary*, III.417). A daughter, Mary, was born there in October 1665 in the very same room where Evelyn himself 'first took breath'; but after the christening Evelyn himself returned to his charges, finding many thousands dead, and 'poor pestiferous creatures, begging alms' in the streets of London. But a year later he still wanted Mary kept safely at Wotton, and after a family celebration at New Year, with 'much, & indeed extraordinary mirth & cheer, all my brothers, our wives & children being together' (*Diary*, III.428), he returned once again to London 'about his Majesties business'.

In the spring of 1666 Evelyn drafted a plan for a new hospital at Chatham, which he had presented to the king (who greeted it 'with great approbation') and was in turn encouraged by the Navy Commissioners to set upon it 'speedily'. The rudimentary plan was for a four-sided infirmary, built around

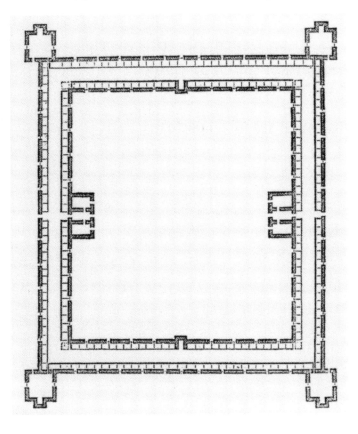

36 Evelyn's plan for a hospital at Chatham, 1666, from William Bray's edition of Evelyn's *Diary and Correspondence* (1887).

a courtyard, with towers at each corner and the corridors lined on both sides with rooms for the wounded (illus. 36). Accompanying the plan was a very lengthy letter detailing the estimated costs of everything from bricks and mortar to window frames and furniture of four hundred beds, as well as the salaries of surgeons, matrons and nurses; estimated costs were to be set against savings and reimbursements (*Particular Friends*, pp. 60–65, with a more simple list of expenditures, pp. 53–4). Once again funds were lacking, yet Evelyn notes how much could have been saved by having had such an 'Infirmary' in the last two years and and how much would be saved in the future (since he wrote this retrospectively, he was presumably thinking of the third Dutch war that broke out five years later).

In 1667 the Dutch navy invaded the Medway, burning English vessels in port (the fleet had not been quick enough to leave) and provoking a panic that the Dutch would sail up the Thames. Evelyn moved 'my best goods, plate &c from my house to another place' (surely Wotton?), and his family were alarmed when an accidental fire erupted in the Deptford shipyard that was assumed (wrongly) to have been started by Dutch invaders. Land forces were moved to defend fortifications in Kent. 'These were sad, & troublesome times', and he was indignant at the overall negligence and the decision to hold the fleet in harbour rather than venture out to sea. He was commanded to search for fuel around London (peat, notably, which he had mentioned in *Sylva*), which he did, but reported that 'nothing was now further done in it'. He visited Chatham to inspect the damaged and still-burning hulks of ships and observed the Dutch fleet blocking the mouth

of the Thames. Peace was eventually proclaimed by August and in the next year he finalized his figures and accounts for the sick and wounded.

In the relative calm between the second and third wars he travelled into East Anglia and stayed a while, somewhat un-happily, while the court hunted, hawked, raced their horses, diced and gambled, taking refuge when he could in his 'pretty apartment'. At Arlington's handsome garden at Euston Hall he advised on 'plantations of firs, elms, limes &c up his park, & in all other places and avenues' (which must have been accomplished by the time Edmund Prideaux drew it in the 1730s, illus. 37), and advised him to bring the parkland up to the house; he also remarked on the 'pretty engine' that raised the water for fountains and a machine to grind the corn. Thence he was taken by Henry Howard to Norwich, where at last he had the chance to meet with Sir Thomas Browne, with

37 Edmund Prideaux, the avenue at Arlington's Euston Hall, Suffolk, *c.* 1735, drawing showing how Evelyn's proposal had matured.

whom he had corresponded: his 'whole house & garden being a paradise & cabinet of rarities, of that the best collection, especially medals, books, plants, natural things'; this 'did exceedingly refresh me', especially in the wake, the night before, of an unseemly dispute between Howard and a carpenter over the measurements of a room.

In June 1669 he returned to Oxford and saw Wren's new-built Sheldonian Theatre, was annoyed by some malicious and hostile remarks against the Royal Society by the Public Orator who conceived of some slight towards the University, but received an honorary degree and was afterwards entertained handsomely at St John's College. And back in Essex a fortuitous encounter with a young Grinling Gibbons in 1671 found him admiring the carving of a crucifix, 'for the curiosity of handling, drawing and studious exactness, I never in my life had seen before in all my travels' (*Diary*, III.567). Evelyn, impressed, acquainted Charles II, who was delighted by the work, and this chance meeting lifted that craftsman into prominence: Gibbons was eventually given work by Christopher Wren at the new St Paul's and at the library of Trinity College, Cambridge, and – as he lived until 1720 – his carving came to decorate country houses: Blenheim, Chatsworth and Petworth. Evelyn may well have admired Gibbons's art also because of the latter's fastidiousness in the woods he chose for his work – lime for fruits and garlands, oak for panelling, boxwood for medallions.

But sea and land battles resumed when another (the third) Dutch war erupted in 1672, provoked by an English attack on the Dutch Smyrna fleet in the Channel and as a result of Charles II's secret alliance with France against the Dutch.

Evelyn himself thought that the conflict 'was slenderly grounded and not becoming Christian neighbours', but he nevertheless had to visit Gravesend to deal with those wounded in that abortive English attack on the Dutch convoy. He sailed to Sheerness to inspect fortifications at Tilbury, and from an Admiralty yacht surveyed 'redouts & batteries' on both sides of the estuary. He was handsomely entertained at Margate, where he took time to remark on the local trade of brewing, with husbandry in the surrounding countryside far exceeding any part of England. He lamented the loss of his friend the Earl of Sandwich, at the sea battle of Southwold Bay, and attended his funeral at Westminster. He organized the funeral of a French rear-admiral commander who died of his wounds and witnessed a double amputation of a gangrened leg, without, in the end, being able to save the sailor: 'what confusion & mischief do the avarice, anger, and ambition of princes cause in the world, who might be happier with half they possess: This stout man, was but a common sailor.'

His correspondence with Pepys resumed as before, as did his journeys to and fro, overseeing prisoners and providing, when he could, funds for both them and the wounded. Pepys himself was moving to higher things, with a seat in Parliament, the Mastership of Trinity House, becoming a governor of Christ's Hospital and in mid-1673 the Secretary of the Admiralty. The war dragged on until February 1674, when the Treaty of Westminster ended the conflict: 'losing so many good men, for no provocation in the world but because the Hollander exceeded us in industry, & all things else but envy'.

Charles II had petitioned Evelyn to write a history of the Dutch conflict; his involvement with the Commission and his obvious literary skill made the request perfectly apt. Charles 'began to tempt me' to write about the Dutch wars after Evelyn presented him in 1669 with *The History of the Three Late Famous Impostors* – namely, two pretenders in the Turkish imperial family (Padre Ottomano and Mahomed Bei) and a Jewish pseudo-Messiah (Shabbethai Zebi) – a book dedicated to Henry Bennet, 1st Earl of Arlington and Secretary of State from 1662 to 1674. His dedicatory epistle asserts that his stories were of 'undoubted verity' and were based upon eyewitnesses, though their names are repressed so they not be 'inconvenienced'. Doubtless this was a sure affirmation of his own historical skills and probity and ensured that he would be continually pressed to narrate the wars with the Dutch. Arlington, on behalf of the king, continued to request such a history, not least because Evelyn's previous request, having been declined, 'was ill taken'.

So, provided with much research assistance from the Secretary's office, Evelyn began work, reported what he had done so far to the king in August 1670 and was 'enjoined' to make his writing 'a little keen [that is, critical], for that the Hollanders had very unhandsomely abused him, in their pictures, books, & libels, &c'. At the start of the next year and again eight months later, Evelyn had his arm twisted once more and was given further materials, but had still not produced the required work. But at some point as early as June 1660 he had annotated his Diary (hopefully or retrospectively) with 'See the whole history of this conflict in my Hist: of the Dutch War', and in 1681 he was still sending Pepys large sea charts and the text of what he had written: 'I transmit the sheets I have long since blotted [that is, completed]

about the late Dutch War' (*Particular Friends*, p. 123). He also
included a map of the Dutch action at Chatham in 1667,
noting the locations of the English ships and the massed
armada of the Dutch at the mouth of the Thames.[4]

But the book, though estimated by its author in 1671 as
being 800 to 1,000 folio pages, was never completed. What
was published in 1674 was his *Navigation and Commerce, their
Original and Progress*, a notice of which also appeared in the
Philosophical Transactions (vol. IX) of the Royal Society, praising
its author as one who 'excites England, and adviseth the most
advantageous preparations for our future defense, and for
aggrandizing our Trade and Commerce'. But what Evelyn had
presented to the king was 'no other than the Preface prepar'd
to be prefix'd to my History of the whole war, which I now
[1674] pursued no further' (*Diary*, IV.41). As propaganda, it
should have been issued before peace was concluded, during
which the king had not only urged him forward but had the
piece read to him. But when even that portion of the history
emerged, the Dutch were deeply offended and demanded
its withdrawal, which was acceded to and copies returned to
the printer.

Yet Evelyn, not surprisingly given his knowledge of the
Netherlands, found their inhabitants skilled in the management of land and in furnishing, through 'commerce alone', the
materials they did not possess – 'grain, wine, oil, timber, metal,
stone, wool, hemp, pitch, nor almost any other commodity
of use' – and he went on to note that the Dutch built 'goodly
cities, where nothing but rushes grew; cultivated an heavy
genius with all the politer arts; enlarged and secured their
boundaries . . .'. As he positions Holland within a survey of

nations, ancient and modern – from Carthage to Venice and Genoa – his argument, while it does not diminish his claims for England and its trade, once again reveals his concern for balance and attempt at evenhandedness (*MW*, pp. 625–86).

Again, one suspects that Evelyn was too scrupulous to proceed rapidly with the work, however much he was interested in that historical moment and his own wish to record his involvements in it. But balancing, on the one hand, commands from Charles II, support from the Secretary of State and demands that he not 'moderate my style' when writing against the Dutch (*Diary*, III.559), and, on the other, his dissatisfaction with both government bureaucracy and the Navy's ineptitude, might have confirmed his own growing sense that the war was both a mistake and not what a Christian nation like England should tolerate.

When writing to Pepys in August 1689, in response to his asking for a portrait to adorn 'your choice library with the pictures of men illustrious', and even when having sat the previous month to have his portrait drawn by Godfrey Kneller at Pepys's request, he demanded, 'what in God's name, should [I] a planter of cole-worts [cabbages] do amongst such worthies?' In this long and extravagant letter (*Particular Friends* pp. 188–204; its editor calling it 'epic') Evelyn seems to be surveying his own role, fame and perhaps uncertain comportment in the world. While 'faces . . . signified nothing to the possessors', he did admire the late Clarendon's decision to collect pictures of 'his own countrymen' instead of 'foreigners'. Evelyn then celebrates the suitable 'faces' of ancient and modern worthies, from Machiavelli and Petrarch to Tycho Brahe and Copernicus, from Vittoria Colonna to Petrarch's

Laura (but not beautiful strumpets); he despises how the court has been corrupted by pimps, concubines and buffoons who devalue English culture, and he promises that truth will out when names are eventually named!

But in the end, lest painted images get banished to 'brokers in every dusty corner', he singles out and praises medals, which should adorn libraries: for their images and descriptions or titles on one side have, on their reverse, notice of what heroic exploits the personages performed, and 'famous temples, thermae, amphitheatres, triumphal arches, bridges, aqueducts, circuses, naumachiae' – all of which have greatly assisted 'the recovery of the ancient and magnificent architecture, whose real monuments have been so barbarously defaced by the Goths'. Medals can elucidate history and chronology, but he forbears discussing their finish or counterfeiting. As with his concern for building collections at the University of Oxford, Evelyn was anticipating the need to found and sustain public museums, as he would later do in forwarding the creation of the first public library in London.

In the remainder of the letter to Pepys, what he calls his 'ramble . . . a deal of ground for so little game', he takes a *tour d'horizon* both of important virtuosi of all ranks and of his own work already published, like *Sculptura*, or perhaps the book he was already envisaging (*Numismata*), his work on preserving the English language and his larger vision or ambition for learning and philosophical collections in England. What is interesting, however, is that he seems to avoid any discussion of his or others' plans for more work on horticulture or gardening. He meanders further through collections of medals and portraits, listing names like Clarendon and dozens of

others that 'I do not at present call to mind', before he focuses
on the establishment of libraries, great collectors, his concern
for the selling or even exporting of book collections, the need
to establish writing academies, which will ensure 'a nervous,
natural strength and beauty, genuine and of our own growth,
without always borrowing, or stealing from our neighbours';
such an assembly would bring into England what Richelieu
had achieved in France to improve 'useful (less mechanical)
conversation, of learned persons'.

Though the printing of his translation of Naudé's book
on libraries (dedicated to Clarendon) had appalled him, he
was still urging that excellent libraries for nobles be created
and maintained; he also urged keeping abreast of 'auctions
[of books that] become so frequent among us' and tended to
scatter in days important holdings that took years to build.[5]
Besides the establishment of noble libraries, he asked that
gentlemen too should have 'competent libraries' to use in
town, for London especially was defective in good libraries,
unlike Paris; yet even if a person did possess a decent library,
he would not have prepared and been willing to circulate a
catalogue, for 'fear of being disturbed'. Oxford and Cambridge
fared better, but he still hoped that some Maecenas would
donate collections of manuscripts especially to colleges,
instancing a great collection of manuscripts of Isaac Vossius
that was in 'danger of being devoured by Mr [Robert] Scott
and other[s] of our auction-men'. Still, he singled out the
magnificent library building that Wren designed for Trinity
College, Cambridge, and listed a handful of other good
libraries in Oxford. But to Pepys, at least in 1689, there is no
mention of 'Elysium Britannicum' or other horticulture work.

At the end of his letter he encourages Pepys to assemble collections of engravings that are cheap, useful and instructive: title pages, heads and effigies of authors, and those who profess arms and arts. These would 'stand in competition with the best paintings'. Pepys's immediate reply noted that in less than five pages, Evelyn had provided him with what, from any other writer, would occupy five volumes.

NINE

Ancient and Modern in Architecture and Gardening

NE DOES NOT GO FAR IN READING Evelyn's writings without realizing how much he was concerned with exchanges between modern ideas and ancient wisdom on a variety of matters. His long, deliberate and pedagogical letter of 1656 to Edward Thurland (*LB*, 1.190–93) is a virtual essay on the subject of prayer, a barrage of citations for and against its topic, from the classics (Silius Italicus, Democritus, Pythagoras, Plato, the Stoics, Cicero), to St Paul and St Augustine, and thence to moderns like Lancelot Andrewes, Henry Hammond and Henry More. While others letters are less instructional, his public writings still dilate upon a similar and pertinent repertory of influences; indeed, he seems unable to write without weighing in with references to relevant authorities. In this seventeenth-century 'battle of ancients and moderns' Evelyn occupies a considerable and visible place as both a careful, yet sometimes awkward, adjudicator of those rivalries.[1]

A crucial and related aspect of the 'battle between ancients and moderns', especially for those committed to the modern, was the appeal to a *progress* of the arts, that is to say a transference, and so an improvement, of ancient ideas now brought into England. But what if the ancients were after all better than the moderns? Nobody who was both a Baconian and a member of the Royal Society is likely to have believed that the ancients were better, but Evelyn was not inclined to dismiss ancient wisdom in matters that concerned him. Charles Perrault's *Parallèle des anciens et des modernes en ce qui regarde les arts et les sciences* (1688–97) maps the progress of the arts with a metaphor that would have appealed to Evelyn's domesticity: 'should not our forefathers not be regarded as the children', writes Perrault, '& we as the Elders and true Ancients of the world?' Such an argument turns the tables on those who wished unreservedly for a new modernity – like Charles's brother, Claude Perrault[2] – by seeing a family relationship, maybe even a physical resemblance, between ancient and modern writers. A similar argument on the progression of the arts is made by the French gardener Jean-Baptiste de La Quintinie, translated by Evelyn in the 1690s: the French text praises the art of pruning as an ancient practice that 'begun not in our days, for it was held ['among the curious'] as a maxim many ages since, as appears by the testimony of the ancients [the margin names Theophrastus, Columella, Xenophon]; so that, to speak the truth, we only follow now, or perhaps improve what was practiced by our forefathers'. After all, the 'Georgical' Committee saw Virgil as both an ancient and yet as a 'child' who needed to be raised to be a 'truer ancient', re-educated in a modern family and culture: Dryden would do it with his translations, as did Pope in his imitations of Horace's epistles and satires. Evelyn was performing the same in his reinvention of Albury's garden terraces. For Evelyn, all wisdom, knowledge and arts from the ancient world, sifted, interpreted and 'translated' in the fullest sense, were no longer the property of a distant past but themselves modern and vital.

To the reader of his *Sylva* he explained that 'to improve natural knowledge, and enlarge the empire of operative phil-osophy [is achieved] not by the abolition of the old, but by the real effects of the experimental; collecting, examining, and improving their scattered phenomena'. While Evelyn may have, too often, enjoyed playing rhetorically with materials in the battle of ancient and moderns, as in his letter to Edward Thurland, he was also keenly alert to the need for his contem-poraries to understand the newness of the past. Horticulture and architecture were obviously and essentially modern, for both were designed for current usage by a process of re-interpretation and renewal. Any recourse to ancient wisdom meant that it needed to be 'read' now, in a contemporary lan-guage. Thus Evelyn, writing to Cowley, saw that the world of nature needed, 'from the variously adorned surface [of the 'Whole Globe'] to the most hidden treasures in her bowels', to be unlocked, and their 'abstrusest things' made 'useful and instructive'.[3] That is what the Royal Society has done: showing that the 'real secrets useful and instructive' were better than anything anyone had done in the 'last 5,000 years', includ-ing Bacon himself. And that contemporary 'showing', that demonstration, was a crucial act of translating the world into words, which is why Evelyn needed a poet like Cowley to pre-pare the prefatory poem for Sprat's *History of the Royal Society*.

Evelyn worked in two ways to make sense of the 'battle' of rival authorities and the progression of the arts. First, by reviewing ancient wisdom and expounding its application to his own country, a form of translation of ancients into modern culture; specifically, of course, by actual translations of texts that lent support to modern work without neglecting what earlier arts had recommended. Second, by his garden and horticultural work, which he pursued both through the Englishing of foreign texts and by his own practical activities. Here there were both successes – *Sylva* above all, along with recommendations made and executed for other landscapes like Albury – and failures, most crucially his inability to bring 'Elysium Britannicum' to a conclusion and publication.

In all these endeavours he needed to adjudicate between ancient authorities (accessed entirely through ancient writings, as few actual sites of gardens existed) and modern work in garden-making, painting, architecture, urban design and engraving, which came as much through images and what he saw around him as through words. All of these, however much these productions acknowledged and borrowed from the ancients, were inevitably modern: gardens may imitate what texts implied of ancient layouts and formal properties, but the plants, the maintenance and their uses were all contemporary, as were the people who designed them. Evelyn's years in Europe gave him confidence to expound modern conceptions and performances in various arts, while his belief in the importance of direct observation during his years abroad reinforced the relevance of what he wanted to recommend in England.

The primacy of modern Renaissance architecture was focused in Evelyn's translation and presentation of Roland Fréart de Chambray's *Parallèle de l'architecture antique avec la moderne* (illus. 38), with its first edition in 1664 and a second issue in 1680; another, posthumous, second edition, planned before

Chambray, Roland Fréart

A
PARALLEL
OF THE
ANTIENT ARCHITECTURE
WITH THE
MODERN,

In a Collection of *Ten* Principal *Authors* who have Written
upon the FIVE ORDERS,

Viz.
{ PALLADIO and } { D. BARBARO and } { BULLANT and
SCAMOZZI, | CATANEO, | DE LORME,
SERLIO and | L. B. ALBERTI and | Compared with one
VIGNOLA, } { VIOLA, } { another.

The three *Greek Orders*, DORICK, IONICK and CORIN-
THIAN, comprise the *First Part* of this *Treatise.*

And the two *Latin*, TUSCAN and COMPOSITA the *Latter.*

Written in *French* by *ROLAND FREART*, *Sieur de Chambray*;
Made *English* for the Benefit of *Builders.*

To which is added an *Account* of *Architects* and *Architecture*, in an *Historical* and *Etymological*
Explanation of certain *Terms* particularly affected by *Architects.*

With *Leon Baptista Alberti*'s Treatise of STATUES.

By *JOHN EVELYN* Esq; Fellow of the *ROYAL SOCIETY.*

The Second Edition with Large Additions.

LONDON, Printed for *D. Brown* at the *Black Swan* without *Temple Bar*, *J. Walthoe* in the
Middle-Temple-Cloysters, *B. Took* at the *Middle-Temple-Gate* in *Fleet-street*, and *D. Midwinter*
at the *Rose* and *Crown* in St. *Paul's-Church-Yard.* 1707.

38 Title page of Evelyn's English translation of Roland Fréart's *Parallèle
de l'architecture antique avec la moderne*, 2nd edition (1707).

his death, did not appear until 1707, and it included additions and paid tribute to Sir Christopher Wren. (In 1665 Wren, whose work Evelyn admired, went to France to observe French architecture at first hand.) Evelyn's version of the *Parallèle* championed modern architecture in opposition to 'the asymmetry of our [ancient] buildings, want of decorum and proportion in our houses', from which 'the irregularity of our humours and affections may be shrewdly discerned [that is, understood]', as he wrote in its dedication to Sir John Denham. The dedication also praises the Frenchman's *Parallèle* as being, more than any other study, a 'safe, expedite and perfect guide . . . where, from the noblest remains of antiquity accurately measured, and perspicuously demonstrated, the rules are laid down; and from a solid, judicious, and mature comparison of modern examples, their errors are detected'. Yet Fréart's conclusion was, in effect, very modern, seeing the arbitrary character of architectural proportions.

Evelyn's determination in his own account of architects and architecture, appended to his translation, also 'addressed the loss of an adequate language', notably in technical or 'mechanical' vocabulary in England compared to that in France.[4] A similar concern with understanding the exactness of linguistic terms also drove his discussion in *Sylva*, where the Advertisement argues that 'it was not written for the sake of our ordinary rustics', but to improve 'the more ingenious'; an exercise, then, in domestication for the 'benefit and diversion of gentlemen, and persons of quality, who often refresh themselves in the agreeable toils of planting, and the gardens'. He admits that he 'may perhaps in some places, have made use of (here and there) a word not as yet so familiar to

the reader; but none that I know of, which are not sufficiently
explained by the context and discourse'. Still, he appended
a list where some curious terms were provided with a more
straightforward, indeed English, gloss: a 'coronary garden' is
a 'flower garden', 'iconography' refers to a 'ground-plot', 'ster-
coration' is 'dunging', 'olitory' is explained as 'salads, &c
belonging to the kitchen-garden, and 'insolation' glossed as
exposure to the sun.

Fréart's *Parallèle de l'architecture* was first published in Paris
in 1650, and a copy of that French edition was catalogued in
Evelyn's library in 1687. He started his 'interpretation' of it
in France in 1652 'to gratify a friend in the country', then laid
it aside, until an architect colleague in England, Hugh May,
who had acquired 'a most elaborate edition of the [original]
plates', urged him to complete it. His edition reproduced
those plates and added his own 'Account' of modern architects and architecture. Copies were given to the king, the
Queen Mother, Wren, John Beale, who had written Latin
verses for it, and Sir John Denham, one of the commissioners of highways and sewers. Its discussion of the Greek and
Roman orders are contrasted and compared in engravings
and adjacent texts, 'made English for the benefit of builders',
a claim that was endorsed by other virtuosi as well. A final
addition takes up Leon Battista Alberti's *De statua* (once again,
noted as 'first introduced into our language'). His tribute to
Charles II, who 'most resembles the Divine Architect' (as he
noted, it was 'hard not to slide onto the Panegyrick' mode),
acknowledged 'the impiety and iniquity of the late confusions' and gloried in the accomplishments that were making
'our Imperial city' great.

Evelyn had clearly appreciated modern architecture in Europe and found occasion to applaud its arrival in England. He admired Inigo Jones's Banqueting Hall in Whitehall and his classical portico (of 1633) for the old St Paul's; the London squares of St James's and Southampton (later Bloomsbury) revealed how elegant townhouses were coming into fashion, and Parliament had sanctioned the 'regularity' of the latter's architecture. The mansion for the Earl of Clarendon (formerly Sir Edward Hyde), designed by Robert Pratt, whom Evelyn had known in Rome and who had an unrivalled knowledge of modern architecture, was (for Evelyn) among the 'graceful and magnificent' examples of English houses (*Correspondence*, pp. 177–8; though later he had reservations about its 'pomp', 'costly & only sumptuous': *Diary*, IV.321, 338). Wren's Sheldonian Theatre, which Evelyn saw finished in 1669, was a thoughtful reworking of Roman models into a suitable assembly house for modern academics. At Wotton Evelyn's brother had designed a Renaissance-style front to the grotto below the mount during the 1650s, maybe at his suggestion. In 1658 his Diary found 'tolerable' the facade of what would later be Northumberland House, finding that it was not 'drowned by a too massy & clowdy pair of stairs' (III.216): 'clowdy', his editor says may be a 'slip', but it does suggest the avoidance of 'clouding' or obscuring a set of stairs with a too-fussy elaboration; as such, it echoes Sir Henry Wotton's advocacy of 'plain compliments and tractable materials'. Evelyn's proposal for a version of Solomon's House (see illus. 24), made before the formation of the Royal Society, was firmly modern, despite its acknowledgement of Carthusian monastic landscapes, and copied a building that

Evelyn had known well, Balls Park, Hertfordshire. And in 1664 he reluctantly admired parts of the house designed by Hugh May, an architect about whom he had reservations, at Eltham Lodge near Deptford, especially its views over the grounds. He accompanied Sir John Denham, famous for the prospect poem 'Cooper's Hill' of 1642 and now Surveyor-General of the King's Works, to Greenwich Palace, which Charles II wanted modernized. But they disagreed on what would be appropriate: Denham wanted a building on piles over the river, Evelyn – which suggests indeed that his judgement of Denham as a better poet than an architect was right – thought a handsome courtyard that saw the Thames as lying like a 'bay' before it would be better. He joined Denham and May on a commission to improve London's thorough-fares; in 1663 he appreciated the installation of new paving stones in Holborn that would save innumerable women and children from injury on the streets. And, in August 1666 with Wren and others, he had surveyed the old 'gothick' St Paul's and realized that it needed to be completely rebuilt. Indeed, it was so dilapidated that an engraving of it by Hollar was inscribed in Latin with the phrase 'daily expecting collapse'.[5]

All of his earlier attention to architecture and urban sites when travelling in Europe and now his translating of Fréart gave him an opportunity, he thought, to intervene in the rebuilding of London after the Fire of 1666. And in doing so, he would be able to put into practice a modern, contemporary vision, and at its core the best elements of the antique, now 'translated'. The Great Fire in the month following his visit to survey St Paul's not only cleared the huddled city of its plague-tormented housing, but inaugurated a complete renewal of the city layout, building practices and a new St Paul's. His Diary (III.459–63) recounts at more than usual length the destruction after the Great Fire: the ruined vaults, melted lead from roofs, calcinated stone, books burning 'for a week following' where stationers had secured their stock in the crypt of St Paul's, fountains dried up yet water still boiling, the chains used as barriers across streets also melted, the lanes filled with rubbish; on top of which came riots, fuelled by rumours that the French and Dutch, with whom England was at war, had invaded. He, Mary and his son John watched the conflagration from the south bank of the Thames, and Sir Richard Browne asked his daughter to send some 'Deptford wherries' or a 'small lighter' to ferry his and others' possessions out of harm's way from his quarters in Whitehall. Evelyn later compared what he saw in the Great Fire to the burning of Troy, from which Aeneas escaped to found, eventually, the city of Rome.

Eleven days after the fire started, Evelyn presented Charles II on 13 September with his 'Londinium Redivivum', a survey of the damage and 'a plot for a new city, with a discourse on it'. Such involvements in civic projects were far more congenial than some of his other civil service work (see previous chapter), yet his vision of a new London was never realized and the plan survived only in manuscript until printed first in 1748 and with its accompanying text appearing in many subsequent versions.[6]

There were many proposals for rebuilding the city: Evelyn noted that 'everybody brings his ideas', and the character of Sir Positive At-all in Thomas Shadwell's *Sullen Lovers* (1668) claimed that he had himself constructed seventeen models of the new city! Plans and proposals came from Evelyn himself, from Wren (who had proposed his own scheme two days earlier), Robert Hooke (curator of the Royal Society), Peter Mills (a former City bricklayer with an architectural career as City Surveyor), another surveyor, Richard Newcourt, and one Captain Valentine Knight, who was arrested after saying that his scheme would much profit his Majesty's revenue. All proposals envisaged a new city of regularity, with straight and radial roads, circuses and open squares, with clear and unencumbered locations of important and key buildings. Out of the 'sad ruinous heaps' Evelyn saw a city emerging that would 'dispute it with all the cities of the world', at once beautiful, rich in health and apt for both commerce and government.

Evelyn's plan has come down in three engraved versions, though they are generally similar in profile (illus. 39). It brings a long, straight avenue from the Strand at Temple Bar in the west to a newly named Charlesgate, 'in honour of our illustrious Monarch', at the east. It first meets a double octagon, from which eight roads emerge like a star, then it crosses the 'new channel' of the River Fleet, passes between a College of Physicians and a Doctors' Commons, and emerges before a new St Paul's, set in an oval plaza from which two main roads go northeast (to the Guildhall) and southeast to meet the Thames. He made the riverbank and quays more imposing, with six openings and wharves facing the water, reminiscent of the harbour at Genoa. The Custom House next door to the Tower was connected inland to a square with the Navy Office and Trinity House. A specially enlarged square on the river held the Royal Exchange, from which another avenue led straight north to Moorgate and Moorsfield outside. The city

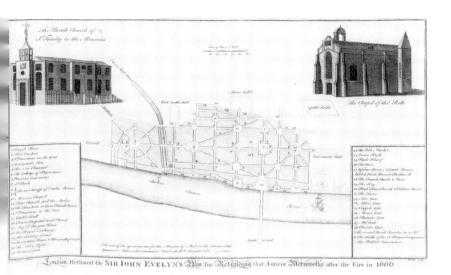

gates would be rebuilt as triumphal arches and 'adorned with statues, relievos, and apposite inscriptions, as prefaces to the rest within, and should therefore by no means be obstructed by sheds, and ugly shops, or houses adhering to them'. Twenty parish churches are marked on the plan with a small cross, and public fountains with a small circle.

The Guildhall is modelled after Amsterdam's Town Hall (1647–55) by Jacob van Campen, and Evelyn's plan owes much to his own knowledge of Rome and its urban planning under Sixtus V and the architect Domenico Fontana, though in London the Italian's 'stational liturgy' was replaced by customary English pageantry. Also implied is the translation of Continental landscape forms into elements of urban lay-outs, though former indigenous place names are retained: a series of rectangular, oval and circular piazzas punctuate the avenues, as they did along Continental garden walks, and

39 Plan of new London, undated, but mid-18th century: as Evelyn was never knighted, this caption refers, by mistake, to a later baronet.

the hemicycle (which Evelyn later adopted in the 1680s reworking of Sayes Court) is used here to enclose the Fish Market that faces over London Bridge. Evelyn's plan and programme were at once modern, attentive to much of what he had seen and admired in Europe, and yet would inspire a 'modern Rome'. Even those who favoured rebuilding the old city on its old foundations wanted it made not with timber, but with bricks, if not with marble.

It was Wren, the accomplished professional, who seems to have made the more thoughtful plan, but he still may have exchanged ideas with the amateur Evelyn, whose scheme got submerged or subsumed under others. Evelyn told Samuel Tuke that 'Dr Wren had got the start of me' (*LB*, 1.421), yet Joseph Rykwert in *The First Moderns* captions an illustration with 'Plan for the rebuilding of London submitted by Christopher Wren and John Evelyn, dated 1748 after Vertue' (though it is not clear to what extent this engraved plan represented that collaboration). Evelyn later acknowledged the aptness of Wren's scheme, where to the east of St Paul's two streets would form a 'Pythagorean Y', and noted that he 'willingly follow[ed] it in my second thoughts'; yet Evelyn hid that Y *behind* a new St Paul's, whereas Wren parted the streets more dramatically in front of it. Wren's streets were wider, and his Royal Exchange was given a prominent position along the northeast bifurcated street leading from St Paul's; whether that was deliberate or not, it was a clear celebration of commerce. Wren also wished to reduce the size of St Paul's and the number of city churches to nineteen from eighty-six to acknowledge their diminished congregations, which Evelyn might not have wished (though he himself brought the number down to twenty, with parish boundaries redrawn). But he would have welcomed Wren's Baroque and geometrical urban layout and the Pantheon-like St Paul's with a dome above porticoes.

Neither scheme for this urban development was fulfilled, not least because of some energetic jockeying in the Royal Society about whose plan would be best – there were three prominent members vying with their own plans. Oldenburg, who managed the Society's *Philosophical Transactions*, saw the process as 'still very perplex'. Evelyn's own was marginalized when plans, which included Wren's, were considered by the House of Commons. A survey undertaken prior to any re-modelling to measure all the original foundations was conducted by Wren and Hooke, the curator of the Royal Society but later appointed surveyor of the City.[7] Now there were hopes of progress. Pepys records in his Diary that Hugh May saw 'the design of building the City doth go on apace', but then hoped that it would not come too late to satisfy the people. The estimated costs, the 'disputes over legal owner-ship, boundaries law and custom' (Darley, *John Evelyn*, p. 223) caused delays. Nor was it easy to make or remake a city after the loss of thousands of buildings. Simply the availability of materials for rebuilding proved a major obstacle, for there was no question that timber was impossible and that bricks and stone would be needed. The Act for the Rebuilding of the City of London was passed by Parliament in February 1667, and a second rebuilding Act followed in 1671; the first of those specified brick. Evelyn, having written about earth and its soils, was much involved in exploring the quality of clays and he investigated the option for kilns to be established at

Deptford; he and a colleague, Sir George Sylvius, sought to obtain, unsuccessfully, the sole licence for inventing new kilns for the manufacture of plaster, tiles and bricks.

Evelyn's disappointment during the aftermath of the Fire and the work on rebuilding was clearly a setback, with his probable financial loss on the kiln scheme, and more crucially with his inability, as a prominent member of the Royal Society, to see his ideas on the rebuilding make headway. But in other respects, he could still take pleasure in work for the Society: in the donation of Henry Howard's library to the Society, and his appreciation of Howard's provision of rooms for the Society in Arundel House in the Strand after Gresham was made uninhabitable following the Fire. Equally, he was pleased by the successful transfer of the Arundel Marbles from the garden on the Strand to the University of Oxford and the display of their inscriptions, bas-reliefs and sculptures around the new Sheldonian Theatre. After the opening in 1683 of the Ashmolean Museum, they were installed there.

If he did not have success in planning and projecting a new London, he cast his mind back favourably to his days in Paris, when advising Pepys in 1669 on his travels through France. He insisted much on what good architecture had been achieved there, though making some positive comparisons with what was new and a-building in England. His long letter (*Particular Friends*, pp. 68–70) advises visits to hospitals, the Palais du Luxembourg, which he thought as 'fine as Clarendon House', the Louvre and the Tuilleries, the Pont Neuf that lacked the houses which so cluttered London Bridge, the Val-de-Grâce ('your eyes will never desire to behold a more accomplished piece'), Mansart's Maisons, where he had once taken his young wife and which, he gathers, has survived better than St Germain-en-Laye, the then as yet incomplete Collège des Quatre Nations, founded by Mazarin, and generally the uniformity of new housing. Beyond architecture, he treasures his memories of gardens outside Paris, the fortifications at Calais, 'many rare Pictures and Collections' and libraries.

His advices and recommendations for Pepys and his wife, whose father had been French, had perhaps been triggered while preparing yet another translation from the French, his version of Fréart's *An Idea of the Performance of Painting Demonstrated* (1668), which he dedicated to Henry Howard in gratitude for the 'never-to-be-forgotten' generosity of gifting his grandfather's collection of both books and marbles; he might also have been acknowledging Howard's patronage for the gardens at Albury and help with gardens in Norwich. In his Preface he protests at the drudgery of translating (perhaps in disappointment at his failed urban involvements), but justifies it by saying that with his discussion of painting he had completed his survey of the arts, after *Sculptura* and Fréart's architectural book. The title page continues Evelyn's determination to draw parallels between ancient writers on lost paintings (the elder Pliny and Quintilian) with the work of modern painters like Nicolas Poussin; Keynes notes that one presentation copy was given to the painter Sir Peter Lely 'from his humble servant J. Evelyn'.

But his concerns with the transference of ancient ideas to gardening at least were still consuming and he continued to urge them, even though he had presumably given up on 'Elysium Britannicum'. Later, during the 1690s, he corresponded with William Wotton, tutor for the children at

Albury, who was planning a life of Boyle, for which Evelyn plied him with information and encouragement: 'the subject you see is fruitful, and almost inexhaustible' (*Correspondence*, pp. 347–52). Wotton had already published *Reflections upon Ancient and Modern Learning* in 1694, and for his second edition (1697) he added a chapter 'Of ancient and modern agriculture and gardening'. Wotton's addition was clearly inspired by his correspondence with Evelyn, who the year before had urged him to read René Rapin's *Hororum libri* (which Evelyn's son had translated, and a copy of which was lent to Wotton) as a source on ancient ideas and practice:

> Concerning the gardening and husbandry of the ancients, which is the inquiry (especially of the first), that it had certainly nothing approaching the elegancy of the present age, Rapinis (whom I send you) will abundantly satisfy you [here he cites the relevant sections of the fourth book]. What they call their gardens were only spacious plots of ground planted with plants and other shady trees in walks, and built about with porticoes, *xysti*, and noble ranges of pillars, adorned with statues, fountains, *piscariae*, avaraies, &c ... Pliny indeed enumerates a world of vulgar plants and olitories, but they fall infinitely short of our physic gardens, books and herbals, every day augmented by our sedulous botanists, and brought to us from all quarters of the world. (*Correspondence*, pp. 363–4)

He also advised Wotton to read the Huguenot gardenist and ceramicist Bernard Palissy, whose *Recepte véritable* of 1563 contained a long description of how to construct a hillside garden;[8] this suggests how much Evelyn was still attuned to early modern garden ideas from France. But in this case it was perhaps less surprising, as Palissy had projected his garden as a physical representation and celebration of Psalm 124 (as a Protestant he wanted the Bible accessible in the vernacular and as authorized text), and Evelyn would have been keen to see such a modern, as opposed to a pagan, garden constructed; yet it is hard to envisage Evelyn wishing to make garden references explicitly to the scriptures in seventeenth-century England.

Wotton was far less cagey than his correspondent, and in *Reflections* he credits *Sylva* with containing things that the 'ancients were strangers to' and that it 'out-does all that Theophrastus and Pliny have left us on that subject'. Similarly, the ancients fell 'far short of the gardens and villas of the princes and great men of the present age' (p. 300), and the moderns excel in plant variety, gravel walks and 'spacious grassplots, edged with beautiful borders'. Evelyn agreed in a letter of 28 October 1696 that modern gardens excelled in 'elegancy' of construction and 'dials'. Nor surprisingly at that date, when his piety had been much exercised, does he resist supplanting pagan ornaments in gardens with Christian and philosophical imagery: the 'obscene Priapus', the 'lewd strumpet' Flora would give way to 'sacred stories' and 'representations of great and virtuous examples', so maybe Palissy had an effect.

To Sir Thomas Browne in 1660 he had written of the need to 'redeem that time that has been lost' during the Interregnum (*Diary*, IV.275) by drawing upon 'all the august designs and stories . . . either of ancient or modern times'. On the progress of gardening from its ancient beginnings until the modern and scientific age, he tries to be even-handed; yet the central ambition of 'Elysium Britannicum' is to 'refine upon what has been said' (*EB*, 253), with that refinement being essentially a modern enterprise. Much later, in *Acetaria* (1699), he noted that the 'artist gardener' takes many ages for his skills to be perfected, which inevitably values the latest perfection. For gardens are always alive, flourishing on the earth, and therefore above all modern. If a writer like Sir William Temple (echoed later by Alexander Pope) could argue that the garden of Alcinous in Homer's *Odyssey* proved all the necessary rules for a fine garden, which Evelyn's letter to Wotton about Pliny (quoted above) seems to reject, then those necessary rules must depend upon their *translation* into modern forms and uses. All good translations require no diminution nor declension of the original, yet a clear sense that the translated 'text' was clearly of the moment: hence Oldham's determination to make Horace 'speak, as if here living and writing now'; hence Evelyn's 1667 reworking of Albury.

TEN

'Elysium Britannicum'

HIS WAS TO BE EVELYN's *opus magnum*, 'my long-since promis'd (more universal hortulan work)', as he wrote to John Beale in 1679 (*LB*, 11.631–3). He probably started the project when settling at Sayes Court in the early 1650s, acquiring ground on which to make his own garden. His memories of gardens in Italy, France and the Low Countries were fresh and exciting, and the challenge to introduce these into England was compelling. Though he had other things on his mind during that decade – not least starting a family, trying to find a way to talk to his countrymen about the 'character' of both France and England, and responding to current philosophical ideas – he must have worked sufficiently on what he called the 'model' of his hortulan work to have drafted a synopsis or abstract. This he circulated to a variety of colleagues at the end of the 1650s.

To one of them, Sir Thomas Browne (whom he had not yet met), he wrote to explain his strategy, wishing to correct 'the many defects which I encountered in books and gardens', where expense was not wanting but 'judgement' was.[1] Though he confessed his youth and 'small experience', he expected that 'if foreign observation may conduce [that is, if he can be led by his observations of foreign gardens], I might likewise hope to refine upon some particulars, especially concerning the ornaments of gardens'; these he later listed as 'caves, grots, mounts, and irregular ornaments' that 'do influence the soul and spirits of man'. There was both a specific English agenda – his 'abhorrency of those painted and formal projections of our Cockney gardens and plots, which appear like gardens of paste board and March pane, and smell more of paint than of flowers and verdure' – and a determination to unite the 'useful and practicable' with the philosophical. His aim was to address the 'universality' of garden-making, including practical matters that also 'do contribute to contemplative and philosophical enthusiasms'. In this endeavour, he explained to Browne, he would invoke classical terms, the 'rem sacrum et divinam' (the sacred and divine) of 'Elysium, Antrum, Nemus, Paradysus, Hortus, Lucus, &c', as well as 'ancient and famous garden heroes'. To that end, 'a society of *Paradisi Cultores*, persons of ancient simplicity, paradisean and hortulan saints' would emerge to constitute 'a society of learned and ingenuous men'.

It was an ambitious project, and one that he had hoped might be published to commemorate the Restoration or to coincide with the founding of the Royal Society in the 1660s. The work drew the approbation of many who looked to his 'finishing of Elysium Britannicum', and a letter to that effect was circulated by Jasper Needham among 'doctors & heads of Houses & others Oxon' in January 1660. Those who joined their signatures to Needham's were the two Bobarts, both named Jacob (the father and son who managed the Oxford Physic Garden), Philip Stephens, who revised its catalogue, Robert Sharrock, who had written on vegetables, and nine other scholars. Having seen the 'grand' prospectus that Evelyn had circulated, they clearly understood its essential ambitions, emphasizing 'matters of great and common use & profit' and themes 'altogether new to our writers as having not been elaborated by any English'. They appealed to the 'munificence of noble persons' to equip the book with 'figures and cuts proportionable to the nobleness & state of the piece'. This plea must have struck Evelyn as essential: both his *Sculptura* (1662) and the first edition of *Sylva* (1664) were to have very few plates, an obvious handicap for such works.

'Elysium Britannicum' was not a book that Evelyn would be able to produce on his own, not only because he needed funds for engraving, but because the range of 'universal' knowledge required him to seek, as he always did, help from many quarters. Travellers in Europe were encouraged to send 'anything of new and rare which concerns agriculture in general, and gardening in particular . . . improvements [that] may be derived to our country' (this request was sent to the tutor travelling with his nephew). Colleagues and friends at home, like John Beale, Hartlib, Abraham Cowley and Thomas Hanmer, all supplied advice and recommendations. Evelyn, busy in other ways, envied some of these colleagues happily withdrawn from the turmoil of court and politics who could concentrate fully on garden matters: he admired Cowley for his freedom 'from noisy worlds, ambitious care and empty show'. Of Beale, he asked, 'who but Dr Beale (that stands upon the tower, looks down unconcernedly on all these tempests) can think of gardens and fish-ponds, and the delices and ornaments of peace and tranquility?'

Though urged on by his peers and horticultural friends, Evelyn never completed the manuscript of 'Elysium Britannicum', a failure that is somewhat hard to explain, given that he managed to produce several books and various more modest pamphlets during his long career. It is also true that he left other works either unfinished (a 'History of All Trades') or unpublished ('A History of Religion').[2] There is perhaps a cluster of explanations for why the gardening manuscript remained unpublished.

One, he could never finally master and then order the myriad details, the scientific and mechanical observations and researches that he had gathered and continued to accumulate during his lifetime through correspondence and personal contacts with many other virtuosi. Simply to look at almost any opening of the manuscript is to see how marginalia, pasted additions (some now unstuck), alternative ideas or words had accrued to augment, if not confuse, his arguments.[3] Further, he found it hard to mesh some of these modern ideas with his wide readings in classical authors: his constant references to Varro, Columella, Palladius, Virgil and Cato seemed apt and still relevant, but they nonetheless smacked of an antiquarian relish that Francis Bacon, for example, would have suspected.

Two, the activity of compiling and ordering a huge book, not simple in itself, was complicated further by his public or civil service commitments after the Restoration and by the loss of some esteemed members of the Royal Society; struggling to put out a third edition of *Sylva* in 1679, he noted how so many 'pillars' of the Royal Society had been lost – notably Henry Oldenburg – taking away some of his philosophical and scientific colleagues upon whose communications he relied. In 1679 he also told Beale that he was much distracted by the Dutch wars and 'three Executorships, besides other domestic concerns, either of them enough to distract a more steady and composed genius than mine'. He continued by noticing also 'the public confusions in Church and Kingdom (never to be sufficiently deplored)'. His work as a Commissioner of the Privy Seal under James II made Robert Berkeley worry that this fresh activity would 'hinder or divert you from finishing your grand design', that is, 'Elysium Britannicum' (Evelyn DO, p. 127). Yet to Beale he added that 'in all events you will see where my inclinations are fixed, and that love is stronger than death and secular affairs, which is the burial of all philosophical speculations and improvements.' Nevertheless, he thought he might rescue a segment of his unfinished book titled 'Of Sallets' and issue it as 'a complete volume', *Acetaria*, but typically noted that it would need to be 'accompanied with other accessories, *according to my manner*'.[4] He did not know how to 'take that Chapter out, and single it from the rest for the press, without some blemish to the rest'. In the end, he did exactly that in 1699, and also appended the outline of the troubled work that would no longer be published. Its abstract or synopsis is reproduced at the end of this chapter. Yet as it does not descend to particulars or arguments, it would not risk offending Evelyn's deeply felt beliefs, which also played a role.

Reason three why 'Elysium Britannicum' remained unfinished and unpublished was that, as the comment to Beale implies, Evelyn did not remain 'unconcerned'. He was unable to ignore any strong philosophical or religious objections to the discussion of natural materials that were at the heart of the

'Elysium Britannicum'. That was clear earlier enough when he was reprimanded by Jeremy Taylor, whom he considered 'my Ghostly Father' in 'spiritual matters',[5] about his villa at Sayes Court and his possessions there, to which Evelyn responded by apologizing for living in a 'worldly manner near a great city'. Taylor had also wanted the book entitled 'Paradise', not 'Elysium', pulling Evelyn towards a more religious than antique position. Francis Harris has also argued that his worldly life and pride in house and garden became 'a matter for confession and self-castigation' in his later years.[6] But while growing old may cause some retreat from the 'gay things', for which he apologized to Taylor even when a young man, that does not seem a sufficient block against putting together a book over which he had laboured so ardently from its inception. In 1679 he had written to Beale of

> this fruitful and inexhaustible subject (I mean of horticulture) not fully yet digested to my mind, and what insuperable pains it will require to insert the (daily increasing) particulars into what I have already in some measure prepared, and which must of necessity be done by my own hand; I am almost out of hope, that I shall ever have strength and leisure to bring it to maturity, having for the last ten years of my life been in perpetual motion, and hardly two months in a year at my own habitation, or conversant with my family. (*LB*, II.632)

He excuses himself by appealing to the work he was required to perform for the king and his other political commitments, as well as his activity in the Royal Society and the pull of family

time – all seem valid enough. Yet the ghostly presence of
Jeremy Taylor (who had died in 1667) that lay behind his
'excuses', together with that strange remark to Beale that 'my
inclinations are fixed and . . . Love is stronger than Death',
suggest a deeper reluctance to tangle any more with writing
a truly scientific treatise on horticulture; even if by 'love' he
means his fondness for philosophical speculations, it is a
reluctance he might also have felt less able to share with
Beale, a fellow member of the Royal Society. And maybe, he
was also nervous that a book subtitled 'the Royal Garden'
consorted uncomfortably with the rise of Catholicism and
the consequent removal of James II in 1688.

His reliance on Roman horticulturalists certainly offered
often precise if not always relevant advice. But another more
'modern' and scientific figure like Lucretius was a less immediate help; he features at least nine times in the text, but in
none of those references does Evelyn, in fact, dwell upon
Epicurean atomism. Yet it seems to have been that Evelyn's
faith did collide with his increasing discomfort with Epicurean philosophy as espoused by Lucretius, and even with his
wish to celebrate a royalist Elysium. So that 'love' or commitment reported to Beale disinclined him to complete the
garden book, not least because he was too honest to fudge
the contradictions involved.[7]

Evelyn had already begun his book on garden matters
when in 1656 he published his translation of the first book of
Lucretius' *De rerum natura*, and several years before he circulated a draft of 'Elysium Britannicum' among fellow
virtuosi. His Diary in 1656 noted that 'Little of the Epicurean
philosophy was then known among us', thereby implying that

it was part of his mission to translate another foreign and ancient work. If he had read, while still in France, the French prose translation of Lucretius' *De rerum natura* by the Abbé de Morolles (1650), that was yet another incentive to take on this task of Englishing it. But what he published was only the first book of Lucretius, and his wavering on whether to go further suggested some real difficulty. When that volume appeared in 1656, he was supremely annoyed by the negligence of the printer who had so mangled his text that in his own copy he wrote that he was 'discouraged . . . from troubling the world with the rest' of the translation (Keynes, *Bibliophily*, p. 42). Authorial pique is one thing (nor was it the only time when he was annoyed with printing of his work); but a growing sense that what he was writing in the 'Elysium' was clearly contrary to his faith and conscience must have eaten away at his resolve to proceed. So maybe he could hide at least his own unease with further publishing by sheltering behind an annoyance with the printer.

Evelyn's interest in Lucretius came before he was involved in the Royal Society's 'Georgical' Committee (see Chapter Seven), but it clearly intrigued him by its concern with matters of nature, and that endorsed his discipleship of Bacon's interest in exploring that world. Epicurus was known to have established his academy in a garden, which Evelyn's friend Sir William Temple knew when later, in 1692, Temple entitled his own essay 'On the Gardens of Epicurus'. As was argued earlier (see Chapter Six), some of the compliments that prefaced Evelyn's translation of the first book of Lucretius were not entirely straightforward, at least to a man as fastidious as Evelyn, and they surely drew his attention to a disturbing new

vision of the world, however much its physics appealed to
men of the Royal Society. We have (in Michael Leslie's words)
'as antipathetic a conclusion as it is possible to imagine for a
man of Evelyn's stamp'.

Clearly, in his often muddled, uncertain and endlessly
corrected text of 'Elysium Britannicum' he struggles with
how to respond to its materials: he is happy to list Epicurus
as a subject of garden statues among the statues of 'moral and
[famous] excellent' figures, several of whom are listed (EB,
p. 210), though he noticeably decided to delete the 'excellent'
to describe him (shown here in the format that Ingram uses).
But he is ill at ease with how to cope with Lucretius' intrusions
into his own arguments when in Chapter III of Book One,
'Of the Principles and Elements in General', he notes (in a
somewhat complicated sentence) his 'desire to *reconcile* whatsoever we may have spoken [my italics]' with 'the well restored
doctrine of Epicurus; from which however, the notions seem
[somewhat distinct &] hermetical and to interfere upon a
superficial view, we neither do, nor intend to recede' (EB,
p. 40); again one notices his withdrawal from the 'somewhat
distinct' to insisting on the hermetical world of Epicurean
ideas. There is also the hesitant formulation of this 'recon-
ciliation' – the corrections to his sentences – which reflect a
constant unease with how he needed to explain himself. A
marginal note, the date of which is of course unknown, reads:
'My purpose was quite to alter the philosophical part of the
first book' (EB, p. 38). Yet after the remark about Epicurus
cited above, when he writes that he will not 'recede', the manuscript continues with the simple phrase, 'But to proceed'. But
in the end he finds he cannot.

It is important to observe that soon after his translation of Book One of Lucretius was published, Evelyn started to compose 'The History of Religions', the title page of which notes that it was begun in 1657, and apparently (and interestingly) this 'History' was revised around 1683; it was first published in two Victorian editions of 1850 and 1859. The manuscript had been preserved at Wotton and was included by Evelyn among his projected works that he listed in 'Memoires for my Grandson'; there he termed it a 'larger book . . . being a congestion, hastily put into Chapters many years since, *full of errors*' (my italics – a familiar refrain). The manuscript itself contains 'a rough draft, a second copy, and marginal notes added during revision'.[8] But as Keynes notes, its interest consists largely not in the historical narrative, but in Evelyn's own observations in a short preface on the decay of religion, first under the Commonwealth, and later following the Restoration, when he was led to 'examine for himself the grounds upon which his religious beliefs were founded'.

Religion, and particularly the version of Christianity embodied in the English state Church that emerged from the Reformation, had always been Evelyn's bedrock. When he noted his careful observations of other forms of belief during his European travels, there was no wavering in his own faith, only a curiosity to observe other encounters and explorations. He had left England dismayed by the Presbyterians, survived the Interregnum's repressions of the English liturgy and Church practice, and once the true faith as he saw it was restored, he maintained it steadfastly, above all in the following years when it was buffeted on all sides by Roman Catholicism, continuing Presbyterianism, and other forms of Dissent ('I am neither Puritan, Presbyter, nor Independent,' *LB*, I.88). So by the last years of the seventeenth century this particular version of Christianity was the one thing he would cling to, not least because he had very early found no ability or 'ambitions to be a statesman, or meddle with the unlucky interests of kingdoms' (*EB*, p. 469 note). And that became his *idée fixe,* a bulwark to be maintained against such modernisms as Hobbes's materialism or Epicurus' atomism, and one which survived as increasingly more important than the Baconian rigour he had espoused until it threatened his faith.

Leslie notes pertinently that while Bacon's essay 'Of Gardens' began with 'GOD Almighty first planted a garden', after this conventional and rhetorical 'flourish' Bacon focused on the very practical details and didn't mention God again. Evelyn by contrast begins two chapters of 'Elysium Britannicum' by invoking God as the 'first gardener', the memory of which 'was not yet so far obliterated' by those banished from its earthly paradise (*EB*, pp. 29, 330). Evelyn's argument, as a devout member of the Church of England, is that he was determined to preserve his faith despite the challenge of rival creeds and new scientific ideas. Yet in the 1650s he had, one supposes, determined that he could still be a good English churchman and accept such modern ideas as those espoused in Epicureanism. Indeed, 1657 saw the publication of Walter Charleton's *The Immortality of the Human Soul Demonstrated by the Light of Nature*, where Charleton makes Evelyn appear as 'Lucretius' to expound Epicurianism. Even as he was working on his Lucretius translation, there appeared a publication of Bacon's juvenile writings that showed how much the younger man had espoused Epicurean and Lucretian ideas, a position that Bacon later worked hard to revoke. And eventually Evelyn himself found, as Leslie notes, that he would rather burn 'all the poems in the world' than allow that 'anything of mine should contribute & minister to vice'.

The omnibus and encyclopaedic effort of 'Elysium Britannicum' would necessarily have included not only good science but a reverence for the natural and physical world that produced and sustained all horticulture. Other members of the Royal Society were less fraught over responding to new ideas and able to sustain their faith, like Nehemiah Grew or Richard Boyle. Grew's work is cited in 'Elysium Britannicum' and his original lectures were delivered before the Royal Society, and indeed he thanked Evelyn when they were printed; but Grew's attitude towards the natural world is that it is able to speak for itself, 'without need of a God to cause plants to be the way they are'.[9] One could observe and report on nature's plants, or on the human bloodstream, without committing oneself to a faithlessness (such a delicate balance has, in fact, sustained many a good scientist in the long years since the seventeenth century). And, while it is palpably clear that Evelyn lost his Baconian edge as he progressed with 'Elysium Britannicum', it is also evident that the text itself, as it survives, does not present so dramatic a threat to faith. He may well have planned, as already noted, to 'quite . . . alter' the philosophical parts of the manuscript, but a close reading of it (though an extremely arduous task) does not confront a modern reader of the text with much sense that Evelyn was dismayed by what he left in the bulk of the manuscript. Most of his endless rewritings and hedging of emphases reveal a stylistic worrier and a conscientious horticulturalist as much as anxious piety, and his serious worries were left unwritten.

Another aspect of his uncertain attitude towards Lucretius concerns not only his work on the text of 'Elysium Britannicum', but what he might 'contribute' to actual gardens too. It has been argued that Lucretius and Epicurus found expression in Evelyn's own garden designs.[10] This seems hard to prove, and suppositions tend to fossilize into statements. R.W.F. Kroll sees that at Sayes Court Evelyn 'express[ed] an Epicurean polity of friendship, though he does not attempt to explain this at the level of specific garden symbolism'. Precisely; it was indeed a place where he could welcome his friends, but friendship is not exclusively Lucretian or Epicurean. Nor is it easy to find adequate symbols in garden elements for that 'polity'; even if it were possible, it would be expressed either in texts outside the garden itself or in calculated iconography within the design, which Evelyn avoids. A key idea of the garden as a respite from the busy world, expressing 'tranquility of mind' and 'withdrawal from public affairs' (A. and C. Smalls, p. 197), certainly emanates from Roman writings, but it was not exclusively Lucretian or Epicurean, and was readily and generally available in English culture during the seventeenth century. Though Evelyn himself envied Beale's and Cowley's escape 'from noisy worlds, ambitious care and empty show', he was incapable of following their example.

An extensive argument has been proposed that three gardens with which Evelyn was connected expressed themes of Epicurus: his brother's garden at Wotton, his redesign of the terraces at Albury for Henry Howard, and his involvement with a younger Howard, Charles, at Deepdene, which

Aubrey credits to Evelyn. In these three Surrey gardens, all designed, write the Smalls, 'before 1660, several specific and quite explicit Epicurean motifs can be detected' (p. 196). But it is not clear that Albury was designed before 1660, while he might have been still translating Lucretius (Evelyn went to Albury in 1667 and wrote that he had designed it, but with no mention of it having been projected much earlier). Similarly, George Evelyn certainly took advice from his younger brother, but it is unclear that Evelyn's 'programme' (p. 200) for the site at Wotton involved explicit Epicurean ideas; even if it did, a statue of Venus as a goddess of gardens was a routine iconographical item, and to say that all the features that were originally there 'formed part of John's overall plan' (p. 201) implies an art-historical rigour that would have been uncharacteristic of him.

Evelyn's use of ancient ideas and themes in his garden designs was in fact eclectic (as the Smalls acknowledge), never precise or symbolic. The Smalls write that he was 'never explicit about the symbolism of his garden designs', but that 'he gave a clear pointer' when he wrote about Albury's inspiration from his visit to Naples (p. 205). I am less sure that this is so 'clear'. He was consciously thinking of his visit and says so explicitly in referring to the Neapolitan *crypta* as a *Pausilippe*; but it is implausible to think such an allusion or gesture involved him in constructing a whole programme – with a Roman bath (which may not be his anyway), a semicircular pool to represent the Lago di Agnano, the Albury gardens as the Elysian Fields which, in Italy, lay between Baiae and Misenum – and that all of that was explicitly Epicurean. And Evelyn's design for Albury (see illus. 33) does not, or at least cannot, make such references clear on paper or in the garden itself.

On the other hand, the Smalls have an ingenious way of finding an Epicurean explanation of the experience of arriving on the Albury terraces through the tunnel under the hillside, as being analogous to the *crypta* in Naples: the optical illusion of emerging from the darkness into the light is discussed in *De rerum natura*, Book IV, and is partly quoted by Evelyn in Chapter X of Book II of 'Elysium Britannicum'. But it hardly seems a Lucretian experience unique to Albury, as that section of his manuscript makes clear; even so, it presupposes that visitors would always arrive from the tunnel into the Albury gardens. In short, Evelyn may well have wished to espouse Lucretian ideas during the 1650s, but even in his own translation and presentation of them he was evasive and uncertain, as unwilling to publish as he was to articulate these ideas in garden forms and elements.

The résumé of 'Elysium Britanicum' that he circulated in 1660 and later appended to *Acetaria* does not correspond to the surviving manuscript that has now been transcribed by John Ingram, to which my references are given. As is clear, the synopsis is divided into three books, but much of Book II and all of III have been lost, with only portions, the *Kalendarium Hortense* and *Acetaria*, alone seeing publication. In the first book are general principles of the four elements,[11] seasonal change, 'celestial influences', soils and their treatment, upon which basis any gardener has to work. The second book provides a very detailed review of what today we would call garden design and garden maintenance: from the requirements of a good gardener to the necessary skills of growing, planting

and transplanting (with a calendar of monthly tasks), from a
variety of pragmatic forms and requirements (fencing, upkeep,
pests), to those garden elements that gave it beauty and ornament, and provide a spectacle for the eye and mind ('Hortulan
refreshments'). Yet for Evelyn the ornamental or 'pleasure'
garden coexists with a cluster of other designed spaces that
yield an abundance of useful items for the table and for medicine, and these he lists: conservatories, a vineyard, orchard, a
vegetable garden or 'olitorie'. The third book moves into a
zone at once scientific and philosophical, cultural and social:
here would be discussed a range of activities that clearly per-
tain to the making of a garden and its adjacent areas and
concerns, like preserving and distilling, or he describes the
representation of plants in paint or other materials, the creation of garlands, and the construction of a library of hortulan
books. Beyond these, the third book opens out finally into a
mare maggiore of themes – from entertainments in a garden to
burials there, from gardens (including Paradise) to morals
and a *lex hortorum* or 'laws and privileges' therein, and finally
(as if the survey had been negligent in some fashion) to a history of ancient and modern gardens and a 'Description of a
Villa'.

Throughout the manuscript that survives, the text is frequently augmented with diagrams, drawings and annexed
explanations of such items as garden tools (illus. 40), perspectives, aviaries, rabbit warrens, beehives (see illus. 17), and of
course plants and insects. The text, as transcribed by Ingram,
is full of phrases or sentences crossed through, marginal
notes added or pasted in, insertions of material too lengthy
to be inserted in the text or written in the margins, some of

40 Page from the 'Elysium Britannicum' showing garden tools, where no. 43 (at left towards the top) is a watering truck or barrel for the garden.

which loose papers have become dislodged from their original location. It has to be said that Ingram's printed text, with its careful recording of all these rewordings and rethinkings (second, third thoughts and so on), is infinitely more accessible to a reader than the actual manuscript. His edition uses modern typographical formats and annotations to present a semblance of the original manuscript which is nonetheless clear and hospitable. On the other hand, something is lost: the original manuscript allows a more authentic closeness to Evelyn's instinctive and ever-changing response to his materials. Yet those authorial revisions, though persistent and endless, do not seem the real basis of Evelyn's eventual difficulty with his book. To have accommodated them, absorbed them into his final draft, would be challenging but not impossible – it is a challenge that many authors have overcome.

The whole seventeenth century was a time of upheavals, not only in politics and religion, with endless challenges to the stability of its population, but in concepts of knowledge and epistemology, with the sciences, especially physics, that underpinned them. If these were not enough for an intelligent and thoughtful, if traditional, man like Evelyn, there was a topic in which the 'Elysium Britannicum' was most involved, namely the making and use of gardens. Everything he had seen in Europe suggested new forms of design, new ways of using garden elements to signify or represent a conspectus of ideas that were not limited to the garden, even if embedded or given voice within them. Furthermore, it was clear to Evelyn that gardens, though still enabling the status of the rich and powerful, began to appeal to others – his time in the Netherlands, above all, made this democratization very clear.

And then his own garden-making at Sayes Court sought to make some foreign ideas acceptable in ways that were clearly not apt for 'royal gardens', though that is the subtitle he gave to the 'Elysium Britannicum'.

One of the difficulties he must have faced was that by the second half of the seventeenth century, garden forms and concepts were taken up and adjusted for a variety of different people and social conditions, in books like John Woolridge's *Systema Horti-culturae: or, the Art of Gardening* (1677), Timothy Nourse's *Campania Foelix: or, A Discourse of the Benefits and Improvement of Husbandry* (1700), and Nehemiah Grew's *Anatomy of Plants with an Idea of a Philosophical History of Plants* (1682). Nor was 'Elysium Britannicum' likely to be a 'universal' work on the subject, as he told Beale, applicable to all; that Evelyn would not live to see books on clergymen's or ladies' gardening, issued by John Lawrence in 1714 and Lawrence again (writing curiously under the pseudonym of 'Charles Evelyn') in 1717, did not mean that these cultural and social changes were not apparent before being announced and published. And the topic of a universal treatise on gardens and garden-making would have been directed obviously to a wider readership in an age of much enlarged literacy and publishing, but also in an age with a wider range of believers, some of whom reverenced gardens but not an English faith, which was another anxiety to overcome.

Though it is hard to show in short space, some examples will serve to illustrate what Evelyn was struggling with, for it should be remembered that the impulse to write the 'Elysium Britannicum' was to make available in England and in the English language the wealth of gardening advices and information that its author had garnered in his travels and from his scrutiny of both ancient writings and contemporary learning. Two major issues confronted Evelyn when composing it: how to interpret ancient writings and relate them to modern practice – this was both semantically and horticulturally necessary; then, how to relate verbal, especially ancient, descriptions to modern visual imagery (on the assumption that his sketches in the manuscript could be adequately engraved, which is what Needham and his signatories were concerned to accomplish).

The first chapter of the first book addresses the first of these issues. Its three and a half pages in manuscript (four in Ingram's transcription) are awash with Greek and Latin phrases, the glossing of which is obsessive, despite his remark that this 'may pass for a conceit of the *etymologist*'. But the adjudication of ancient languages (a minimum of twelve classical authorities are cited) is but a step toward understanding what the terms mean in the modern world. There is little sense, in his universal *tour d'horizon* of gardens, that there is any cultural or social difference between God's original Paradise, Adam's postlapsarian need to 'improve the fruits of the earth', the Roman Horace, or the modern makers of the 'four or five' sorts of garden. To 'define a garden *now*' (my italics) is to subsume it into 'a type of Heaven', which is what worthy and illustrious kings, philosophers and wise men mean when they 'describe a garden, and call it Elysium', hence not one specifically adjusted to cultural locality. Evelyn's need to secure the roots of his discussions in etymological research hampers his presentation of the material in modern times and terms, and one wonders how much his contemporaries needed to share his endless anxiety with origins. Indeed, much later (*EB*, p. 410), when he appeals to the 'curious reader' and promises to report on 'wonderous and stupendious plants', he asserts that he wishes to explain them 'not in lofty words, but plain & veritable narrations, & in such language as will become [that is, suit] both our [modern] wonder and astonishment'. That emphasis, reminiscent of Sprat's call for plainness of speech, is not compatible with the style of the opening chapters.

It comes, however, at precisely the point where he concludes his chapter on 'the Philosophical-Medical Garden' by sketching a garden of simples based on what he had seen in Paris (see illus. 9, 10). This representation 'in perspective', he explains, will clarify the many species of plants 'for the most part strangers to our Elysium as yet'. It may be that Evelyn, unable to abandon his beloved etymology and verbal classicism, seeks to achieve something more direct and practical through images. The dialogue, or *paragone* (contest) if you will, between word and image, is also between the image and the various versions of the word that it illustrates. This is intimately aligned with his similar need to explore a universal Elysium as well as a modern and practical garden culture. Now it is perfectly possible to generalize about garden-making, and we all do it. But there is also the required understanding that each garden is different on account of its formal design, its climate and soil, its planting, and the social needs it serves. Evelyn certainly realized that during the years in which he gardened at Sayes Court and while visiting a variety of gardens in England (some of these are recounted in Chapter Eleven). Other late seventeenth- and early eighteenth-century garden books, noted above, equally made clear that different assumptions underlaid and promoted gardens for a range of social classes and uses, not least those close to the metropolis as opposed to those in more distant counties. That particular social understanding was not adequately registered in 'Elysium Britannicum', though he was surely aware of them. Even when he received Beale's careful account of Backbury Hill, he shifts it into both an *exemplum* of an ancient British or maybe Roman garden and lauds it as 'no phantastical *Utopia*, but a real place' (*EB*, p. 97). Yet his version *is* truly utopian, and he removes from his text any suggestion of its actual location in Herefordshire and makes analogies between it and Mt Sinai, the Garden of Semiramis in Media, and Paradise. It is clear, writes Alessandro Scafi, that Paradise is a flexible site:

> Just as many international frontiers were originally zones of transmontane communication rather than clear-cut lines of sharp division, so Paradise seems to constitute a permeable boundary zone, a place where human space and time mix with divine infinity and eternity. Seen this way, Paradise is itself a boundary.[12]

What does, however, become clear is that it is in Evelyn's sketches, presumably intended for reworking by a competent engraver, that he addresses horticultural particulars in a true Royal Society spirit. The images concentrate frequently on issues of planting, grafting, transplanting and transporting of specimens, just as his text in Chapter XVI of Book II is extremely detailed on the scope and contents of flower gardens. A crude sketch of a 'coronary garden' is labelled and the text shows how even an accomplished gardener, 'master

& general of all this multitude', must be helped by depicting its exact delineation, its contents listed (and relisted when changes were made), so that he 'shall have an immediate survey of your whole garden, & know what is planted in every bed'. Other sketches treat of rabbit warrens, aviaries modelled after the Roman Varro's verbal description (a pattern of birdcages still found today), beehives that are transparent (see illus. 17) and are vertical, or horizontal and segmented, furnaces to warm silkworms, seed troughs, and a conspectus of garden tools. For a demonstration of how to render an illusionary landscape on a blank wall, a perspectival device that he had admired in Europe and thought would enhance a small space, he instances a garden in Ripon, Yorkshire, where at the end of a closed walk a perspective is contrived by placing 'a looking glass set so declining as to take in the sky, having a landskip painted under it, which made a wonderful effect' (*EB*, p. 218).

One example of a European garden element that is both 'healthful' and 'more frequented in foreign countries than our own' was to convert walks into 'palle mailles', namely long, or sometimes bent, alleys with boards along their sides and iron hoops at the end where bowls were played. (Pepys records his first view of a 'Pelemele' in April 1661, and the word survives today in London's Pall Mall, which was established on the site where James II would play.) Evelyn's sketches two examples he had seen in Paris, at the Arsenal and the Tuileries (illus. 41); the text notes others in Tours and at Genoa, and in each case their forms are accommodated to the specific site. The text is an extremely detailed explanation of both their construction and the equipment used (the wood for the

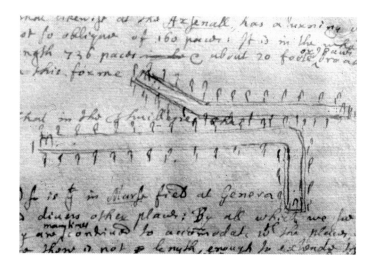

balls is French box; the mallet is ash, bound with leather). His final word, unsurprisingly, also concerns trees: some of these pall-malls have double or even triple ranges of 'most lofty & shady trees', designed for the 'grace and magnificence of the walks and to refresh our active gamester'.

The verbal descriptions make good sense of this conjunction of word and image, linking an example to its more conceptual and theoretical explanations. One section is especially intriguing as it addresses a matter that is usually evaded in garden discussions, namely sound.[13] Moving water in gardens is an obvious auditory source, and Evelyn's chapter IX of Book II takes on the provision and manipulation of waterworks of various kinds. But the following sequence, 'Of artificial echoes, music', explains how music can be made in a hydraulically operated cylinder, with a page of music appended (EB, 234–6), how water can imitate birdsong, and how water in hydraulically worked trumpets will sound the times of day;

41 A sketch from the 'Elysium Britannicum' showing walks for 'pell mell'.

there is further, in a chapter on insects, music that will tempt a tarantula spider out of its 'fits' into an 'amicable concert', though should the musician make a discord, the spider will 'grow mad again'!

Evelyn's concern for a modern England was to marry garden use and practice with philosophical and imaginative resources. Central to this is his determination to bring into modern gardens the rich repertory of garden ornaments, which he lists as 'caves, grots, mounts, and irregular ornaments' that 'do influence the soul and spirits of man'. That was a very contemporary design vocabulary, visible enough in Europe but rarer in most Elizabeth and Jacobean gardens. It allowed him to provide specific particulars while elaborating on the universality of garden experience. But the point of those features, as he constantly advised, was that gardens represent, via their various ingredients, a world that is outside and bigger than one single garden: he is endlessly concerned to underline that the collaboration of nature and art in garden-making was but a local and careful intimation or representation of larger cultural and primitive natures outside them. I have discussed these ideas at length in an earlier essay;[14] I would, however, add that the point I was making in 1998 was perhaps too inclined to emphasize the efficiency of a universal theory in Evelyn than to see how his seventeenth-century context determined his theories. In the next century or so after Evelyn, notions of representation changed radically, yet gardens never lost the need or obligation to speak of things beyond themselves. That is why Evelyn's is still a work that teaches how we should understand those connections; that he did not, could not, anticipate how things would in fact

OUTLINE OF 'ELYSIUM BRITANNICUM' (1699)

THE PLAN OF A ROYAL GARDEN:

Describing, and Shewing the *Amplitude*, and *Extent* of that Part of *Georgicks*, which belongs to *Horticulture*;

IN THREE BOOKS.

Laudato ingentia rura,
Exiguum colito.

change, does not make him less important, but only allows us to see him carefully in and of his time.

That dialogue or balance of these two competing instincts in garden-making – the particular and conceptual, the local and the general – is hard to adjudicate, probably unnecessary. My sense now is that it is with particulars that Evelyn makes his best case, and that it did not depend upon ancient lore or authority, though he loved to think it did. In 1998 when I first wrote about the 'Elysium', I wanted to find in it an idea or theory that held general application; Evelyn himself asks for an 'incomparable use' of his ideas to be a 'fit at all seasons' (*EB*, p. 134, though he was writing specifically of garden walks). His was not, as he told Beale, a 'steady & composed genius', and his work remains fragmentary and palimpsestic. But his genius still grasped some of the ineluctable truths of garden-making and articulated their worth for England. That he could not shape them into a coherent whole and that his country-men never got to read it before their gardens were taken over by the *furor* of so-called English landscaping in the eighteenth century is an unhappy trick of history.

ELEVEN

Last Decades of the Seventeenth Century

EVELYN'S BIOGRAPHERS have tended, understandably, to emphasize the first two-thirds of his life more than the last; the three decades at the end of the seventeenth century seem patchy, less able both for Evelyn himself and for his biographers to discern much structure, private vitality or new excitement, even though more information is now available. Thus 'life went on', wrote John Bowle in 1981, 'the life of official London carried on', yet Evelyn was 'ubiquitous' (*John Evelyn and His World*, pp. 185, 89, 204), and Gillian Darley in 2006 entitled one of her last chapters in *John Evelyn: Living for Ingenuity* 'Perpetual Motion'. It is true that this 'chameleon', as he has been called, seemed less able to find a centre for his turning world. During the last decades there were often tense and dispiriting interconnections between his personal, domestic life and public affairs, though not entirely of his own choosing.

His faith and family had always been important. The first became something of an obsession in the last decades of the century, first as he involved himself during most of the 1670s with an extremely pious young maid of honour at court, Margaret Blagge, which somewhat discomforted Mary, and then with his larger unhappiness at the rise of Roman

Catholicism, as he watched the forced departure of James II and the arrival of William and Mary to the throne.

The growing family was also shadowed by illness, and the deaths of his father-in-law and two daughters; Sir Richard Browne, grumpy, ill, living now at Sayes Court and frustrated with his failure to obtain the monies that were owed him and thinking, along with his daughter, that Evelyn ought to have done more to pressure the government to reimburse them. By accident, that involved Evelyn battling with a powerful official, Sidney Godolphin, his friend and the widower of Margaret Blagge, whose life Evelyn was writing after her untimely death in childbirth.

Thus faith, family and government interacted, and not without unhappiness and frustration on all sides. The base of family life, Sayes Court, was devastated in the winter of 1685–6, and he set himself to refashion it. But a combination of having to rethink the garden, his old age, other disappointments with life in Deptford and – another accident – the reversion to him of Wotton after his brother's death without male offspring, all ensured the family's removal in the mid-1690s from Sayes Court to residence at Wotton. Yet even that happy and unexpected outcome was dogged with legal and financial troubles.

By the end of the century he did publish again – the modest verses of *Mundus Muliebris* by his daughter Mary, who had died of smallpox in 1685, preceded by his own preface and a burlesque 'Fop-dictionary'. Others were more substantial, like his *Numismata* (1697) and *Acetaria* (1699), and his last, important translation, of La Quintinie's *The Compleat Gard'ner* (1693). This turned out to be his final venture into garden matters, for 'Elysium Britannicum' continued to languish, with only *Acetaria* rescued for publication from its accumulating pile of manuscript drafts; as an addendum to that work he had added his 1699 outline of the 'Elysium'. That failure was due undoubtedly to both a public and a personal debacle.

He still relished the advice he could give on others' gardens and continued his visits and comments on what he observed there, at least in his Diary. At Cliveden, the 'stupendous natural rock, wood & prospect' of the Earl of Rochester, he was reminded of the Villa Aldobrandini at Frascati, a romantic place that solicited ekphrastic poetry: Cliveden had been created at 'extraordinary expense', with grottoes in the chalk hillsides, 'cloisters, descents, gardens, and avenues through the wood august & stately'. In contrast, and on the same excursion, he found and much preferred both the painter Antonio Verrio's 'pretty garden, with its careful choice of flowers and curiosities' near Windsor, and his cousin George Evelyn's flat site of Huntercombe Manor – 'with sweet gardens, and exquisitely kept, though large'. He visited Cassiobury Park in Hertfordshire at the invitation of the Earl of Essex, and admired the house, especially the carving of Grinling Gibbons, whom he had discovered earlier; its landscape setting was immense, cut through with avenues and elaborate tree planting, especially firs, under the care of Moses Cook. On another occasion, the wealthy merchant Sir Josiah Child, who had established his estate from scratch on a barren site in Epping Forest, Evelyn saw as typical of 'those over grown and suddenly monied men'. To Althorp, he was invited by the Countess of Sunderland, one of the intellectual women he always admired, and while reserved about her husband's

Catholicism, he applauded the avenues, canals, fishponds and game preserves that were 'all managed without any show of solicitude'. By 1700 Pepys had moved to Clapham, where Evelyn's visit found him happy and the house furnished with Indian and Chinese curiosities, with gardens and buildings admirably suited for pleasurable retirement, which by then Evelyn was himself trying to enjoy at Wotton.

He was also, during these years, still active on projects that grew out of his European experiences and enthusiasms, working for the Council for Foreign Plantations, lately Council of Trade and Plantations, where John Locke was now secretary.[1] He was grateful and curious to learn about the immense vegetation that was reported in Virginia, and shared a correspondent's worry that scientific pursuits there were being submerged in the zeal for making money. At the Royal Society, he continued to attend meetings, present papers and chair committees, but the institution was in need both of more useful members and more funds, and Evelyn was distressed at the king's failure to support it; he also engaged himself to find it a permanent home. He took on the secretaryship there for a while, but refused its presidency when he was nominated in 1690 and again in 1693, wishing to 'avoid it in this ill conjuncture of public affairs', all the while hearing sermons on 'the different ends of the upright and wicked', or 'the falsehood & vanity of evil courses', while noting 'exceeding great storms & yet warm season' in November 1690. He enjoyed the sight of a young rhinoceros ('or unicorn' – 'more resembled a huge enormous swine'), the first to be seen in England, which he described in great and careful detail; also a 'living crocodile' from the West Indies (*Diary*, IV.390–91).

And notwithstanding his aversion to military service, he was delighted by the re-enactment at Windsor Castle of the battle of Maastricht ('artificially designed'). It was more serious than the modest effort by Uncle Toby and Corporal Trim, described later by Sterne in *Tristram Shandy*, to represent the siege of Namur, and it was an uncanny precursor of modern re-enactments. The Windsor event still delighted this member of the Royal Society for what he took to be accurate manoeuvres and displays of military engineering – a 'formal siege, against a Work with Bastions, Bullwarks, Ramparts, Palizads . . . hornworks, Counterscarps &c'. He was happy to note that, with guns fired on both sides, the grenades, exploding mines, parties advancing, prisoners taken, 'what is most strange, [it was] all without disorder, or ill accident'.

On a more practical bent, he found opportunity to advise (negatively) the Lord Treasurer on the purchase of books from the library of the deceased Earl of Bristol, but was far more concerned to see that a public library be established. He was always eager to promote libraries (and the index of his published Diary has two columns of references about them), but he was particularly eager to see books in the hands of those not able to afford and maintain one. He worked with Thomas Tenison and Wren to erect a library 'for public use' in the parish of St Martin-in-the-Fields, and in planning a hospital for disabled soldiers at Chelsea, designed by Wren, he recommended a library and even suggested books that the inhabitants might find suitable even if they were not 'studious'. Wren's handsome design for the Royal Hospital, the foundations of which were laid in 1692, had gardens and canals towards the Thames, reminiscent of Maisons, one of

Evelyn's favourite French landscaped sites. Evelyn had hoped that he could become its governor, but eventually accepted the offer by Godolphin to be its treasurer.

His meagre salary as treasurer did not arrive, and lack of sufficient funds provided a leitmotif in many letters dispatched especially to Godolphin in pursuit of either monies to reimburse his father-in-law or to obtain salaried positions for him and his family. His sense that Godolphin was 'My dearest friend', as he frequently addressed the man who had married the sainted Margaret Blagge, encouraged him to deluge him with lengthy, carefully argued requests that Godolphin, now more and more an established figure in government, must have found both embarrassing and impossible personally for him to respond to without consultation. Evelyn even lamented in 1679 the fact that Godolphin's dedication of 'yourself so profitably to the benefits of the public' in 'all your moments' (LB, 11.634) had lost him 'the most sensible effects of that endeared friendship I once enjoyed, without envying the felicity of one that is now in Heaven [that is, Margaret]', and then proceeded to seek help for his brother-in-law, William Glanville!

Even now well advancing in years, Evelyn was still ambitious for some more settled and congenial government work, though as early as On Liberty and Servitude (1649; MW, pp. 27–37) he had resisted enslavement of a courtier's mind and body by political business; now his needs were as much for funds as for obtaining a post. Nonetheless, he accepted the invitation to join James II's Privy Council, hoping for some useful role in government, both for himself and for obtaining a post for his son. Yet, as noticed in the previous chapter, Lord Berkeley worried that his appointment to the Privy Council would obstruct completion of the work on 'Elysium', and Evelyn himself found that it involved uncomfortable decisions. While he apparently did not dislike James personally, he found his Roman Catholicism abhorrent in a public figure. As the unease and discomfort grew in the nation, and finally into its rejection of a Catholic monarch, Evelyn was also wavering about the country's future. However, keeping in touch with government circles perhaps offered him also a chance to finally resolve the issues of both Sayes Court, still leased, and the payments owed to Sir Richard by his father-in-law's former trustee William Prettyman, as well as the funds that Sir Richard thought were owed to him from his post in France; both were eventually settled, but only after protracted and expensive court proceedings.

In 1695 Evelyn, again through the offices of Godolphin, was appointed Treasurer to the Royal Naval Hospital at Greenwich, which was being projected with Wren as architect. It replaced an abandoned palace and it would, thought Evelyn, be the British equivalent to the Invalides in Paris. His salary was small (£300 per annum), though, more crucially, funding for this project was forever difficult and never appeared when it was needed. A subscription list was formed to raise money, but many who pledged did not contribute; yet the foundation stone was laid on 30 June 1696. In April 1700 William III was presented by Wren and Evelyn with a model and engraved plans of the Hospital, and three years later Evelyn, now 83, resigned the treasurership to his son-in-law, William Draper. (An engraving of this handsome complex was published in 1725 in Colen Campbell's *Vitruvius*

Britannicus, a vision that would have delighted Evelyn for its classical proportions, its quads reminiscent of Oxford and Cambridge, its truly British splendour and its dedication of the nation's naval traditions, as well as its landscape situation; he would also have applauded Campbell's title.)

If his research, scholarship and hopes for employment lacked clarity and direction, so at times did his private life. The family took care and attention – and he was nothing if not stern and advisory when it came to dealing with his surviving son, who did not match the vision he had once envisaged for the five-year-old Richard before his early death in 1678; the same stricture that his father-in-law had expressed then – that Evelyn was 'over charging' the young boy, whose 'tabula rasa [was] easily confounded' – could be applied now to John, who seemed unable to match his father's hopes for success in the world.

Two daughters also died. Mary, the eldest and dearest, born in 1665, died from smallpox, aged nineteen. Her father's Diary is remarkably eloquent on her accomplishments,

> curious of knowing everything to some excess, had I not sometimes repressed it [*sic!*] . . . She had read an abundance of history, and all the best poets . . . all the best romances and modern poems; she could compose happily, and put in pretty symbols, as in the *Mundus muliebris*, wherein is an examination of the immense variety of her modes and ornaments belonging to the sex; but all of these are vain trifles to the interior virtues which adorned her soul (IV.420–22).

Five years after her death he published her poem on the world
of women as the *Mundus foppensis, or the Fop Display'd*, addressed
to a one who has not travelled and, not having read Cicero's
Offices, 'sets up for a beau'.[2]

A preface, presumably by himself, remarks 'how the world
is altered among us, since foreign manners, the luxury . . . has
universally obtained among us, corrupting ancient simplicity'.
Mary obviously had a shrewd wit, a keen and sceptical view of
the fashionable world, though her verses make a poor burlesque; her title page carries two lines of Juvenal and a taut
English translation (by Evelyn?), nicely turned to the world
she tried to satirize: 'Such care for a becoming dress they take,
/ As if their life and honour were at stake'. Evelyn's affection
for Mary is touching, and his own contribution, more trench-
ant than her octosyllabics, is appended as *The Fop-dictionary, or
'An alphabetical catalogue of the hard and foreign names and terms of
the art cosmetic, &c together with Their Interpretations, for instruction
of the Unlearned'.* Ever eager to instruct, it contrives a few hits
at *précieuse* follies: 'MOUCHOIRE. It were rude, vulgar, and
unseemly to call it handkerchief,' or faux Frenchifed pronun-
ciation in 'TOILET. Corruptly called the *twilight*, but ordinarily
signifying a little cloth.'

Another daughter, Elizabeth, distressed by her sister's
death yet excluded from her parents' grief, had eloped with
a man working at Deptford dockyard, married, and fallen ill,
again with smallpox. She was nursed by her mother once again,
until God was 'pleased to take her out of this vale of misery'.
The father of Evelyn's wife also died suddenly, aged nearly
eighty, in February 1683. But Evelyn's surviving daughter,
Susanna, was married in April 1693 to William Draper, a

marriage welcomed by all the family.[3] The modest ceremony was held at Holborn, not Wotton, and was conducted by an Evelyn friend, Thomas Tenison, Bishop of Lincoln, with Francis (Margaret Godolphin's son) as one of the pages, and a young Tuke, though Catholic, as bridesmaid.

But his son John was Evelyn's gravest burden. By the time he died in 1699, aged 44, though depressed and gloomy, he had much redeemed himself in his father's eyes. In his youth he left Evelyn frequently distressed by his lack of application, his debts, his drinking (even taunting his father with tales of excessive drinking at Wotton), his unhappiness when forced to be at Sayes Court, his inability to be what his father wanted – a better version of the five-year-old Richard whose virtues were celebrated in Evelyn's *The Golden Book*. John received the best education from tutors, being first taught by Milton's nephew, Edward Philips, and then by Ralph Bohun, who became a good family friend and looked after him at Oxford, and with his father organized John's educational regime. John was admitted to the Middle Temple, but gave up his studies, evidently lacking any self-discipline. He also seems to have been socially self-conscious, suffering from crooked legs, the irons on which he depended concealed beneath long coats. In 1675 John was dispatched to Paris in the company of Lord and Lady Berkeley on their diplomatic mission, under the watchful eye of his father's friend Margaret Blagge. But he was bored by life there, apparently treated almost as a servant and not involved in any of the various Berkeley activities. Professing an interest in languages, he asked leave to travel, as his father had once done through Europe, but Evelyn refused and brought him home. Evelyn was clearly thinking of John in 1679 when he dispatched a long letter to the Countess of Sunderland (*LB*, 11.625–8) that argued, contrary to his own earlier advocacy of the virtues of travel, that, at least for her own sons, travel abroad of 'susceptible youths' found them quickly involved in 'profane and filthy communication, atheistical, negligent and extravagant talk, which passes now amongst our most generous youth'. He lectured John endlessly, with instructions on morality, the need to find employment outside the court and eventually, when he got married to Martha Spence, with marital advice and the seriousness of the sacrament he was undertaking.

The marriage settled John, and he resumed his studies at the Middle Temple, leaving his wife and son at Sayes Court. An early venture into translation, whether inclined or pushed by his father, of Rapin's poem on gardens, was followed in the 1680s by translations of a volume of Plutarch's *Lives* and *Grotius, his Arguments*. Government posts were hard to obtain, yet he obtained one briefly in the Treasury, then a more permanent posting in 1692 to Ireland in Customs and Excise through the good offices of Sidney Godolphin; John left his son, Jack, in Deptford with his parents, but took his young daughter and wife with him to Ireland. He developed a love of books and paintings, and his own Jack promised exceeding well, and would eventually go to Eton and Oxford. But John had never been in good health and was often depressed by the time of his death in 1699. Knowing by then that he would have no son to succeed George at Wotton, Evelyn saw his grandson Jack, born in March 1682, as the inheritor of his own taste and of the family estate.

While Evelyn had always been willing to observe other faiths during his tour of Europe, he was steadfast in his dedication to the English Church. Yet the slow, but increasingly obvious, growth of Roman Catholicism at the court and among the king's advisers offended him deeply: 'the truth is, the Roman church [is] exceeding bold, and busy everywhere.' His Diary records Parliament 'being now alarmed with the whole nation, about a conspiracy of some eminent papists, for the destruction of the king, & by introducing popery' (IV.153–4). This was the Popish Plot, fabricated by Titus Oates and a confederate, but it was nonetheless capable of inflaming a real anti-Catholic fervour against the Jesuits, whom Oates had said were trying to kill the king. Evelyn had already translated *The New Heresy of the Jesuits* in 1667 and, though suspicious of Oates's veracity, was exceedingly worried when a Jesuit secretary of the Duchess of York accused the queen of wanting to kill the king. The secretary was tried and executed, and Parliament passed a Test Act to exclude all Roman Catholics from sitting in the Commons or the Lords, with the exception of the Duke of York himself, well known to be a Catholic. When the Commons later voted against York's 'recusancy', James retreated with his duchess to the Spanish Netherlands. A further scare, the 'Protestant Plot' of 1683, disturbed Evelyn even more, and he blamed the English for having betrayed the Dutch in the late wars.

In February 1685 Charles II died, and Evelyn heard from Pepys that he had received the Catholic last rites, though doubted the evidence that he was shown. On the day of Charles's funeral, the new king, the former Duke of York, shocked Evelyn by attending Mass, and in March Evelyn saw an oratory set up in the king's lodging – 'mass being publically said, & the Romanists swarming at Court' (*Diary*, IV.419). Though James professed his willingness to defend the Church of England 'as by law established', rebellions in the Highlands and by the Protestant Duke of Monmouth in the West Country did not augur a smooth reign, though they were quickly put down. Evelyn seemed pleased at first with the king's person, but lamented the larger political scene and wished that James 'were of the national religion' (*Diary*, IV.230). He feared for the French Protestants after the Revocation of the Edict of Nantes in 1685, and as a Commissioner for the Privy Council he refused permission to publish popish books, or managed to absent himself from crucial meetings to deny it a quorum. A new Catholic Chapel at Whitehall was opened in 1687 with unabashed ritual and homage to the papacy. James tried to court nonconformists and Quakers to include them with Catholics in a general toleration, and required all bishops to read his Declaration of Indulgence; many refused. There seemed no prospect of a peaceful resolution and increasingly there was fear that another civil war was brewing. James, realizing that his own daughter was married to a possible successor, the Protestant William of Orange, fluctuated between allowing a restoration of ejected Protestant fellows in Oxford and staffing his army with Catholic officers, mainly from Ireland. James shifted as best he could. People switched religions according to pressure and circumstance, hence the satire of the Vicar of Bray, who altered his religion when the monarch changed his.

The final months of James's reign were messy and muddled, and the result – the Glorious, but bloodless, Revolution

– is well known. Long before this was accomplished, overtures had already been made to William of Orange in the Netherlands and his English consort, Mary. Evelyn was, as usual, somewhat uncertain about the likely outcome, and prayed that God would step in and 'settle truth and peace amongst us again'. A variety of different political suggestions were being aired as to how England should be governed. But as Bowle notes in *John Evelyn and His World* (p. 201), 'events were making up Evelyn's own royalist mind'. He was undoubtedly glad both that civil war was avoided, though armies were moved about England without engaging, and that a Protestant prince and his English wife had come to the thrones of Great Britain. He sent his son John to greet the Prince of Orange, and watched James II, guarded by Dutch soldiers, taken to a boat and dispatched via Rochester for France. The Commons addressed 'the great question of Government' (*Diary*, IV.616) and urged the Lords to crown William of Orange; the Lords tried for a regency of twelve bishops, but this was narrowly defeated. The arrival of William and Mary was feted in Deptford and across the land, and George Evelyn's son, also George, died from an 'apoplectic fit' after drinking to celebrate the Glorious Revolution. Nobody exactly knew where James had got to, and not all the bishops were happy with this disposal of a consecrated monarch; even Evelyn thought the 'temper' of the new king 'slothful sickly'. Evelyn, now aged 69 in September 1689, was not optimistic ('what government next? Regal or by Election?').

An essential component of Evelyn's domesticity, as he knew well himself, had been his wife and her own resolute faith and domestic probity. Their early marriage, when Mary was thirteen and he twenty-six, proved both a success and a lifelong support for him, though Darley (*John Evelyn*, p. 95), foreswearing hindsight, calls it a 'gamble'; maybe Evelyn himself realized shrewdly how good a choice he had made. His zeal to instruct surely imposed much pedagogical earnestness upon her, and his desire to do so that is apparent in his early letters, as well as the *Instructions Oeconimiques*, leads Darley (p. 73) to write that it was more 'suggestive of those between a school master and pupil than young lovers'. But Mary possessed something from the start that never left her: a social ease and intellectual skill learned in the cosmopolitan world of France, Paris especially, where she much enjoyed herself and which she was reluctant to leave, not least because her new husband was being urged to stay out of England. Her portrait by Robert Nanteuil, taken while she was still in France, gives nothing away about her future, except perhaps her youthful and steady gaze, which she inherited from her parents (illus. 42).[4] Yet in 1657, when William Rand was translating Gassendi's *Life of Peiresc* and dedicating it to Evelyn, he also went out of his way to celebrate Mary for her 'English gravity, being moderately [that is, in moderation] allayed, sweetened and spirited, by the mettlesome air and education of France', which has brought her to 'such a perfection, as to be no hindrance, but a meet help to her beloved lord, in his most many concernments'. Dedicatory epistles, especially then, could be overwrought; but this seems nothing but an inspired appreciation of genuine worth, and Rand's testimony was to be constantly confirmed.

Mary was both independent and dutiful, a combination that takes real skill at any time. Impatient with any intellectual or social affectation, she was forthright and often witty in

writing to family, like her cousin, the Catholic Samuel Tuke,
or her son's former tutor at Oxford, the bachelor Ralph Bohun,
a fervent anti-papist.[5] Wry and solicitous in ways that may
still surprise us, she is coolly dispassionate in describing to
Tuke her solitary life at Sayes Court ('a philosopher, a woman,
and a child, heaps of books'); but she could also tell Bohun
of her exasperation at her husband's need to satisfy 'his seraphick who deserves that and anything a thousand times better'.
Yet after the death of the 'seraphick' Margaret Godolphin
(née Blagge), Mary could evenhandedly note that, though 'not
in the first rank of [Mary's] friendship', Margaret 'combined
the grace of a lady of the court with the sincerity and innocence of a primitive Christian' (Darley, *John Evelyn*, pp. 232,
252). That 'primitive' is both shrewd and graceful and yet
extremely sharp. She was loyal too in ways that others might
have found unconventional: after the death of Pepys's wife,
whereupon Pepys cohabited for the rest of his life with Mrs
Skinner, his housekeeper, Mary joined her husband in meeting and always greeting the pair kindly. She alone seems to
have forgiven her daughter Elizabeth for eloping, which
Evelyn never did, even after her death from smallpox.

On her return to England with John, Mary failed to obtain
a position at court with the Portuguese queen (a lost opportunity that she may eventually have appreciated), and this gave
her the chance to involve herself wholly in the life of Sayes
Court, not neglecting her friends, but producing four sons,
only one of whom survived into adulthood, and three daughters. When her husband was frequently away, especially
during the Dutch wars and during his necessary attendance
at court, she managed the property, some of the interior

42 Robert Nanteuil, *Mary Evelyn*, née Browne, late 1640s.

rebuilding with extreme care, as well as directing garden maintenance. As daughter, wife, mother and companion, she seemed a perfect example of an intelligent and accomplished seventeenth-century woman – a painter and miniaturist; a musician; an elegant writer who involved herself in her husband's work by helping him with his translations from the French, which she spoke fluently, and talking with him about the sick and wounded during the Dutch wars; and capable of designing the frontispiece for his translation of Lucretius as well as being skilled in the domestic realms of kitchen and household medicine. It is difficult for anyone in the twenty-first century to gauge her completely within her own context. Evelyn said she was 'the best wife in the world, sweet, and (though not charming) agreeable and as she grew up pious, loyal & of so just a temper'. Darley (*John Evelyn*, p. 73) writes that this 'hardly does her justice', and it was not particularly fulsome; but I like that phrase – '(though not charming) agreeable', since it speaks of *her* potential to be wry and even ironical as well as agreeable, which her letters often reveal. Bohun got it absolutely right, though, when he acknowledged, with a wit she'd have appreciated, that 'you perform that [that is, your wifely duties] in a silent closet which whole courts and theatres would unanimously applaud' (quoted Darley, *John Evelyn*, p. 95). That opposition of self-performing stage and sycophantic court to the home (and its fleeting allusion to a closet or cabinet, which she herself possessed) is particularly telling. She was tolerant, wry, in private even satirical, about some of her husband's female friends, especially Margaret Cavendish, Marchioness of Newcastle. But she faced her greatest challenge in dealing with the other Margaret, in which she surpassed herself. This episode has elicited a variety of explanations and narratives about the middle-aged Evelyn, but it bears some examination for the light it can throw upon aspects of his domesticity.

The friendship with Margaret Blagge was a 'seraphic love', platonic, yet suffused with Christian values. 'Seraphic love' had been discussed, among others, by Evelyn's Royal Society colleague Robert Boyle in *Some Motives to the Love of God, better known as Seraphick Love* (with four editions in the 1660s). But Boyle, as a bachelor, managed the discussion more easily than Evelyn would do in practice: Darley rightly observes that such love was easier 'to define on the page' than to navigate through the realities of emotions and 'sexual attractions' (*John Evelyn*, p. 240). The relationship became an unexpected disruption of Evelyn's family life.

Margaret Blagge was a maid of honour at court when Evelyn first met her in 1669, and found her (as he would write of her in his *Life*) 'humble, religious and serious', not liable to tease (for he seems to have feared mockery). His short yet sustained and passionate friendship with her was subsequently narrated in *The Life of Mrs Godolphin*, after her marriage to Sidney Godolphin and her death in childbirth a few years later; this manuscript – more a hagiography than conventional biography – was eventually given to her widower, but published only in 1847. The narrative was composed with the hindsight of being able to give his own role in their friendship a suitably pious and ethical perspective, though he was at times honest enough to realize the extent to which he or their joint friendship had been fraught. This revisionism was in tune with some of his own attempts to shape his story towards the end of his life, variously in recasting his Diary retrospectively and in establishing the carefully edited and annotated letterbooks.

When published in 1847, *The Life of Mrs Godolphin* was welcomed by its readers as a truly Victorian tale of manly piety and decorous friendship towards a woman marked by her conscious devotion to God and the queen she served.[6] Subsequent responses have been made in the light of a different readership, hence Virginia Woolf's tart and somewhat trivializing essay of 1920, 'Rambling Round Evelyn' (published in *The Common Reader*, 1925), with its 'Poor Mrs Godolphin . . . whom he celebrated in a sincere and touching biography' and whose 'habits of an angel' did not present her friendship with Evelyn in 'an alluring light'. Keynes thought the *Life* 'charming and a characteristic production', which is somewhat anodyne. Hence, too, W. G. Hiscock's Freudian *John Evelyn and Margaret Godolphin* of 1951. In 1981 Bowle, by contrast, moves smoothly and quickly through this whole episode, noting their almost childish companionship while visiting the poor together, viewing cabinets and an exhibition called 'Paradise Transplanted and Restored', their shared devotions, his willingness to help her with finances and making a will, and Evelyn's being persuaded by her to manage the elaborate affairs of Lord Berkeley, when he and his wife were sent, along with Margaret and accompanied by his son John, on an embassy to Paris. After Evelyn belatedly learned of her marriage to Godolphin, and found his complacency was 'shaken', he nevertheless renewed their friendship, helping them to refurbish an apartment in Whitehall. She died horribly, aged 25, 'in raging delirium', and after despairing for this 'most excellent, and most estimable friend that ever lived' he continued a relationship with the widower. Evelyn's narrative, Bowle writes, 'reveals himself rather more than in most of his generally guarded writings' and emphasizes his 'extreme humility'.

Twenty years further on, Frances Harris's *Transformations of Love* brings into play a more feminized view, where both Evelyn himself and the male culture of the Restoration court become central. Her narrative of the friendship and life of Evelyn and Margaret Godolphin is based on an intimate knowledge of the relevant material, and with a keen and shrewd eye for court culture.[7] Darley, writing four years after Harris, brings to this 'affair' a tact and brevity that both defers to Harris and yet moves past it quickly. In the end, and at this distance and with the opportunity to (mis)read Evelyn's *Life*, much remains obscure or ambiguous, caught between Hiscock's unconvincing Freudian version of Margaret's neurosis and our own scepticisms with 'seraphic' love. Yet the narrative is still frustrated on many counts: by the obliquity of some of the letters between them, by the lacunae that are inevitably found in written communications between people who talk frequently to each other, the unwritten thoughts they might have intuited, and by the tensions between a married man and a woman already promised to another man; these were tensions that both tried to understand but did not fully articulate. Today, all of this must be fleshed out with due narrative smoothness, hence our recourse to the 'perhaps', the 'must have', the 'suggests', by which a story is allowed a completeness and convincing authority in the twenty-first century.

What is clear, though, is that it was undoubtedly a deep and platonic friendship, what Jeremy Taylor in his 'Discourse on

Friendship' deemed 'the nearest love and the nearest society of which the persons are capable'. A 'seraphic' relationship could yet from time to time be misjudged by either of the parties or even misappropriated in local conditions or events. Evelyn first noted Margaret in his Diary of 28 June 1669: 'my wife being gone a journey of pleasure down the river as far as the sea, with Mrs Howard, & her daughters the Maids of Honour, amongst whom, that excellent creature Mrs Blagge'. He celebrated her wit and intelligence, her obvious piety and her careful measuring of her life at court, where as a maid of honour there were responsibilities above all to herself, but also to the court, and to obtaining a husband (one of the prime occupations for a maid of honour, especially when the resources of her royalist Suffolk family made that acquisition imperative). By 1671 she was committed to a marriage with Stephen Godolphin. Yet he was much involved with finding a place at court or in government administration – which he eventually would do with various and important posts in the Treasury after her death, but was meanwhile absorbed in precisely the activities (gambling and racing horses) that Margaret Blagge found reprehensible and wished he would reform before their marriage. At times she committed herself simply to wait 'till God is pleased to dispose of me, one way or the other' (quoted in Harris's *Transformations of Love*, p. 213).

On Evelyn's part, he always found congenial the role of pedagogy or instruction, not least because he had been himself largely self-taught and wished now to help others. This propensity revealed itself in several lengthy and careful pieces of advice that he composed, not only for his wife, but for others: for his wife on their marriage he addressed his *Instructions*

Oeconomiques, later for his daughter he wrote 'Directions for the Employment of your time', and similar advices for his son before his marriage to Martha Spencer; he also penned a small volume for John on his departure for a post in Ireland in 1692, with advice on religion and 'profitable Entertainment'; and when he knew he would be leaving Wotton to his grandson, Jack, he wrote 'Memories for my Grand-son'. The letterbooks of the 1680s and 1690s contain many communications of moral, ethical and religious direction, career suggestions and careful admonishings, as well as warm, exemplary and elaborate expressions of sorrow for deaths of people Evelyn had known, both within the extended family and in society at large. Much inclined to be *in loco parentis*, with a family to groom and especially a son whom he assumed would continue the cadet branch of the Evelyn family, it was a role he could readily assume with Margaret Blagge.

It was also natural enough that in 1676 he would, though at her request, address Margaret Godolphin with his lengthy 'Oeconomics to a Newly Married Friend', attaching Mary Evelyn's own advice on housekeeping; he wrote that Margaret herself had told him, 'You are the first friend I ever had and ever shall be so.'[8] Margaret was an adult and gifted young woman, whereas his own girls had come late into his family, and were still young. He would also find out that Margaret's own birthday was exactly the same as that of the much lamented Richard, so she became a substitute offspring. And since Evelyn was also in need of some formal role in government administration, it was inadvisable to cut himself off entirely from the royal circle; so her life at court gave him some opportunities for them to meet, some sense of proximity to

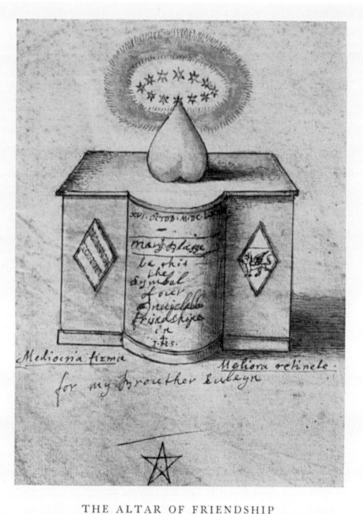

THE ALTAR OF FRIENDSHIP

From a drawing between the pages of Evelyn's MS. diary

43 'The Altar of Friendship', drawn by Evelyn and inscribed with 'be this the Symbol of our Inviolable friendship' by him and Margaret Blagge, from the 1939 edition of the *Life of Mrs Godolphin* by Harriet Sampson. A manuscript copy of this *Life* in the Houghton Library at Harvard (see illus. 44) does not include this image.

the court and reasons for judging it, even discovering in her life there some possibility of right conduct; as he noted, an English churchman could still manage to become a courtier. And his frequent friendship with other women – Lady Sylvius, Lady Sunderland, Lady Arlington – with names sometimes taken from pastorals and conducted with spirit, tact and deliberate self-consciousness, was also something of a precedent. But Margaret Blagge's need for a high-minded and yet emotional friendship at the age of twenty and for the guidance that she herself sought were intense and were readily, if slowly, answered on his part. His claim that she first solicited his friendship and help is of course made in Evelyn's own life of her, but is a piece, writes Darley (*John Evelyn*, p. 240), of 'matchless self-delusion', though Evelyn himself recalls that Margaret's invitation was 'her very expressions to me'; that again could be post-rationalization.

This relationship, as Frances Harris has well documented, was at the time seen as 'seraphic'. Such a relationship was idealistic, and as idealism it could be contaminated by misunderstanding and circumstance: 'Blameless innocence' (Evelyn's phrase) is beset by experience, as William Blake would know. Margaret could treat him at first as her 'most constant and loving playfellow', but for both of them, though in different ways, this lightheartedness moved into something deeper and perhaps 'uncontrolled feeling' (*Transformations of Love*, p. 164); long letters were exchanged (some of hers she asked later to be returned). Evelyn, 'not satisfied with a verbal pledge' of friendship from Margaret (*Transformations of Love*, p. 151), himself made a drawing of an 'altar of friendship' (illus. 34) and invited her to inscribe it as a 'symbol of Inviolable Friendship', and date and sign it 'for my brother Evelyn'.[9] After she decided to leave the court and take up residence with the Berkeleys, Evelyn accompanied her everywhere; they exchanged portraits, and he helped her to cultivate her private devotional faith. All the while Margaret was urging Sidney to become a more responsible and pious person, and Mary was keeping a careful eye on her husband's activity. Of course, the closer and more intense these meetings became, the more opportunity there was to quarrel, to be bewildered, or even to strain against the careful disciplines of a seraphic friendship.

While Evelyn urged her often to think of marriage to Godolphin and found pious reassurances to recommend it, she herself worried about whether even marriage was to be preferred to some, always unspecified, cloistered retreat (not being a Catholic, a nunnery abroad would not serve). When she did suddenly take the plunge, it was after an obviously painful role in a court masque, when rehearsals endlessly distracted her from her own devotions: to act as the chaste Diana in a court that was conspicuously lewd and corrupt was not a role she relished, even if she could remain slightly aloof from the performance. This episode is fully and convincingly narrated by Frances Harris.[10] From this unappetizing court entertainment Margaret fled into a quickly arranged and private ceremony with Godolphin that none of her family, nor Evelyn, were told of until later. Darley (*John Evelyn*, p. 246) also seems to think that the 'catalyst' for her sudden decision to marry was that being required to accompany Lord and Lady Berkeley to Paris she would be leaving Godolphin behind. Soon afterwards, when she left with the Berkeleys, Evelyn accompanied her to Dover, where, still unaware of her new status and with Godolphin remaining at court, Margaret actually told him in parting that 'if ever I return again, and do not marry, I shall retire,' a harmful yet necessary deceit when the marriage had still not been announced. But Evelyn would later write that it was the only time she had ever 'prevaricated with me'. She must eventually, upon returning to England, have told her sisters that she was married, and one of them, either deliberately on her behalf, or by accident, told Evelyn. He was inevitably much distressed; I would venture that distress was caused as much by her lack of confidence in him as by his repressed and perhaps frustrated love for her as a 'daughter'.

During this extended friendship Mary Evelyn knew and met Margaret on several occasions in London and at Sayes Court. All along Margaret had been a friend of Evelyn's family, with Mary always welcoming her and Godolphin at Deptford, though privately and occasionally caustic, as when she commented to Bohun that Margaret's role of Diana in the court masque must have constrained her 'severity' (*Transformations of Love*, p. 231). On one occasion at least she made clear, yet with some irony, that her husband show his presence at Sayes Court and not in the 'glorious court' and that she herself had 'a little interest in you, and possibly, am kindly thought of by you'.[11] Evelyn's own piety escalated in step with Margaret's: at the height of the friendship he asked Mary to let him sleep apart so as to 'vacate to holy and solemn offices' (quoted *Transformations of Love*, p. 202). But once Margaret's marriage to Godolphin was announced and recognized, Mary was welcoming and, at the time of Margaret's own confinement, fever and final death, she was a visitor and helper in finding doctors and midwives. Mary was genuinely touched by Margaret's death in childbirth and careful to send Godolphin her support and yet her hope that he had not hurt himself by too much brooding on his sorrow.

At her own insistence Margaret was to be buried at the ancestral Godolphin home in Cornwall, and Evelyn took care of the arrangements in London, engraving the brass plate on the lead coffin and inscribing it with the pentacle by which he had always signalled his seraphic friendship and the motto 'Un Dieu, Un Amy' (one god, one friend). He followed the hearse and its six horses as far as Hounslow, and then turned back, not to Sayes Court but to London, where he helped Godolphin, who felt unable to make the journey, to clear their lodgings. He pledged his friendship to Godolphin in person and by letter once he had returned to Deptford. Godolphin asked him to continue to supervise the finances for Margaret's little boy, even as he was himself pulled back into the affairs of court and eventually into a commission at the Treasury. In that position, as he had promised Evelyn all along, he would endeavour to assist him with the financial matters relating to both the lease of Sayes Court and the monies owed to his father-in-law.

Godolphin's eagerness for life in government administration and his relish of courtly activities had been a contested area with his late wife. But it pulled him again, if reluctantly and perhaps guiltily, into circles around the court. Yet his work in the Treasury actually caused a severe rupture in his good relations with Evelyn that was never wholly mended. An administrative decision taken by the Commissioners refused to convert the lease of Sayes Court into freehold, which greatly annoyed Evelyn, not least because his own family

The Life of M:rs Godolphin
Written att the request of my ⟩ By a Friend
Lady Sylvius _____ ⟩

Vn: Dieu ✶ Vn: Amy

Madam:

J am not vnmindfull of what your Lady:sp lately suggested
to me concerning that blessed saint now in heaven. doe you —
beleive J need be incited to preserve the memory of one ___
whose Jmage is soe deeply printed in my heart. Butt you
would have a more permanent Record of her perfections
and soe would J. not onely for the veneration wee beare her
precious ashes; Butt for the good of those who emulous of
her vertues would pursue the Jnstance of it in this, or
perhapps any age before it; Tis certaine the materialls J
have by me would furnish one who were master of a stile
becomeing soe admirable a subject; and wish'd J have a
thousand tymes the person in the world who knew her best
and most she loved would give vs the picture his pencill
could best delineat if such an artist as he is decline the
vndertakeing, for fear that even with all his skill he should
not reach the orriginall. how farr short am J like to fall ___
who cannot pretend to the meanest of his talents; Butt
as indignation (they say) sometymes creats a poem ✓

44 Opening page of a manuscript of Evelyn's *Life of Mrs Godolphin*
(1684), written at the request of Lady Sylvius.

could not believe that a powerful friend like Godolphin had not helped him. It not only soured any relationship with Godolphin, but forced him to reconsider exactly what his relations with Godolphin's wife had been before and after her marriage. Despite further entreaties, Evelyn found no immediate help in that quarter, though later it was settled, perhaps with Godolphin's assistance.

An early request by Godolphin for Evelyn to compose a memorial for Margaret did not progress – doubtless evidence of Evelyn's own ambivalence on what exactly he would write. But a request by one of her friends in 1684 settled him to the task once again. He addressed the *Life* specially to her, Lady Anne Sylvius, née Howard (illus. 44), and handed his manuscript to her in December of 1684. Four years later he retrieved it, made a presentation copy of it in his own hand, and eventually gave it to Godolphin in 1702.[12]

With the latter he maintained an uneasy relationship: Godolphin was unwell after his wife's death, but later returned to the Treasury under William III, rose to be prime minister under Queen Anne, and became good friends with the Duke and Duchess of Marlborough. Contact with Evelyn was infrequent and stilted, though the young John was helped to a post by Godolphin.

Yet Evelyn still harped on some further connection with Margaret: he had once told Mary that he would have loved it if one of his granddaughters might be married to Margaret's son, Francis. In the end, he achieved something of a similar match by seeing his grandson Jack, of whom he was especially fond, marry Anne Boscawen, in whose company Francis had grown up.

TWELVE

At Last: Wotton, 'reckon'd among the fairest of Surrey'

ARLY IN THE 1690S, John Evelyn knew that he would be inheriting Wotton. His brother George, after the loss in 1692 of his only surviving son, also called John, had no surviving male heirs, so the estate would pass by entail to Evelyn. Yet his first thought was to comfort his brother on his loss. He eventually confirmed formally the reversion of Wotton to himself; later, since he would also himself lose his only surviving son, John, in 1699, he realized that Wotton would go eventually to his grandson, Jack.

Thus when George himself died later that year, on 4 October 1699, Evelyn now found himself with home, house, gardens, woodlands and an estate estimated at 7,500 acres and with a useful rent roll – 'Far from my least expectation, or desert'. At the same time, he had a double obligation to see that Jack was instructed in the importance and significance of his inheritance and that the estate was to be left in a better condition than when he inherited it. Evelyn made a new will,[1] and in 1704 compiled his 'Memoires' for Jack (his last flourish of instructional family advice): this is a veritable manual of domestic probity, of estate management and – by the end – of theology and of what books of devotion to be read. It is a document that, though intended to ensure that Wotton would be in good hands and well maintained, must have been somewhat unnecessary for a 22-year-old, who had absorbed much of these matters already.

On 4 May 1694 Evelyn's Diary records that

> I went this day, with my wife & 3 servants from Sayes Court, & removing much furniture of all sorts, books, pictures, hangings, bedding &c: to furnish the apartment my brother assigned; & now after more than 40 years, to spend the rest of my days with [my brother] at Wotton, where I was born, leaving my house, & 3 servants at my house in Deptford (full furnished) to my son-in-law Draper.

Later he told Pepys that 'I pass the day in the fields among horses and oxen, sheep and cows, bulls and sows,' and that the family was enjoying a 'very sorry conversation among the bumpkins', and they were devouring 'plum-pie, pottage and brawn all holy-days'; but in the cold of January they had the comfort of 'luculent fires in most of the rooms'; otherwise, 'we live in heathen-darkness . . . and shall become barbars in a short time' if he did not receive any letters'.[2] He did however find pleasure in communicating with William Wotton, tutor at nearby Albury, a prodigy whose friendliness and learning he greatly appreciated and with whom he shared ideas of ancient and modern gardening (writing to Pepys, *LB*, 11.1027). But Evelyn missed being closer to London, though he managed to return there from time to time. Later he and Mary would keep themselves informed by taking turns to 'read the packets of all the news sent constantly from London, which serves us for discourse till fresh news comes' (Introduction by the editor, *Diary*, I.89).

William Draper, his son-in-law, managed Sayes Court for a while, though the family envisaged renting it to anyone who would maintain the garden. Eventually it was let first to Admiral Benbow, from whom a short lease was obtained by Peter the Great, who wished to reside nearby when inspecting the shipbuilding at Deptford. Whether or not the tsar did indeed push a wheelbarrow through Evelyn's holly hedges, as was reported, when he left Sayes Court it was badly damaged inside and out, and on behalf of the Treasury Christopher Wren and George London were sent to assess the costs to be awarded to Evelyn and to Benbow for damaged furnishing. Evelyn also made a visit in June 1698 to 'view how miserably the Tsar of Moscovy had left my house after 3 months', and he reported the damage in the revised 1706 edition of *Sylva* that he was preparing. He visited Sayes Court again in March 1701, when the property was again rented, this time to Lord Carnarvon, and once more in June 1705 to visit another tenant.

Before George Evelyn died, short of funds, he asked John to pay rent for the family's apartment at Wotton. But there were debts that John also needed to pay off, as well as providing a dowry for his daughter Susanna in her marriage to William Draper in 1693. Further, as Evelyn's debts now belonged to the Wotton estate, they were also being pursued by George, and the entail was even called into question by his daughter, Lady Mary Wyche. George's son-in-law, Sir Cyril Wyche, filled Wotton with his servants and horses after returning from a post in Ireland in 1695. So Evelyn and Mary took refuge for a while with their son in London. Nor, when George died in 1699, did he leave Wotton without further complications, having bequeathed to his brother only his personal possessions, library and family portraits, while appointing his daughter, Lady Wyche, as his executrix. She organized a vast funeral, writing over 2,000 local gentry, the extravagance of which shocked Evelyn, who retreated again to London. In January 1701 he returned to find the house emptied, cleared by sale or disposal of George's furniture. With a solicitor's assistance he was able to argue that the fishponds and pigeon-houses always went with inheritance, and that no 'fixed vessels' (cisterns or copper basins) were in fact 'moveable' items. Yet he was forced to buy back equipment for the farm, along with cocks, hens, hogs and ducks to stock it.

So the return to Wotton, much as it pleased him and had been urged upon him by his son John, was not altogether straightforward or pleasant.[3] What concerned him deeply, despite the problems in resuming the family home, was to establish it as a model of architecture, gardening and estate management, yet also one that respected its appropriate status and place in the world. He had told George in 1692 that all he wished for at Wotton was to care and supervise the gardens and to bring it, after so many years of abandonment, to be worthy of the family estate.

The estate and garden at Wotton had declined considerably by the end of the seventeenth century, with much woodland felled and not replenished; Evelyn told his grandson in 1704 that Wotton was 'naked and ashamed almost to own its name' (that is, its toponym about woods). Yet at the start of his stewardship, George had done well. A record of the large Tudor house 'as it was in 1640', before he revised

the garden, was sketched by his younger brother (illus. 45).
It shows a rambling sequence of gabled roofs and chimneys,
mullioned windows, and a note to indicate the room in which
he was born. A walk across the front of this southern aspect
leads from a pavilion in a small garden at the east towards 'a
pheasant garden' on the west; a little summerhouse overlooks
the moat, and facing the house is a mound of trees (on which
is noted 'here is now the grotto'[4]); on one side of and beyond
the building are 'meadows' and an 'upper garden'. Another
sketch (dated 1653, or perhaps noting retrospectively that the
new garden was created that year) was 'taken in perspective

45 Sketch of Wotton Park as it was once.

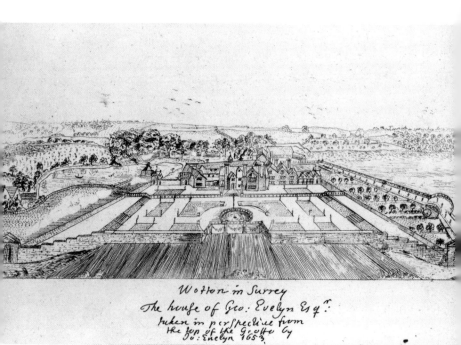

Wotton in Surrey
The house of Geo: Evelyn Esqr:
taken in perspective from
the top of the Grotto by
Jo: Evelyn 1653.

from the top of the grotto' (illus. 46). It shows that George
had filled in the moat, and in its place established a parterre
stretching from the platform of the house to the base of the
grotto mound; George himself had wanted a bowling-green,
but his wife seems to have wanted a garden. Along both sides
of this central space are terraces with steps leading down onto
the parterre, and a fountain is in its centre. Beyond the immediate garden are a pond to the west and a fruit garden to the
east, with hilly, wooded countryside beyond. Another sketch
taken from the east (illus. 47) shows the triple platforms of
the mound above the grotto, which is faced with a classical
facade of four pillars. The parterre is regular, but not particularly 'Italianate' (as it has been described), with geometrical

46 Wotton, from the top of the mount, in an etching of 1653 by
John Evelyn.

beds marked by columns or plinths at the corners and with lateral terraces of the sort that were by then common in England.[5] The grotto and steep mounds are, however, more Continental; the grotto front and what appear to be matching entries at either end of the mount (as in illus. 47, though these no longer exist) are also classical, and the clearest evidence of a 'color Romanus'. George's hopes for the grotto interior and his soliciting of help for its decoration from John show clear evidence that Evelyn had understood grotto work in both France and especially in Italy and advised his brother accordingly; the latter worried that such materials were not easily obtainable in England, and, in the end, the interior did not get built as they had envisaged.

By the 1690s Evelyn's concern, as he explained to his brother in 1694 with an accompanying sketch, would be to have a grove of evergreens, and the need to build a modest conservatory to shelter oranges and myrtles during the winters. In 1695 he listed the 'tools bought since I came into Surrey for my garden grove at Wotton' – usual items, like a wheelbarrow, hoes, rakes, spades, with a 'quadrant level for

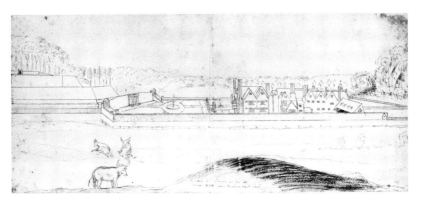

47 Distant view of the mount at Wotton Park.

banks & alleys', a foot measure and a 'large wooden compass';[6] this suggests some further ambition to reorganize or rectify the garden and establish a new evergreen grove. He was still planting an elm walk in 1701.

Evidently around 1700 Evelyn envisioned remodelling or replacing the old Tudor house with a modern front that echoed the earlier mount, which his sketch shows in the background across the parterre (illus. 48). It is a quasi-Palladian scheme with lateral wings, out of which spring two matching ranges of offices on two sides of a courtyard, through which a drive leads across a road and through a hemicyclical '*base court*' (reminiscent of what he had inserted into Sayes Court after the bad winter of 1685–6). This scheme, which would have brought his earlier enthusiasm for modern, European architecture to his family home, was never implemented. A later painting of 1739 by George Lambert (illus. 49) reveals what the house and gardens still looked like during the tenure

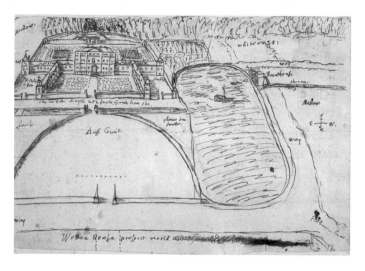

48 A proposed modern revamping of Wotton House.

of Wotton under his grandson, 33 years after Evelyn's death. It is indeed striking that we have a useful collection of images of Wotton house, gardens and their setting within a wooded landscape (see also illus. 2–3, 6), but none of Sayes Court except the important plans of his design of the grounds (see illus. 17, 20): at Sayes Court he was focused therefore on its design and planting, but at Wotton it is both the complex itself and his wish to memorialize it that seems to have mattered.

In these last years he was once again working on publications. In 1693 appeared the translation of La Quintinie's *The Compleat Gard'ner*, and four years later his book on medals, *Numismata*. Both return to some of his early enthusiasms: most obviously to ideas of foreign gardening layouts and maintenance and their usefulness in England, but also to a related topic that he had raised with Pepys in an extremely long letter of 1689 on medals and how a library might best be adorned

49 George Lambert, *Wotton in Surrey*, oil painting of 1739.

with historical and instructive images of illustrious men (*Particular Friends*, pp. 188–204).

La Quintinie's *Instructions pour les jardins, fruitiers et potagers* was published first in 1690, with a second edition two years later. It was a topic of particular interest to Evelyn, but the author had died before completing it, which prompted Evelyn to add a piece on melons, and a translation of La Quintinie's 'Treatise of Orange Trees'; he had known La Quintinie, the chief gardener of Louis XIV, since he visited Sayes Court in 1670, as he notes in his own section on melons. Evelyn's is a handsome folio in two volumes, but now well illustrated, with eleven full-page or folding plates, eleven engravings (illus. 50) and four woodcuts. The frontispiece is a portrait of La Quintinie, and the first folding plate, immediately before his initial chapter, is a plan of the Jardin du Roi at Versailles, where he was director; this is captioned and numbered to indicate the sites where the various fruits and vegetables were grown and maintained. And that now is evidently Evelyn's central concern, a book (he told his brother in March 1693) that was 'for use not for show & parade' (BL, Add. MS 78291). Indeed, the book he translates and introduces largely eschews many of the materials on design or the significance of gardens that he projected for 'Elysium Britannicum'; a similar emphasis sustains the publication in 1699 of one segment of that magnum opus, his *Acetaria*, a work that concerns 'salads' and 'pot herbs'. So he is promoting his translation of La Quintinie's book, which had been justly praised in France, so that 'we can and are able to perform matters that have amenities and advantages peculiar to *our own* [nation], which neither France, nor any other country can attain to' (my italics).

To help with the new section on melons, he had long since asked his brother-in-law William Glanville for assistance while in France in 1669;[7] Glanville professed himself something of a philistine in matters of horticulture, but was received civilly by the French gardener, who managed to convey some information on the topic of raising and pruning melons that Evelyn could later use. He also obtained help in translating what was, at his advanced age, a formidable task; he told his brother that 'I do not attribute the whole to myself', but his publishers had allowed it to proceed 'under my name' (Keynes, *Bibliophily*, p. 224). His assistant in the work was probably George London, who had been apprenticed to John Rose, the nominal author of *The English Vineyard* (1666); London had later studied at Versailles, returned to be gardener for the Bishop of London and thereafter founded Brompton Nursery.[8] The translation was never republished as a whole. But London, along with his Brompton Nursery partner, Henry Wise, published an abridged, one-volume

50 An engraved headpiece from Jean de La Quintinie's *The Compleat Gard'ner*, translated from the French by Evelyn (1693).

edition in 1699, though without acknowledging Evelyn;[9] it offered itself as 'now compendiously abridged, and made of more use, with very considerable improvements'. This went into five subsequent editions between 1701 and 1719.

Evelyn's 'Advertisement' is essentially a puff or promotion for Brompton Nursery. He salutes London and Wise for their achievements, which are superior to anything 'I have hitherto seen, either at home or abroad; or found by reading many books published on this subject'. A walk there on a fine day, he suggests, will show 'what a magazine these two industrious men have provided . . . such assembly I believe, as is nowhere else to be met within this kingdom', and one that has supplied materials – particularly fruit trees – to many gardens throughout England. Yet he does note, in passing, their capabilities for design: they have attained

> a sufficient mastery in lines and figures for general design, and expeditious methods for casting and leveling of grounds: and to bring them into the most apt form they are capable of; which requires a particular address, and to determine the best proportions of walks and avenues, stars, centres, &c. suitable to the lengths; and how, and with what materials whether gravel, carpet, &c. to be laid.

But they are no less capable 'in that most useful (though less pompous part of horticulture) the *potagere, meloniere,* culinary garden'.

By contrast, *Numismata* seems an extremely odd book, and was never reprinted in any form after 1697. It was dedicated to the son of Margaret Godolphin, Francis, whose education at Eton and King's College, Cambridge, Evelyn had supervised. That dedication, one supposes, was not undertaken lightly, yet Keynes notes that Francis, though a young man not yet twenty, might have found puzzling his former tutor's book, which Keynes calls 'garrulous and digressive' (Keynes, *Bibliophily*, p. 233); and Keynes then quotes Horace Walpole's criticism of its index under the letter 'N' – for how could a discourse of medals direct even its most curious reader to such topics as 'Nails of the Cross, Narcotics . . . Neapolitans, their character . . . Noah, Noses . . . Nurses, of what importance their temper and disposition?'

Yet it is both ambitious and a work of some erudition, an attempt to narrate a history of modern England through a discussion of medals, 'as they relate to history, chronology, and other parts of erudition'. Evelyn is arguing what Joseph Addison would later explain in his dialogues *Upon the Usefulness of Ancient Medals* (1726): that a fund of money is a fund of knowledge. This goes some way, surely, to explain the 'digressive' tendency of the story, but 'garrulous' it is not, given the format of the lengthy section on 97 medals. Portraits on one side have iconographical images on the reverse; the figures are described and identified, their costumes explained (Roman dress, for example), and the inscriptions around them and on the reverse, along with the iconographic items, are annotated and sometimes glossed with quotations from Virgil or Camden. It is in fact an economical way of expounding events, and, unlike written or painted imagery, which might be lost or destroyed, they can expound histories 'in more lasting monument than painted cloth' (p. 161). On one occasion,

when rehearsing a segment of national history during the
Civil Wars, in which Evelyn was personally involved, he uses
a medal of Charles I and Henrietta Maria that was discovered
'on a field of mine' (p. 110; it is more likely to have been
Wotton than Sayes Court, because its estate featured more
conspicuously in the wars than Deptford).[10] Besides the elaborate notes interpreting the medals of kings, bishops and
soldiers, with their historical role and symbolic significance,
Evelyn adds chapters on 'other persons and things, worthy
the memory and honor of medals', on the usefulness of inscriptions, on how to collect and procure them, on makers
of them, and one that urges collectors to find occasion to
display their holdings. There are lists of scholars and divines
('English, Irish, Scots, &c'), historians, antiquarians, philosophers, physicians, mathematicians, lawyers, 'poets and great
wits', musicians, worthy benefactors, great travellers, and
'imposters' (Evelyn had himself written about these in his
History of Imposters, 1669). In short, a conspectus of all those
who contributed to the nation of modern England; in many
cases, it is precisely those who were members of the Royal
Society. Towards the end he concludes with praise of those
'men of genius who have made this age as great as any, by
experimental knowledge' (his italics). It suggests that Evelyn's
endeavour, at an advanced age, was the need to plot, if not
narrate, a turbulent history of his own country, with attention to matters religious, political, cultural and philosophical.
In addition, his title page announced 'A digression concerning Physiognomy'; it explains how different nations and cli-
mates influence how people look and behave, how different
topographies produce different types (mountain people

versus folk of the valley, or plains). That is a conceit that still animates W. H. Auden's 'In Praise of Limestone', where different geologies have encouraged various types of human behaviour.

Stumbling and haphazard as *Numismata* seems, it can be read as an attempt to fulfil what ten years before he had proposed to Pepys in his lengthy discourse on medals and images of the famous. That letter had revealed an astonishing range and grasp of the topic, even if it was offered in a 'rambling' way. He may modestly have not wanted his own 'shallow-head' adorning Pepys's library of worthies, but he thought that medals, and engravings, would 'stand in competition with the best paintings', and he urged a wide assembly of persons in both 'Armes and Arts . . . Wit and Learning . . . and other instructive types': there he lists a miscellaneous group of 'effigies and icons of those who have made such a noise and bustle in the world, either by their madness and folly'; nor would he stop there, but would attend to many more classes of activity, such as those who fought battles, organized 'funerals and other pomps, tombs, trials, animals, monsters; stately edifices, machines, antique vases, reliques . . . ruins and landscapes', to some of which activity *Numismata* gestures in its survey of persons and iconography.

'To the Reader' of *Numismata* notes that he had started upon this book 'almost five years since', but finding others were addressing the subject (perhaps Obadiah Walker's book on ancient coins) he abandoned it for a while. Then he decided that 'there were yet some corner and little wastes' that could be 'dressed' by a new approach (the landscape metaphor is telling), since 'they relate to the conformation of some remarkable matter of fact, [they can] discover the genius of the age, and link the history of divers notorious passages of the latter centuries and revolutions'. In doing so, he may incite others 'who have better store and opportunities of perfecting what I have first begun', to augment his narrative.

And this is precisely what a later reader of Evelyn's book did, though alas anonymously, with his copy of *Numismata* that is now in the Houghton Library at Harvard University. He annotated the text profusely in all the blank spaces – in the margins, between engravings of the medals and commentaries upon them – but not always legibly. A note by Guy de la Bédoyère (dated 1977), kept at Harvard, thinks that the annotator could be William Wotton or Ralph Thoresby, both of whom corresponded with Evelyn about medals, but decides that it is somebody who did not know him, and is therefore likely to be of the mid-eighteenth century and writing from 'a detached and . . . scholarly point of view'. On the last page of the index, this anonymous reader has started a list of Evelyn's writings (again barely readable), where he notes Cowley's verses for *Sylva* and that he himself values the works that treat of gardening, which itself suggests an eighteenth-century reader. So he has brought his own researches and reflections on English history to extend Evelyn's narrative, even annotating the index of *Numismata*. His reading of the book suggests (*pace* Walpole) that he recognized Evelyn's attempt to narrate a much larger cultural history of England through the medium of coins and medals, to which the elaborate (and now annotated) index can be a rich and fertile introduction.

In 1704 Evelyn started to write *Memories for my Grand-son*, Jack being then 22; to this he added a series of 'Promiscuous

Advices' (*Memories*, pp. 75–90), adding that it would not be 'time lost sometime to read over & seriously to consider them' – such apothegms as 'He who has a soul to save, a family to provide decently for and a severe accompt [accounting] to give of his actions, needs few diversions to pass away time,' or 'Suspect everything that is too prosperous,' or 'Too much raillery diminishes respect.' All those precepts speak to his own character.

In the main memoir, following the example of 'My Lord Chancellor Bacon' (p. 40), Evelyn insists upon studying subjects both 'social, but all practical'; mathematics, in particular, 'sharpens and settles the judgment'. He urged 'dexterity of pen' and the study of 'the Latin and modern tongues', especially French and Italian, but not neglecting Spanish and 'the Saxon' (German). Keeping commonplace books is encouraged, and maintaining cabinets of both pictures and rarities and 'natural curiosities'. In particular, he advises on 'library apartments', 'which require your especial and constant inspection, nothing more becoming a person whose education has been something above the ordinary'. Reading lists of both ancient and contemporary authors are supplied, and Evelyn does not 'restrain him for the translation of others' works' (that is, he could undertake translations). A library, not 'great' as long it is not 'contemptible', is the 'most desirable furniture and ornament of all' (since it furnishes the mind and also distinguishes its owner). At one point Evelyn itemizes all the materials that a library should contain and that belong to writing: book presses, 'standishes' (ink stands), desks, stamps, scales, binding materials, map cases, penknives, erasers, wax, mathematical and surveying instruments, globes, microscopes, optic glasses and levels. Earlier at Sayes Court he had written instructions for a new gardener; now he has to address personnel at a much larger estate, like a steward with more detailed responsibilities, including the need to review expenditures and wages, seeing that garden and field tools are repaired and oiled, keeping locks on the boat-shed, and making sure that everything from walking sticks, fishing rods and 'traps against vermin' are kept in their proper places. And he advises Jack to 'read Cato, *De re rustica*, Columella and the Geoponiks' (that is, agricultural writers).

A fascination with detail colours all of his recommendations; he is nothing if not obsessive on matters from the choice and conduct of a wife, to the raising of children, where Jack is instructed in the rearing of infants to accept 'precepts, examples, restraints, and encouragements, things useful, delightful and not trifling of the nursery'. Care of Wotton's woodlands and the conduct of a household and its servants are all carefully explained, and on the issue of 'recreation' he recommends 'gardening, groves and walks and other innocent amenities, so far as to preserve that which is already planted and improvable without suffering it to run to ruin' (p. 16). Towards the end he lists some of the archives now at Wotton — his writings, 'several unpolished draughts' of other books, devotional writings, the unpublished parts of Lucretius, materials pertaining to Margaret Blagge, medical recipes and 'other books of mechanics', along with a note that he has annotated 'with my black-lead crayon' some hundred authors in his library (p. 68).[11]

It reads like some résumé of Evelyn's own life, hopes and relationships. Perhaps it also served as some comfort 'after so many of my dear children have been taken away & miscarried' that at least one male Evelyn would continue and cherish the family's ideals of a fulfilled and useful domestic life. He hopes that Jack will endow six poor people in the parish of Wotton and Abinger (though that did not happen). He began his 'Advises' by hoping that Jack will marry or 'adopt 'some honorable and worthy person' in order to perpetuate the name Evelyn (p. 5); but halfway through (p. 69), for he has obviously been drafting his notes randomly, he salutes Jack's marriage to Anne Boscawen. His last page is dated 'Ætat.85'.

The care and attention paid now to the future of the Wotton estate, in the hands of an extremely well-instructed Jack, augur how well the Evelyns now felt themselves at home there, despite the earlier inconveniences, the legal concerns and the death of John, who might otherwise have inherited. The family was beginning to enjoy life at Wotton, the gardens were improving, and more of their belongings were moved from Sayes Court; inventories were made of the contents in 1702 – something that implies a commitment to their life there. These are exceptionally detailed, a personal résumé, as it were, of the material aspects of their two lives: a 'cabinet' or 'closet of curiosities' both literal and metonymic.[12] Jack was now married to Anne, niece of Lord Godolphin (as he was by then). And Bohun was appointed to the living of Wotton, though one sermon inveighing against extravagant clothing annoyed Evelyn, who must have felt it was directed at the only two well-dressed women in the family, Susanna and Mary.[13] An old man, especially in that period, suffered from a catalogue of illnesses, and Evelyn had excruciating piles, kidney disorders, gout, the stone, and – a hard fate for a gardening man – he broke his shin while walking in Brompton Nursery in March 1703; and he even fell asleep now during sermons. He prayed God to make his infirmities bearable and grant him a peaceful life thereafter. Weather was still an object of worry and an occasion once again for indulging in prognostications. From nearby Albury, William Wotton wrote to him on 22 January 1702 after a particular wretched and destructive storm to cheer him up about how Wotton's 'charming groves' made it such a delicious seat, 'the greatest ornament of the finest county in England (*Correspondence*, p. 385). He was alert enough to follow military and political events abroad, including Marlborough's victory at Blenheim, and seemed to worry about the succession to the throne, for if Queen Anne was to die without issue, George of Hanover would likely assume the throne.

While wintering in London in 1706, John Evelyn died at Dover Street, aged 85, on 27 February, and was buried at Wotton on 4 March. Mary died two years later, at the age of 75, also in February. Jack was awarded a baronetcy in 1713, became a member of both the Royal Society and the Society of Antiquaries, and also lived into his eighties, dying in 1763.

Postscript

HIS BOOK HAS SOUGHT to narrate the scope of Evelyn's domesticity. His last years, spent largely at the home he finally and unexpectedly inherited, were much focused on domestic concerns, with some attention in his publications to larger and national matters. The interest in Evelyn's life always extended beyond the personal to the public, as he connects local place to national circumstance, practical gardening to the spiritual health of the world. If *oîkos* meant home for Evelyn, the Greek word would also come to mean *ecology* in the nineteenth century, and that was also a necessary part of the larger realm of *polis*. Evelyn's explanation of the significance of gardening and horticulture also realized that the local, the domestic and, specifically, a proper attention to how trees and plants flourished in England was intertwined with the political. And, as noted in discussing 'Elysium Britannicum', he saw that the individual and the local garden always sought to represent or exemplify the larger world that contained it. That is still a useful lesson to have learnt from his life and contacts, for (in its turn) it transcends a concern with just one life.

Yet it is sometimes hard to seize what could be significant or even useful about John Evelyn beyond narrating the local and biographical – for he is not an easy person to assess, and the materials of his life are vast and sometimes unwieldy. Virginia Woolf's scepticism finds others in agreement with her judgement, and the conventional contrast of the diaries of the dry, conservative, pious Evelyn with the outgoing, lively Pepys does him little good. So perhaps a different comparison may serve here at the end: with John Aubrey.

They worked together on the 'Georgical' Committee of the Royal Society, though in 1672 Aubrey was still asking whether 'Mr John Evelyn . . . has written on planning and gardening', so clearly he did not know Evelyn well enough at that date; but four years later he was pleased to note that 'my friendship with Mr Evelyn has grown since I sent him my notes on Surrey.'[1] And Evelyn's commentary on Aubrey's Surrey material begins to draw a useful distinction between them. They both contributed to the cultural revolution that marked the English Enlightenment, a strange mixture of local enthusiasms and a keen (if pious, in Evelyn's case) empiricism. And they both saw themselves, as we can now, as transitional figures in an early modern world.

Aubrey was a master of 'observables', whose 'industry' in his study of Surrey Evelyn clearly appreciated, though he was able himself to provide further material on the 'county of my birth, and my delight' that he thought Aubrey had missed: so he lists over a dozen 'observable places, which I doubt not but you reserve for another perambulation'. But he then moves quickly in his letter to celebrate Wotton, its 'boscage' and water, its prospects ('one of the largest prospects in England'), its solitudes and its various topography. For what excites him and distinguishes him from Aubrey is the history,

the setting and the cultivation of this family estate. While
Evelyn eventually inherited Wotton and meanwhile had created his garden at Sayes Court, Aubrey was forced to sell his
family home at Easton Piers in Wiltshire, and for the rest of
his life only managed to project on paper an elaborate garden
and landscape *all'italiano*; he forever regretted that he had not
travelled to Italy ('my longed for tour of Italy'), and he could
only record his dreams in his 'Designatio de Easton Piers' (now
in the Bodleian Library, MS 17). While both men had been
assiduous collectors of 'observables' throughout England, only
Evelyn had been lucky enough to 'make' both gardens and
books.

Aubrey filled his 'Natural History of Wiltshire' and his
'Monumenta Britannica' with wonderful and careful descriptions, though neither were published before his death in 1697,
the year of Evelyn's *Numismata*. Aubrey, like Evelyn, was fascinated with soil, trees, the remains of Avebury and Stonehenge,
visits to older gardens at Blenheim, Thomas Bushnell's her-
mitage, Danvers's garden at Chelsea, Deepdene, and Bacon's
house, garden and parks near St Albans; he was inspired by
reading Bacon's publications, pursued 'experimental philosophy' at Oxford, read Sir Thomas Browne's *Religio Medici*, and
taught himself to draw and to map, insisting on the importance
of chorography. Both men, in Aubrey's words, were happy to
have rescued 'what I could of the past from the teeth of time',
and both accumulated more materials than either could easily
manage and make accessible to a larger readership. Aubrey
seemed to be acquainted with everybody either in person, or
(like an indigenous Hartlib) by a cultural osmosis through
which he acquired materials for his 'Brief Lives' and other

projects; yet his last years are filled with notices of their deaths
and his failure to make useful contacts with them, whereas
Evelyn moved in circles where he could make more use of his
many contacts, and he was undoubtedly proud of his wide,
and often distinguished, aristocratic company.

Aubrey borrowed money from friends, especially Robert
Hooke, and sold his books to repay some of the loans; and he
was forced to shift his lodgings frequently, without being able
to assemble and keep his library. While Evelyn maintained
what William Rand had called his 'concernments' – concerns
for faith, family, country, friends and a place where these could
be cherished – by contrast Aubrey lamented his inability to
have many of them, including a wife. Aubrey's only publication in his lifetime was *Miscellanies: A Collection of Hermetick
Philosophy* of 1696, a strange assemblage that the eighteenth
century would deem the work of a madman, or what Ruth
Scurr terms 'hocus-pocus': in short, there was nothing in that
book that these days makes him a considerable presence in the
long history of England as 'biographer, antiquarian, archaeolo-
gist and historian of nature, science, mathematics, language,
folklore and architecture' (Scurr's list). Evelyn by contrast
managed more publications, of which *Sylva* in particular ranks
highly.

If both men were able to rescue the past, perhaps a more
useful discrimination is to distinguish between Aubrey's
detailed, laborious and fascinating conversion with that past,
and Evelyn's attention to bring what he knew of the past into
a useful and promising future. His notes for Jack point by
implication to his concern for the development of English
gardens and estates, his editions of *Sylva* argued especially for

a more rigorous and up-to-date agenda for woodlands, and his translation of La Quintinie makes real claims for garden-making (both pragmatic and philosophical, even 'pompous'). *Numismata* was certainly, in part, a narrative of the past, but it was also devised to make sense of an extremely fraught, yet important, period of contemporary English history. That 'Monumenta Britannica', like all of Aubrey's best work, did not see publication certainly meant that Evelyn was unable to direct future thinking about gardens and their design, though his synopsis of that work did circulate and must have provoked new thinking. He would not have known of Vanbrugh's creation of the gardens and landscape at Blenheim, nor other early English gardens, nor that one of his granddaughters married the owner of Nuneham Courtenay in Oxfordshire, another memorable eighteenth-century landscape.

There is no time or occasion here to undertake what might be an interesting research – tracking how much Evelyn's garden ideas percolated through to others, besides Switzer. This could fill an interesting lacuna in garden history, prior to the *furor hortensis* of the English landscape garden, by seeing how his understating of natural processes could be translated and adapted in the making of new gardens.[2] For landscape design is essentially a 'translation' of nature that is well observed into forms that would be more noticeable, more understandable, to more people. It was an instructional as well as an aesthetic act. Like many in the late seventeenth century, Evelyn observed the workings of nature and wrote about them; but he was also given the opportunity to formulate or transform them into 'built' work in actual garden-making. As a pragmatic and philosophical gardener, Evelyn saw a means of using

51 The emblem on the title page of Evelyn's *Kalendarium Hortense* (1664).

and lending his observations on the making of gardens, at once literal and metaphorical, to others. His careful attention to where garden and horticulture might lead puts him with a cluster of others in the seventeenth century, historical figures certainly; but he was also capable of envisaging, as promised in his *Kalendarium Hortense*, that local labour (illus. 50) can encourage universal peace and plenty. The making of English gardens was a supreme instance of his domesticity.

CHRONOLOGY AND MAJOR PUBLICATIONS

1620   Born in the family home of Wotton, Surrey, the younger son
        of Richard Evelyn

1620s   Lives in Lewes, Sussex, with his grandmother; attends the
        town's free grammar school

1637   Goes up to Balliol College, Oxford, as a Fellow Commoner,
        but leaves without a degree in 1640 and enrols reluctantly at
        the Middle Temple, London, to study law

1641   Spends some months in the Low Countries before returning
        to England, where the Civil War looms

1642   Briefly joins the king's army

1643–7 Travels in Europe, through France, Italy and Switzerland

1647   Marries Mary Browne, daughter of Sir Richard Browne,
        the resident ambassador in Paris

1649   Execution of Charles I

1651   After several visits back and forth to England after his
        marriage, settles at Sayes Court, Deptford, at first sharing
        it with Mary's uncle, and begins to lay out his garden there

1652   His first child, Richard, born; publishes *The State of France*

1656   Publishes his translation of the first book of Lucretius,
        De rerum natura

1658   Death of his son Richard, aged five; starts to translate St John
        Chrystostom's *Golden Book Concerning the Education of Children*;
        publishes his translation of *The French Gardiner* by Nicolas de
        Bonnefons

1659   Publishes *A Character of England*

1660   Return of Charles II to England, where Evelyn witnesses
        his arrival in London

1661   Foundation of the Royal Society, with Evelyn appointed
        by the king to its council; publishes *Fumifugium*

1664   Publishes his discourse on arboriculture, *Sylva*, having
        previously delivered a talk on this topic to the Royal Society

1665   During the Dutch wars is appointed a Commissioner for
        the wounded and prisoners of war

1666   The Great Fire of London

1671   Appointed by the king to the Council of Foreign Plantations,
        and a year later adds Trade to its agenda

1672   Appointed Secretary of the Royal Society

1685   After the death of Charles II is appointed Commissioner of
        the Privy Seal under James II

1688   James II flees to France; William and Mary proclaimed king
        and queen

1691   With the death of his elder brother's only son, Evelyn became
        the heir to Wotton

1693   Publishes his translation of La Quintinie's *The Compleat Gard'ner*

1697   Publishes *Numismata*

1701   Treasurer of the Royal Naval Hospital

1706   Dies in London, buried at Wotton

REFERENCES

1 Domesticity

1 Published only in Victorian times, this *Life* has become something of a battle-ground for understanding what that relationship actually was (see below in Chapter Nine). It reminds me of the *bon mot* that 'hindsight is a fine thing, and hindsight about a bit of foresight is even better when it comes to storytelling' (Michael Wood, *London Review of Books*, 18 February 2016).

2 London, BL, Add. MS 78392, f. 36. The text of his *Instructions* was written out by his scribe, Richard Hoare. Evelyn would have known that in Xenophon's *Oeconomicus* the husband instructs the wife on home management.

3 BL, Add. MS 78440.

4 BL, Add. MS 78441.

5 The term is used by my old friend Douglas Chambers in his mammoth undertaking to transcribe and explain Evelyn's letters. See Chambers, '"Excuse These Impertinences": Evelyn in his Letterbooks', in *John Evelyn and his Milieu*, ed. Frances Harris and Michael Hunter (London, 2003), pp. 21–36, and then his edition, with David Galbraith, of *The Letter Books of John Evelyn*, 2 vols (Toronto, 2014). I am myself more convinced that Evelyn did have a more holistic sense of what he was up to, which both the term 'virtuoso' (though of less force today) and my own theme of domestication attests.

6 All my quotations from *New Atlantis* are referenced to the edition by Alfred B. Gough (Oxford, 1915).

7 In a letter written to Lord Burghley, Queen Elizabeth's chief minister, and cited in the Introduction to *New Atlantis*, p. ix.

8 Michael McKeon, *The Secret History of Domesticity* (Baltimore, MD, 2005), p. 40. This is an omnibus of a book, subtitled *Public, Private, and the Division of Knowledge*, that sorely needed severe copyediting; not all of McKeon's excursions pay fruit in regard to Evelyn (who is cited only three times; Pepys has more). But McKeon offers a history of the term that has some relevance to my project.

9 John Locke, *An Essay Concerning Human Understanding* (1690), Bk 2, chap. 1, sec. 2 (my italics).

10 Elizabeth Yale, *Natural History and the Nation in Early Modern Britain* (Philadelphia, PA, 2016).

11 The introduction to the Chambers and Galbraith edition of the letterbooks offers a clear and useful overview of the role and styles of letter-writing that Evelyn employed. This emphasis has a long history: Plato saw the house as a small city and the city as a big house. In 1657 (*LB*, I.212) Evelyn thanks Jeremy Taylor for sending *A Discourse of the Nature, Offices and Measures of Friendship, with Rules of Concluding It* (1657), and to Benjamin Maddox the next January he urged 'above all, procure acquaintance, and settle a correspondence with learned men; by whom there is so many advantages to be made and experiments gotten' (*LB*, I.220).

12 Quoted by Ruth Scurr, in her remarkable and wonderful *John Aubrey: My Own Life* (London, 2015), p. 5, during her discussion of Aubrey's books and manuscript collections.

2 Early Life in England

1 I cite the modern edition of *The Diary of John Evelyn*, ed. E. S. de Beer, 6 vols (Oxford, 1955). For the actual composition of the Diary and its editorial rearrangements, see the useful synopsis in *LB*, I.xxii and note. De Beer explains that early parts of the Diary were a free copy from his much earlier notes, to which he added from or drew upon other books, newspapers and maybe manuscripts; this rewriting was undertaken between 1660 and 1665; therefore all citations from the early Diary were in many respects retrospective and concerned to shape his legacy. Later parts dating from July 1649 were written after 1680. After about 1684, the Diary consists of periodical entries and not fair copy.

The evidence is set out by de Beer in volume 1, along with an early version of the Diary, 'De Vita Propria'. The sixth volume has an incomparable index, so that I will throughout not cite individual references, except where a long passage is invoked. I have also throughout used modern spellings of Evelyn's orthography (except for his ampersands!) and expanded his abbreviations.

2 See Mary Dobson, *Contours of Death and Disease in Early Modern England* (Cambridge, 1997).

3 John Bowle, *John Evelyn and his World* (London, 1981), pp. 12–13.

3 'The fruit of travel': Continental Europe, 1641 and 1643–7

1 See George B. Parks, 'John Evelyn and the Art of Travel', *Huntington Library Quarterly*, X (1946–7), pp. 251–76. A general account of European travels can be found in Chloe Chard, *Pleasure and Guilt on the Grand Tour: Travel Writing and Imaginative Geography, 1600–1830* (Manchester, 1999). Evelyn often advised friends on the 'fruit of travel': see *LB*, I.237–80.

2 Anthony Radcliffe and Peter Thornton, 'Evelyn's Cabinet', *Connoisseur*, 197 (April 1978), pp. 256–61, which included details of the brass reliefs of animals along the base of illus. 6; this concerns the one made for Evelyn in Florence. His wife would eventually order her own cabinet in France, which is now in the Geffrye Museum, London. And in 1704 Evelyn urged his grandson to preserve several different cabinets at Wotton (see Chapter Twelve). On cabinets generally, see *The Origins of Museums: The Cabinet of Curiosities in 16th- and 17th-century Europe*, ed. O. Impey and A. MacGregor (Oxford, 1985). Among Evelyn's letters of 1665 is a catalogue of the 'precious treasures and curiosities' that the keeper of the king's cabinet should consider (*LB*, I.356).

3 Browne as the English Resident in Paris had served in other quasi-diplomatic roles. For more on Browne see Darley, *John Evelyn*, pp. 37ff.

4 And he would find in books he later owned that other virtuosi were fascinated by 'natural' echoes: Robert Plot's histories of both Oxfordshire and Staffordshire contain entries on echoes, the former with eight entries in its index. And clearly this idea

travelled, for an artificial echo was constructed in the grounds of David Meade in Kentucky – see James D. Kornwolf, 'David Meade II: Pioneer of *le jardin anglais* in the United States', *Journal of the History of Gardens*, XVI (1996), p. 265.

5 Evelyn corresponded with the artist and engraver Hendrik van der Borcht, who accompanied him on the visit to Fontainebleau and reminded Evelyn to send any sketches of it so they could be engraved by Wenceslaus Hollar: see Robert Harding, 'John Evelyn, Hendrick van der Borcht the Younger and Wenceslaus Hollar', *Apollo*, CXLIV (1996), pp. 39–44, specifically p. 42 (letter to Evelyn of 17 October 1645).

6 In this 'civil' letter to his cousin Keightly (*LB*, 1.86–9), who had converted to Catholicism while in Rome, Evelyn engages with another member of his large family by explaining that his curiosity led him to inquire into religious customs in Italy, but that Keightly could 'seriously weigh the real foundation, with the superstructure, and tried [that is, drew] the pure gold from the dross (and other her adulterate ingredients) [and then] certainly you cannot but acknowledge that the metal is foully mixed, and all is not gold that glisters'. Another letter to John Cosin, son of the Bishop of Durham, in 1652 (*LB*, 1.105–11) considers at length his conversion to the Catholic faith; 'for mine own part, I am satisfied in my religion, and have nothing to do to judge of others . . .', yet embarks on a lengthy critique of Catholicism. Cosin eventually reverted to the Church of England.

7 Evelyn in 1659 wrote of Browne's 'incomparable elucubrations . . . a magazine of all erudition' (*LB*, 1.251). My colleague and friend the late C. A. Patrides described this work's 'breathtaking range of interests and stupendous learning', some samples of which he provided in his Penguin collection of Sir Thomas Browne, *The Major Works* (London, 1977), pp. 163–260. In his Diary (II.397–8) Evelyn expressed his annoyance that he had not taken more seriously a 'Mountebank' who demonstrated a phosphorescent ring; yet elsewhere he was both inquisitive and sceptical in equal measure. In the large folio notebook 'Adversaria. Historical, Physical, Mathematical, Mechanical, &c' (BL, Add. MS 78333), he notes 'superstitions still remaining among us'.

8 In March 1645 he wrote in Italian from Rome to a former
   schoolfriend in Lewes, Robert Heath, to describe his visit to the
   Naples area, and his verses 'On Travel to R. Heath Esq.' are in BL,
   Add. MS 78357, fol. 41.

4 Marriage, and the Interregnum

1 It was ultimately transcribed by John Ingram and published by the
   University of Pennsylvania Press in 2001. I take up this large topic
   and possible reasons for its incompletion in Chapter Ten.

2 As Evelyn explained to his father-in-law in January 1649: BL, Add.
   MS 78221, fol. 30ff.

3 Quoted in Michael Hunter, *Science and the Shape of Orthodoxy:
   Intellectual Change in Late 17th-century Britain* (Woodbridge, 1995),
   p. 70.

4 Darley, *John Evelyn*, gives an account of this, pp. 75–6, 80–82.

5 This 'merriness', though surprising perhaps to those who think
   of Evelyn as a sombre and even sometimes melancholy person,
   was not unusual: see the 'spirit of mirth' from Evelyn and the
   company's almost 'dying of laughing' at his antics in September
   1665 in *The Diary of Samuel Pepys*, ed. R. Latham and W. Matthews
   (London, 1970–83), VI.220, which interestingly did not get
   recorded in Evelyn's own Diary.

6 Keynes (*Bibliophily,* p. 35) suspects that the regicides were too
   preoccupied to pay attention to an unknown author. The
   pamphlet is scarce, but Keynes notes that it was still being
   advertised in 1656 and 1658.

7 I interpret 'theatre' here as the theatre or stage of the world in
   England; but the editors of *LB* gloss the same word in a different
   context as 'into the issue' (I.169).

8 Darley, *John Evelyn*, p. 115, speculates that the dedication to 'your
   honor', to whom he is indebted for 'so many signal obligations',
   was his father-in-law.

9 Keynes, *Bibliophily*, p. 36, thinks that some copies with this
   monogram may have been printed especially for Evelyn.

10 *LB*, I.92 (writing to John Cosin, ejected from the Mastership
   of Peterhouse in 1644).

11 *Diary*, III.1. He had visited Maisons before in 1649, apparently alone (*Diary*, III.563, from which I have taken some of his observations); he was showing Mary what he clearly regarded as rewarding new architecture and landscape.

12 Aubrey also, in 1634, thought it might be 'possible to count and number the stones. I will do so one day': Ruth Scurr, *John Aubrey: My Own Life* (London, 2015), p. 24.

13 Hartlib is a truly fascinating figure to whom I cannot do justice here. See Charles Webster, *Samuel Hartlib and the Advancement of Learning* (Cambridge, 1970), and *Samuel Hartlib and Universal Reformation: Studies in Intellectual Communication*, ed. Mark Greengrass, Michael Leslie and Timothy Raylor (Cambridge, 1994), which gathers eighteen essays on this man and his work. Darley, *John Evelyn*, has useful accounts of the contacts between Hartlib, Evelyn and many others. I take up later Hartlib's specific contributions to Evelyn's garden work and what he learned through him.

14 See F. Sherwood Taylor, 'The Chemical Studies of John Evelyn', *Annals of Science*, VIII/4 (1952), pp. 286–92. This is a detailed account of experiments, diagrams of vessels, sketches of the layout of rooms, furnaces and so on. A chemistry book in the British Library (Add. MS 78345) is partly filled with diagrams, notes on the distillation of vegetables and spices, and 'chemical processes experimented by me'. See also his chemical studies in BL Add. MS 78335.

15 *Correspondence*, pp. 114–15; secondly to William Wotton, p. 391.

16 Evelyn recalls his recollection of Hartlib for William Wotton in 1703: *Correspondence*, p. 391, and earlier for Boyle in 1659, ibid., p. 115.

17 Leslie discusses in detail the relations between the two men in Evelyn DO, pp. 131–52, whose pages I quote here; interestingly Beale also shared his reservations about Hartlib, while remaining in contact with Evelyn after Hartlib's death.

18 Evelyn thanked Creech in 1682 for sending his translation (*LB*, II.689 and note). Howard Jones, *The Epicurean Tradition* (1989) provides a useful survey of the tradition and (in a final chapter) its fortunes in England, on which I draw; here p. 204. See also T. F. Mayo, *Epicurus in England (1650–1725)* (Dallas, TX, 1934), and Michael M. Repetzki, *John Evelyn's Translation of Titus Lucretius Carus* (Frankfurt,

2000). It is useful to recall that Lucretius wrote during the
Roman Civil Wars, and Evelyn started his translation during the
Interregnum in the aftermath of the English Civil Wars; but with
that unrest behind him at the Restoration, Evelyn may have felt
it less useful to pursue the task of publishing more.

19 This is a line from Lady Margaret Cavendish's *Poems and Fancies*
(1653), quoted by Jones, *Epicurian Tradition*, p. 198.

20 Fanshawe's response to his sending the manuscript is answered by
Evelyn in a rather florid and convoluted manner that also suggests
some embarrassment about the project: LB, 1.137–8. Fanshawe's
letter: *Notes and Queries*, CXCVI (1951), pp. 315–16; Taylor's and
Evelyn's response: *Correspondence*, pp.72 and 73ff.

21 I am indebted for this point to Darley, *John Evelyn*, p. 145, where
she notes that Evelyn never mentioned this 1657 book. However,
a 'dialogue' between discussants allows a measure of openness in
the matters raised.

22 Stuart Gillespie writes on 'John Evelyn's Occasional Poems and
Translations' in the TLS (30 January 2015), but does not address
the quality of the Lucretian verses, though they are mentioned
once in passing.

23 See H. Jones, *Pierre Gassendi, 1592–1655: An Intellectual Biography*
(Nieuwkoop, 1981).

24 Michael Leslie, in his '"Without Design, or Fate, or Force":
Why Couldn't John Evelyn Complete the *Elysium Britannicum?*',
in *Gardens, Knowledge and the Sciences in the Early Modern Period*, ed.
Hubertus Fischer, Volker Remmert and Joachim Wolschke-
Bulmahn (Springer, 2016). Darley, *John Evelyn*, chap. 8 also notes
Evelyn's probable concerns with giving a classical author like
Lucretius a proper and solid Christian interpretation. Carola
and Alastair Small, 'John Evelyn and the Garden of Epicurus',
Journal of the Warburg and Courtauld Institutes, 60 (1997), pp. 194–214,
make some sweeping claims for the influence of Lucretius on
Evelyn's gardening projects (see Chapter Ten). Michael Hunter
also discusses this book in Evelyn DO, pp. 96–101. See also the
collection of essays *Lucretius and Modernity: Epicurean Encounters across
Time and Disciplines*, ed. Jacques Lezra and Lisa Blake (Basingstoke,
2016).

25 His harping on the 'villainy of the printer' continued through several letters (*LB*, 1.177–8, 195, 201), as did also his waverings about Lucretius: see *LB*, 1.176 (to Taylor), his father-in-law about a better edition (1.195) and William Rand (1.201), and thinking nonetheless to proceed with it to Elizabeth Mount, Lady Cary (1.189). Much later in 1674 he wrote to Meric Casaubon that the continuation of the translation was 'long since escaping me', and that it was perhaps his youth, rashness and ambition that made him undertake this 'poor essay' in the first place (*LB*, 1.557).

26 For more, see Walter E. Houghton Jr, 'The History of Trades: Its Relation to 17th-century Thought as Seen in Bacon, Petty, Evelyn, and Boyle', *Journal of the History of Ideas*, 11 (1941), pp. 33–60, and Hunter, *Science and the Shape of Orthodoxy*, pp. 74–82.

27 An insight into Evelyn's faith and its practices can be gathered from *A Devotional Book of John Evelyn*, ed. Walter Frere (London, 1936), an editor who has written widely about the state of religion in England during the seventeenth century.

28 *MW* dates this to 1651, but there is no evidence for this; it was published in 1659, at the very end of the Interregnum. Given its topic, it may well have been initiated while Evelyn was still in France, and it certainly offers an ironic and satirical riposte to his 1652 book on France itself.

29 Some similar comments on the social and sartorial habits in Hyde Park were written by Evelyn to his cousin Sanders: *LB*, 1.144–7.

30 See again the book by Mary Dobson, *Contours of Death and Disease* mentioned above in Chapter Two, n. 2. In the late seventeenth century, for example, Queen Anne, after seventeen pregnancies, had only one child survive past infancy.

31 Quoted Darley, *John Evelyn*, p. 149.

32 His tomb was recorded and transcribed by John Aubrey in his *Natural History and Antiquities of Surrey* (1718), IV.137–42, where he also reprinted a long quotation from Evelyn's translation of the *Golden Book*.

33 *MW*, pp. 169–92, with numerous footnotes added, being taken from the fourth edition; Keynes (*Bibliophily*, p. 71) says the pamphlet was reprinted four times. This was republished, along with Evelyn's *A Panegyric to Charles the Second* of 1661, by the Augustan

Reprint Society, 28 (Los Angeles, CA, 1951), with an introduction
by Geoffrey Keynes.
34 The text is reprinted in *MW*, pp. 193–204, and in running
footnotes it reprinted Needham's diatribe.

5 Sayes Court

1 This first remark, from Evelyn to Sir Thomas Browne, means,
surely, that there are Continental details that the English have not
fathomed or 'descended to', but Evelyn will do so, if he can. The
second motto is from *Kalendarium Hortense*, p. 55, as published in the
first edition of *Sylva* in 1664.

2 For whatever reason, but mainly increased taxes under the
Commonwealth, he was forced to sell two other properties in
August and September, the first being a newly acquired estate
that he had destined for Mary. But throughout his tenure of Sayes
Court, he was preoccupied with funds: indeed, his ongoing quest
for remunerative employment for himself and his father-in-law
was as much the need for regular funds as his wish to find a useful
public role.

3 Letter from Mary Evelyn in June 1685, quoted in Prudence Leith-
Ross, 'The Garden of John Evelyn at Deptford', *Garden History*,
XXV (1997), p. 146. That Mary would help to tend the garden
when Evelyn was involved in civil services duties did not deter her
prevent her writing to a close friend that the garden required 'no
end of improvement' and that the 'fancies of men have the reward
of praise, when poor women are condemned for altering their
dress' (quoted in Darley, *John Evelyn*, p. 183).

4 Frances Harris, *Transformations of Love: The Friendship of John Evelyn and
Margaret Godolphin* (Oxford, 2002), p. 300.

5 The 'particulars' are difficult to read but have been transcribed by
Leith-Ross, 'The Garden of John Evelyn at Deptford', pp. 138–52,
to which my text makes occasional reference.

6 Southeast of Surrey Quays Underground station is Evelyn Street,
which leads to Deptford and thereafter changes into Creek Road
and continues into Greenwich. There are moves to recreate his
garden: see www.sayescourtgarden.com.

7 This was the task originally taken up by Mark Laird, 'Parterre, Grove and Flower Garden: European Horticulture and Planting Design in John Evelyn's Time', Evelyn DO, pp. 171–219; since then in three further essays he has pushed his subject into the effects of storms and 'chaos' at Sayes Court, in both 'Sayes Court Revisited' in *Milieu*, pp. 115–44, and 'Greenhouses and the Great Storm', in *Celebration*, pp. 99–119. A final approach, something of a 'conclusion', comes in chap. 2 of Laird's *A Natural History of English Gardening, 1650–1800* (New Haven, CT, and London, 2015).

8 I wish here simply to signal how I understand garden 'translation': in my *Garden and Grove: The Italian Renaissance Garden in the English Imagination, 1600–1750* (London, 1986; Philadelphia, PA, 1996), I showed that Italian ideas were adapted in England – referential, for sure, but also often explicitly 'naturalized' or 'domesticated'; in chapter 12 of *The Making of Place* (London, 2015) I argued that reinvented gardens, however faithful or facsimiled, were also new recreations and susceptible to 'the day's predilections'.

9 Letter to Sir Thomas Browne in 1657. Douglas Chambers, in his essay in Evelyn DO, tracks Evelyn's thinking about 'Elysium Britannicum' through his correspondence, not always identifying it by that title. Many learned and ingenious commentaries have sought to make connections between what he wrote with what he did on the ground at Sayes Court, but given the difference between a gentry and a royal garden, which he must himself have realized, such connections are hard to accept.

10 Mark Laird has published a conjectural reconstruction of the oval garden and also of the grove in *A Natural History*, plates 1 and 24. This may be compared with the plan in illus. 13. Laird also discussed this and its planting in Evelyn DO.

11 On 'dials' see the index references in the modern EB, this being an essential item for telling the hours of the day; in his garden retreat and his poem 'The Garden', the poet Andrew Marvell salutes the 'skillful gardener' for providing a 'dial' of 'flowers and herbs'; this is presumably a floral sundial that serves as both a daily and a seasonal clock, depending on the times of day and year in which flowers bloomed.

12 He had used the term 'villa' about the estate at Albury belonging
to the Earl of Arundel in a letter of August 1646: *LB*, 1.66. And
John Aubrey, without the advantage of visiting Italy, also used
the term frequently, especially about his hope to make one at the
Aubrey family home in the hamlet of Easton Piers, Wiltshire: see
Ruth Scurr, *John Aubrey: My Own Life* (London, 2015), pp. 180–82,
and Hunt, *Garden and Grove*, pp. 153–7.

13 Quoted in Harris, *Transformations*, 22, citing BL, Add. MS 78340,
fol. 88v. Evelyn would take up this need to deal with the soil in
his *Discourse on Earth* (see Chapter Seven).

14 Leith-Ross, 'The Garden of John Evelyn', p. 145.

15 Quoted in Laird, in *Celebration*, where he discusses Evelyn's
attention to greenhouses and solar heat. See also Douglas
Chambers, 'John Evelyn and the Invention of the Heated
Greenhouse', *Garden History*, XX/2 (1992), pp. 201–6.

16 For more on this 'chaos', Laird's essays in *John Evelyn and his Milieu*
(London, 2003), ed. Frances Harris and Michael Hunter, and
Celebration, can be consulted, as can Leith-Ross's articles.

17 The planting annotations on the plan are discussed by Prudence
Leith-Ross, 'Fruit Planting around a New Bowling Green at John
Evelyn's Garden at Sayes Court, Deptford, Kent, in 1684/5', *Garden
History*, XXXI/1 (2003), pp. 29–33.

18 It saw three editions by 1792, and also appeared in *MW*, and a
reprint of the first edition by the Women's Auxiliary, Brooklyn
Botanical Garden in 1937. See also Graham Parry, 'John Evelyn as
Hortulan Saint', in *Culture and Cultivation in Early Modern England*, ed.
Michael Leslie and Timothy Raylor (Leicester, 1992), pp. 130–50;
I quote him here from p. 147.

19 *Diary*, III.72. Jonson was both a pious man and a member in the
1620s of Gresham College. The poem was first published in 1616.
See Don E. Wayne, *Penshurst: The Semiotics of Place and the Poetics of
History* (London, 1984).

6 The Restoration

1 This was not a chore that Evelyn relished. He wrote that it was
'published' in 1661, but Keynes, *Bibliophily*, pp. 100–101, notes

that it may not have been printed, as no copy has been seen or described, nor is it recorded in the catalogue of his own library. Maybe by 'published' Evelyn meant 'circulated'.

2 For the coats of arms see Michael Hunter, *Establishing the New Science: The Experience of the Early Royal Society* (Woodbridge, 1989), plate 1 and pp. 41–2.

3 The phrase on 'domesticity' is taken from a book on Robert Hooke by Michael Cooper, *'A More Beautiful City . . .'* (Stroud, 2003), where Hooke's life and apartment in Gresham College is discussed and illustrated (pp. 66ff), and has some interesting similarities to Evelyn's project. In BL, Add. MS 78344 Evelyn sketches this new college (fols 112 verso and 113 recto) and notes the groves of trees and the individual gardens there.

4 I have consulted Charles Webster, *The Great Instauration: Science, Medicine and Reform, 1626–1660* (London, 1975), and *Samuel Hartlib and the Advancement of Learning*, ed. Charles Webster (Cambridge, 1970). Also major works on the Royal Society by Michael Hunter, *Science and Society in Restoration England* (Cambridge, 1981), *The Royal Society and its Fellows, 1660–1700: The Morphology of an Early Scientific Institution* (British Society for the History of Society, 1982 and 1985), his essay on 'John Evelyn in the 1650s: A Virtuoso in Quest of a Role', in Evelyn DO, pp. 79–106, and *Establishing the New Science*. For work on precursors of the Royal Society and non-members in touch with it, see *Samuel Hartlib and Universal Reformation: Studies in Intellectual Communication*, ed. M. Greengrass, M. Leslie and T. Raylor (Cambridge, 1994), and the CD-ROM edition of *The Hartlib Papers: A Complete Text and Image Database* (Ann Arbor, MI, 1995, and www.hrionline.ac.uk/hartlib). For the Society's involvement in landscape and agriculture see *Culture and Cultivation in Early Modern England*, ed. Michael Leslie and Timothy Raylor (Leicester, 1992), a topic that is taken up in the next chapter (see n. 16).

5 The lists in Hunter's *The Royal Society and its Fellows*, pp. 133ff., are illuminating, and I have pulled a few names from among the early elected fellows. The list also shows the offices they held, like Evelyn's secretaryship and his frequent membership of its Council (pp. 142–3).

6 On this project, see Michael Hunter, in Evelyn DO, pp. 87–95.
   It corresponds to many of Hartlib's activities in Evelyn's response
   to technological and mechanical matters, though he would later
   find them either too uncongenial for an aristocratic virtuoso, or
   maybe a betrayal of trade secrets. But many of Evelyn's activities
   (engraving, arboriculture, buildings, shipping) had relevance to,
   or impinged upon, a history of trades.

7 For a larger survey see Christine L. Cotton, *London Fog: A Biography*
   (Cambridge, MA, 2015).

8 *Evelyn's Sculptura. With the Unpublished Second Part,* ed. C. F. Bell
   (Oxford, 1946); the first text is also in MW, pp. 243–336. Bell
   did not think Prince Rupert was the inventor of mezzotint,
   though presumably Evelyn thought so at the time; but later
   in his *Numismata* of 1697 (p. 283) he ascribed it, correctly, to
   Ludwig von Siegen. See Anthony Griffiths, 'The Etchings
   of John Evelyn', in *Art and Patronage in the Caroline Court: Essays in
   Honour of Oliver Millar,* ed. David Howarth (Cambridge, 1993);
   for other advice I am indebted to Peter Parshall's unpublished
   lecture on *Sculptura.*

9 In contrast, Christopher Hussey, *English Gardens and Landscapes,
   1700–1750* (London, 1967), p. 15, finds *Sylva* a major influence on late
   seventeenth-century English gardens, and John Bowle's *John Evelyn
   and his World* (London, 1981), pp. 114–21, is excited when detailing
   some of its contents.

10 This is admirably discussed by Douglas Chambers in chapter 3
   ('A Grove of Venerable Oaks'), *The Planters of the English Landscape*
   (New Haven, CT, and London, 1993).

11 Prudence Leith-Ross, 'The Garden of John Evelyn at Deptford',
   Garden History, XXV (1997), pp. 146 and 148.

12 Evelyn seems the first to have used this word 'avenue' in
   his Diary of 25 August 1654, though having admired the
   'extraordinary long walks set with elms' at Maisons in France.
   See S. Couch, 'The Practice of Avenue Planting in the Seventeenth
   and Eighteenth Centuries', *Garden History,* XX/2 (1992),
   pp. 173–200.

13 Evelyn was also presumably the translator in 1660 of Le Gengre's
   La Manière de cultiver les arbres fruitiers, first published in France in

1660: see Keynes, *Bibliophily*, p. 83, where Keynes records John Beale assuming that *The Manner of Ordering Fruit-Trees* is 'I guess from the style of Mr Evelyn'; but Evelyn does not record this in his Diary.

14 Chambers, 'A Grove of Venerable Oaks', cites Traherne, p. 32. A modern discussion of ancient groves is Patrick Bowe, 'The Sacred Groves of Ancient Greece', *Studies in the History of Gardens and Designed Landscapes*, XXXIX/4 (2009), pp. 235–45. A more modern and even philological attention to how we talk about or name aspects of landscape comes in John Stilgoe's *What is Landscape?* (Cambridge, MA, 2015).

15 Respectively *Correspondence*, p. 226, and Pell's letter in the Bodleian Library, MS Aubrey 13, fol. 93v.

7 The 'Georgical' Committee

1 R. Lennard, 'English Agriculture under Charles II: The Evidence of the Royal Society's Enquiries', *Economic History Review*, 4 (1932), pp. 23–45. Douglas Chambers pursues the theme of the 'translation of antiquity', in particular Pliny and Virgil, in *The Planters of the English Landscape Garden* (New Haven, CT, and London), chap. 2.

2 Ruth Scurr, *John Aubrey: My Own Life* (London, 2015), p. 145.

3 I have explored the substantial effect of these travel volumes on a variety of English explorers of Italy, including Evelyn, in my *Garden and Grove: The Italian Renaissance Garden in the English Imagination, 1600–1750* (London, 1986; Philadelphia, PA, 1996).

4 This sketch is not dated, but suggests Kent's continued interest in how English landscape and history was described after his own return from Italy: see John Dixon Hunt, *William Kent: Landscape Garden Designer* (London, 1987), cat. no. 62.

5 On Enlightenment geography see Rhonda Lemke Sanford, *Maps and Memory in Early Modern England: A Sense of Place* (New York, 2002), and *Geography and Enlightenment*, ed. David N. Livingstone and Charles W. J. Withers (Chicago, IL, 1999).

6 Scurr, *John Aubrey*, respectively, pp. 23, 26, 91; other instances are frequently recorded throughout his writing.

7 *The Works of Francis Bacon,* ed. James Spedding, Robert Ellis and
   Douglas Heath (London, 1860), pp. 252–70. Bacon's *Sylva silvarum;
   or, A Natural History* was published posthumously in 1616.

8 See Scurr, *John Aubrey,* pp. 114, 143, 150–54.

9 See Gwyn Walters, 'The Antiquary and the Map', *Word and Image:
   A Journal of Verbal/Visual Enquiry,* IV/2 (1988), pp. 529–44, to which
   I am indebted here.

10 Royal Society Classified Papers, XIX, no. 43. Also published in
   Robert Boyle, *General Heads for the Natural History of a Country, Great or
   Small; Drawn Out for the Use of Travellers and Navigators* (London, 1692).

11 Aubrey's involvement in the natural histories of English landscapes
   is well discussed in Michael Hunter, *John Aubrey and the Realm of
   Learning* (London, 1975), and he had himself been endlessly curious
   and sharply observant of British landscapes and antiquities, as the
   material set out by Scurr, *John Aubrey,* makes clear: see his remarks on
   Avebury Circle (which he preferred to Stonehenge), p. 75, or notes
   on his extended visit to Bacon's house, garden and park (pp. 85–7).

12 Bodleian Library, Oxford, MS Ashmole 1820a.

13 See John Rogan and Eric Birley, 'Thomas Machell, the Antiquary',
   *Transactions of the Cumberland and Westmorland Antiquarian and
   Archaeological Society,* LV (1956), pp. 132–53.

14 Aubrey's 'Monumenta Britannica' was published in an edition
   by John Fowles, 2 vols (Sherborne, Dorset, 1980–82). Even
   earlier manuscript examples were George Owen's 'Description
   of Pembrokeshire' (1607), published and edited later by Henry
   Owen in *Cymmrodorion Record Series,* I (1892), and Rice Merrick's
   1578 'Booke of Glamorgan', published in 1825. The rapid increase
   in the study of English landscape and antiquities during the late
   seventeenth century took those early inquiries far beyond books,
   ancient manuscripts and coins to encompass a much larger social
   and cultural topography.

15 A very useful volume on Royal Society membership is Michael
   Hunter, *The Royal Society and its Fellows, 1660–1700: The Morphology of
   an Early Scientific Institution* (Oxford, 2nd edn, 1994).

16 The draft plans are reprinted as an appendix to *Culture and
   Cultivation in Early Modern England,* ed. Michael Leslie and Timothy
   Raylor (Leicester, 1992); the long letter similarly in an appendix

to *Samuel Hartlib and Universal Reformation: Studies in Intellectual Communication*, ed. M. Greengrass, M. Leslie and T. Raylor (Cambridge, 1994); the letter must have been passed to Evelyn from Hartlib. I discuss them also in Chapter Ten. I have written about these variously in both volumes. Those who want to see the letter as unproblematic pleas for 'natural gardening' are Peter H. Goodchild, 'No phantasticall utopia, but a real place', *Garden History*, XIX (1991), pp. 106–27, and Timothy Mowl, 'New Science, Old Order: The Gardens of the Great Rebellion', *Journal of Garden History*, XIII (1993), pp. 16–35.

17 See Michael Leslie in *Culture and Cultivation* on his tentative animism, and Will Poole, 'Two Early Readers of Milton: John Beale and Abraham Hill', *Milton Quarterly*, 38 (2004), pp. 76–99.

18 For an extended discussion of this notion of a hierarchy of land use and formulation see chapters 3 and 7 of my *Greater Perfections: The Practice of Garden Theory* (London, 2000).

19 Ernest A. Kent, 'The Houses of the Dukes of Norfolk in Norwich', *Journal of the Norfolk and Norwich Archaeological Society* (1931), pp. 73–87.

20 Sally Jeffery, '"The Flower of all the Private Gentlemen's Palaces in England": Sir Stephen Fox's "Extraordinary Fine" Garden at Chiswick', *Garden History*, XXXII/1 (2005), pp. 1–19.

21 Reported in Aubrey's *Natural History of Surrey* (1718), IV, pp. 66–7; there are many references to Arundel in Evelyn's Diary. My discussion here is drawn from what I wrote in *Garden and Grove*, pp. 148–52, and from Douglas Chambers, 'The Tomb in the Landscape: John Evelyn's Garden at Albury', *Journal of Garden History*, I (1981), pp. 37–54. Hollar's engravings are illustrated in John Harris, *The Artist and the Country House* (London, 1979), pp. 30–31. Evelyn's design for Albury was first published, with a commentary, in Evelyn DO by Michael Charlesworth, pp. 289–93.

22 The list of recommendations given to Evelyn when leaving Padua on his way north is printed in Mary F. S. Hervey, *The Life, Correspondence and Collections of Thomas Howard, Earl of Arundel* (Cambridge, 1921), pp. 449–53.

23 Cited in Michael Hunter, *Science and Society in Restoration England* (Cambridge, 1981), p. 101.

8 Work as a Civil Servant

1 Brian Vickers, ed., *Public and Private Life in the Seventeenth Century* (New York, 1986), p. xxvii.

2 Guy de la Bédoyère, ed., *Particular Friends: The Correspondence of Samuel Pepys and John Evelyn* (Woodbridge, 1997). Darley, *John Evelyn*, pp. 193–202 has a useful, detailed account of this work for the Commission, and the ill-health he suffered doing it. See also her essay '"Action to the Purpose": Evelyn, Greenwich, and the Sick and Wounded Seamen', in *John Evelyn and his Milieu*, ed. Frances Harris and Michael Hunter (London, 2003), pp. 165–84.

3 *The Diary of Samuel Pepys*, ed. Robert Latham and William Matthews (1972), VII.49 and 112.

4 This redrawn map is reproduced in Bédoyère, ed., *Particular Friends*, fig. 4, p. 337. The stained, faded original is held at Princeton University in the Pforzheimer collection (item 28620).

5 He is still harping on this topic in 1679 (Keynes, *Bibliophily*, p. 105), writing to the Provost of Eton.

9 Ancient and Modern in Architecture and Gardening

1 See Joseph M. Levine, 'John Evelyn: Between the Ancients and the Moderns', in Evelyn DO, pp. 57–78.

2 Claude Perrault's *Ordonnance for the Five Kinds of Columns after the Manner of the Ancients* (Santa Monica, CA, 1993), pp. 57ff., makes clear his objection to an 'exaggerated respect for antiquity' by those humanists who can only 'reason in anything other than a theological way' – an approach that might have given pause to Evelyn.

3 Letter to Cowley in March 1667, asking for a poem to preface Sprat's *History of the Royal Society*: LB, 1.434–6.

4 His *Account, Br*. I am using the posthumous second edition of Evelyn's *Parallel* here, since it usefully addresses issues of ancient and modern with the hindsight of the works done in and around London that are acknowledged in 1707, where Evelyn cites his recent visit to the new St Paul's and the encouragement of men who worked there who profited from his first edition. Difficulties delayed the second edition until after his death of this, 'Evelyn's

most splendid book' (Keynes, *Bibliophily*, p. 166). Evelyn's contributions are printed in MW. There were two issues of the first edition, in 1664 and (with a new title page) in 1680; that of 1707 augmented his 'Account of Architects and Architecture', added a new title page and a dedication to Wren. Another, posthumous, third edition of 1723 added Wotton's *Elements of Architecture* (1624), to which the second edition refers. Rudolf Wittkower, in *Palladio and English Palladianism* (London, 1974), thinks the work was 'a somewhat incongruous brew' (p. 102).

5   See Gillian Tindall, *The Man who Drew London: Wenceslaus Hollar in Reality and Imagination* (London, 2002), p. 128.

6   See John Evelyn, *London Revived: Consideration for its Rebuilding*, ed. E. S. de Beer (Oxford, 1938). I have also been helped by passages in Kerry Downes, *Christopher Wren* (London, 1971), and Adrian Tinniswood, *His Invention So Fertile: A Life of Christopher Wren* (Oxford, 2001), pp. 150−57, including Wren's plan, and Joseph Rykwert, *The First Moderns* (Cambridge, MA, 1980), pp. 144−8.

7   See Michael Cooper, *'A More Beautiful City': Robert Hooke and the Rebuilding of London after the Great Fire* (Stroud, 2003). Evelyn's own assessment of Hooke was that he and two others (John Wilkins and William Petty) were 'three such persons together not to be found else where in Europe for parts and ingenuity' (*Diary*, III.416).

8   There is a modern edition of Palissy's *Recepte véritable*, with a preface by Frank Lestringant (Paris, 1996), and an English version of the garden project was published, in a limited edition, as *A Delectable Garden,* translated and with an introduction by Helen Morgenthau Fox (Peekskill, NY, 1931).

10 'Elysium Britannicum'

1   *The Genius of the Place: The English Landscape Garden, 1620−1820*, ed. John Dixon Hunt and Peter Willis (London 1957, revd edn Cambridge, MA, 1998), pp. 57−8, where the correct date of the letter should be January 1659/60. The following letter from Jasper Needham and Oxford fellows can be found as Appendix II in *EB*, pp. 460−61. All quotations from 'Elysium Britannicum' refer to pages in Ingram's

edition, where he also provides the relevant folio or page number in the MS.

2   Hartlib saw Evelyn working on the 'History of All Trades' in 1653, when he visited him in Deptford, while also describing him as a 'chemist'. The 'History' was to be the collection of all information about the 'Circle of Mechanical Trades' that Evelyn talked about at the Royal Society in January 1660 (*Diary*, III.268). A manuscript preserved in the Royal Society is entitled 'History of Arts Illiberal and Mechanical' (Keynes, *Bibliophily*, p. 116). A detailed account can be found in Michael Hunter's *Science and the Shape of Orthodoxy: Intellectual Change in Late 17th-century Britain* (Woodbridge, 1995), pp. 74–82. For the unpublished 'History of Religion' see Keynes, *Bibliophily*, p. 251.

3   Furthermore, two manuscripts at the British Library (Add. MSS 78342 and 78343) contain vast collections of notes relevant to and (in the latter) 'Rude collections to be inserted into Elysium Britannicum, referring to the several changes of what is beg[un]', including texts now missing from the former. This complicated archive is described in the BL online catalogue of the Evelyn Papers. It is clear enough how much work was needed to bring the text into publishable form.

4   My italics: what he calls his 'manner' of proceeding suggests an instinct for accumulating addenda and glosses, something he shares with John Aubrey, among others. But it was also a necessary early modern approach that accompanied the need for careful observation, the sharing of information and experiments. In this respect see Elizabeth Yale, *Social Knowledge: Natural History and the Nation in Early Modern Britain* (Philadelphia, PA, 2016).

5   A collection of Taylor's sermons and other writings in *The Golden Grove,* ed. Logan Pearsall Smith (Oxford, 1930), affords a rich canvas of his ideas, including some letters sent to Evelyn, and has a useful introduction.

6   Frances Harris, *Transformations of Love: The Friendship of John Evelyn and Margaret Godolphin* (Oxford, 2002), p. 300.

7   Michael Leslie, '"Without design, or fate, or force": Why Couldn't John Evelyn Complete the *Elysium Britannicum*?', in *Gardens, Knowledge and the Sciences in the Early Modern Period*, ed. Hubertus

Fischer, Volker Remmert and Joachim Wolschke-Bulmahn (Basel, 2016). Leslie kindly shared these ideas with me before its publication. He has also suggested to me that Lucretius, writing during the Roman Civil Wars, made it appropriate for Evelyn to translate during the Interregnum, but afterwards found it more uncomfortable after the Restoration. Darley, *John Evelyn*, also notes Evelyn's probable concerns with giving a classical author like Lucretius a proper and solid Christian interpretation: pp. 102–3, 137–8, 141–7.

8 My information and quotations come from Keynes, *Bibliophily*, p. 251.

9 Leslie, '"Without design, or fate, or force": Why Couldn't John Evelyn Complete the *Elysium Britannicum?*', note 6, has a very useful examination of Grew's work, from which I quote.

10 R.W.F Kroll, *The Material Word: Literate Culture in the Restoration and the Early Eighteenth Century* (Baltimore, MD, 1991), pp. 165–6. Also the article by Alastair and Carola Small, 'John Evelyn and the Garden of Epicurus', *Journal of the Warburg and Courtauld Institutes*, 60 (1997), pp. 194–214, to which references are given in my text. I discuss two of these gardens where Evelyn was involved, to a lesser or greater extent, in chapters Nine (on Albury) and Twelve (on the Wotton grotto).

11 It would also have been difficult to accept the four elements, as Boyle argued that the classical four elements have to be repudiated, as they do not stand up to scientific scrutiny – that is what *The Sceptical Chymist: or Chymico-Physical Doubts & Paradoxes* (1661) is about; *The Sceptical Chymist* is set in a garden. Evelyn clearly loves the notion of the four elements; but could he publish it when one of his best friends, a fellow member of the Royal Society, had debunked it? I am grateful to Michael Leslie for pointing this out to me.

12 Alessandro Scafi, 'Mapping Eden', in *Mappings*, ed. Denis Cosgrove (London, 1999), pp. 57–8.

13 However, a recent symposium from Dumbarton Oaks does address this topic; see *Scent and Sound in the Garden*, ed. R. Didi Ruggles (Washington, DC, 2016).

14 John Dixon Hunt, 'Evelyn's Idea of the Garden: A Theory for All Seasons', in Evelyn DO, pp. 269–93.

11 Last Decades of the Seventeenth Century

1 Darley, *John Evelyn*, p. 280, notes how much Evelyn appreciated
   Locke's *Essay Concerning Human Understanding* of 1690 for its
   confirmation of God's existence and authority, his zeal to
   remove medieval jargon and above all his celebration of modern
   'mechanical arts, and experimental philosophy' rather than
   subscription to ancient learning.

2 It is an 'uncommon trifle', say Keynes, *Bibliophily*, p. 213, although
   it was published three times in 1690. The first edition was
   republished in MW, pp. 697–713.

3 On Susanna, see Carol Gidson-Wood, 'Susanna and her Elders:
   John Evelyn's Artistic Daughter', in *John Evelyn and his Milieu*
   (London, 2003), ed. Frances Harris and Michael Hunter (London,
   2003), pp. 233–54.

4 Nauteuil's portraits, reproduced in Darley's biography, are
   standard and conventional, except perhaps the unflinching looks
   that the artist gives to Mary and her two parents; the eyes of
   Evelyn himself are slightly more hooded, reserved.

5 Francis Harris, 'The Letter-books of Mary Evelyn', *English Manuscript
   Studies*, VII (1998), pp. 204–23, offers a shrewd assessment of both
   her letter-writing and her 'secluded domesticity'.

6 His *Life* was composed to make the best of his 'friendship', which
   includes, as Harris argues, 'his fantasy of a pious infant beauty
   bringing religion to a corrupt court (p. 113). There are several
   manuscripts of the *Life*, one of which is illustrated here as illus.
   33. It was edited in 1939 by Harriet Sampson (Oxford University
   Press), with a useful and straightforward introduction by Margaret
   Blagge herself.

7 This episode certainly needs consideration in any discussion of
   Evelyn's domesticity, which I try and do here; but for a much fuller
   and carefully modulated narrative Frances Harris's *Transformations
   of Love: The Friendship of John Evelyn and Margaret Godolphin* (Oxford,
   2002) remains the best and provides full references to the
   considerable archival materials.

8 For Evelyn's 'Oeconomics', see Frances Harris, *Transformations of
   Love*, pp. 247–57; for Mary's advice, BL, Add. MS 78386 and 78392.

Evelyn writes to Pepys in *Particular Friends: The Correspondence of Samuel Pepys and John Evelyn*, ed. Guy de la Bédoyère (Woodbridge, Suffolk, 1997), pp. 160–61, and notes how Margaret Blagge had been 'known to me, and my wife in particular'.

9 Harris, in *Transformations of Love*, argues that this drawing, made in October 1672, required more forethought than the sketch and the circumstances of drawing and exchange of it on the spur of the moment would suggest; she sees the lozenge of the Evelyn coat of arms, its 'perspective properly observed' and shaded washes ('clearly applied before the inscriptions were added') as evidence of a preconceived move; surely such graphic skill is something he'd readily have done, given his own skills, while making the simple sketch before their inscription. But the imagery itself, even if carefully composed, is equally telling: the heart in not pierced by any arrow shot by cupid, and it rests (unconventionally) on a double base with its pointed end toward the stars, where it is encircled with an enormous halo.

10 Ironically, this masque, *Calisto*, was something that Evelyn might have appreciated, being a representation of 'the Splendour & Grandeur of the English Monarchy' and a demonstration of the usefulness in England of European ideas, though one marvelously inept stage direction announces 'The Genius of England enters and is reassuring'! It was equally a *reprise* of the glorious and more intellectual masque tradition of the early Stuarts' world under Inigo Jones and Ben Jonson.

11 This letter is quoted in full in Harris, 'The Letter-books of Mary Evelyn', p. 212.

12 For details about the manuscripts of the *Life*, see Appendix A in Harris, *Transformations of Love* (pp. 304–5), as well as Harris's four-page discussion of Hiscock's writings on the subject in Appendix B (pp. 306–9).

12 At Last: Wotton, 'reckon'd among the fairest of Surrey'

1 This is printed in Helen Evelyn, *The History of the Evelyn Family* (London, 1915), p. 54.

2 *Particular Friends: The Correspondence of Samuel Pepys and John Evelyn*, ed. Guy de la Bédoyère (Woodbridge, Suffolk, 1997), p. 256.

3 The family quarrels continued to disturb their arrival at Wotton but are not mentioned in his Diary, but they are chronicled briefly in Keynes's notes to his edition of the *Memories*, pp. 93–4, where it notes that a printed broadside directed to the House of Commons has Evelyn affirming that he and George had a 'perfect understanding' of this inheritance and that the trouble caused by George's litigious son-in-law, Dr Fulham, a clergyman, is simply in his imagination and can be ignored.

4 There is some discussion as to who was responsible for this revision, whether George, another cousin George who had travelled in Europe, or John himself: it was attributed to the last, citing his Diary of 22 February 1652, by the Smalls (see Chapter Ten, n. 9, but the suggestion that he did not want to acknowledge his role in the garden's reformulation was due to his rejection of Epicurean ideas is far from plausible). Whether or not it was John Evelyn's work, this sketch was surely drawn *after* the work was done, as his note on it reads 'here is *now* the grotto' (my italics), which means that he is aware of how the moat would have been filled in and the mount itself cut back for a hundred yards to insert the parterre. If it was indeed his 'brother's work' undertaken at his suggestion or that of cousin George, the sketch is retrospective, a memory of the site before the work was embarked upon. We know from George's letter to his brother in Europe that John would have supplied ideas and materials for the work, notably plants and items to decorate the grotto – this is admirably explained by Harris in *Celebration*, pp. 58ff. Evelyn's later objections to the grotto columns came in the *Memories for my Grand-son* and seem to be his more nuanced understanding of the classical orders, as a result of his own 1664 *Parallel of Architecture,* then in the process of being revised in the early years of the eighteenth century while at Wotton.

5 As at Sir John Danvers's Chelsea garden or Lucy Harrington's Moor Park, Hertfordshire: I discuss these in my *Garden and Grove: The Italian Renaissance Garden in the English Imagination, 1600–1750* (London, 1986; Philadelphia, PA, 1996), pp. 126–39.

6 This note is printed in the *Directions for the Gardiner at Sayes-Court
    But which may be of use for other gardens,* ed. Geoffrey Keynes (London,
    1932).

7 He was writing to La Quintinie in April 1669 (*LB* 1.43–4) about
    the visit of Granville.

8 Douglas Chambers, *The Planters of the English Landscape Garden* (1993),
    p. 44 and note 51 (p. 197) makes this a firmer attribution. The
    book was dedicated by its publishers to Baron Capel, a Privy
    Councilor, whose famous gardener, Moses Cook, had moved by
    1681 to join the Brompton Nursery founded by London; Evelyn
    records (*Diary,* v.176) taking the secretary of the Royal Society,
    Richard Waller, there in 1694.

9 One wonders whether London and Wise neglected to use Evelyn's
    name on the abridged 1699 issue of La Quintinie because of some
    resentment that London's name had been less visible on the first
    issue.

10 A manuscript or draft of this book is held in the British Library,
    Add. MS 78350. Sean Silver, 'John Evelyn and *Numismata*: Material
    History and Autobiography', *Word and Image*, XXXI/3 (2015),
    pp. 331–42, uses this one medal to show how it can illuminate
    what he calls the 'belletrist'(!) Evelyn's own life. Using several
    modern writers, especially Roland Barthes, to link autobiography
    to his life (as Silver presents it), the article lacks any sense that the
    thrust of *Numismata* is Evelyn's attempt to explore a large narrative
    of English history rather than his own.

11 Two articles in Frances Harris and Michael Hunter, eds, *John Evelyn
    and his Milieu* (London, 2003), attend to these library matters: Giles
    Mandelbrote, 'John Evelyn and his Books' (pp. 71–94)
    and Miriam Foot, 'John Evelyn's Bindings' (pp. 61–70).

12 Two inventories were made: a general one, BL, Add. MS 78403,
    and one for Mary, Add. MS 78404. And also 1696 inventories for
    'stuff' left at Sayes Court.

13 See John Bowle, *John Evelyn and his World* (London, 1981), p. 241. On
    the same page he writes that Evelyn 'stumbled in *his* garden' (my
    italics) and broke his shin; but it seems to have been at Brompton
    that the accident occurred (see Darley, *John Evelyn,* p. 303), which
    suggests Evelyn's continuing interest in that nursery.

Postscript

1   I am much indebted to Ruth Scurr's *John Aubrey: My Own Life*
    (London, 2015), from whom I have drawn some remarks on his
    own life. Evelyn's letter to Aubrey was published eventually in *The*
    Natural History and Antiquities of Surrey, 5 vols (1718–19; republished
    Dorking, 1975), and a section of it in *Celebration*, pp. 268–9.
    Monumenta Britannica was eventually published, edited by J. Fowles
    (Boston, MA, 1980).

2   Recently David Jacques has attempted this narrative in his *Gardens*
    of Court and Country: English Design, 1630–1730 (New Haven, CT, 2017).

FURTHER READING

John Evelyn's many works have been catalogued and described by Geoffrey Keynes in *John Evelyn: A Study in Bibliophily*, with a bibliography of his writings, 2nd edn (Oxford, 1968); what follows are both publications available outside rare-book collections and a few modern republications or editions of his works. Otherwise, Keynes is the first stop for further enquiries.

Acetaria: A Discourse of Sallets, ed. Christopher Driver (Devon, 1996). Another edition was published by the Women's Auxiliary at the Brooklyn Botanical Garden (1937)

Diary and Correspondence of John Evelyn, ed. William Bray, 4 vols (London, 1857), of which the third volume contains Evelyn's correspondence

The Diary of John Evelyn, ed. E.S. de Beer, 6 vols (Oxford, 1955). This is extensively annotated and makes a rewarding approach to Evelyn's multifarious interests. If a simple text would be more useful in the first place, see other editions, like that published by Everyman's Library (1973)

Directions for the Gardiner at Sayes-Court, ed. Geoffrey Keynes (London, 1932)

Elysium Britannicum; or, the Royal Gardens, ed. John E. Ingram (Philadelphia, PA, 2000)

Evelyn's Sculptura, With the Unpublished Second Part, ed. C. F. Bell (Oxford, 1946)

Fumifugium: or The Inconvenience of the Aer and Smoak of London has appeared in modern editions (1930, 1933), plus one published by the

National Society for Clean Air (1961) and one by the National
   Centre for Atmospheric Research (Colorado, 1969)
Jean de La Quintinie, *The Compleat Gard'ner*, trans. by Evelyn, reprint
   (New York, 1982)
John Evelyn in the British Library, 2nd edn (London, 1995), reviews the
   holdings in the Evelyn archive now held there
John Evelyn's Translation of Titus Lucretius Carus, ed. Michael M. Repetzki
   (Frankfurt, 2000)
The Letterbooks of John Evelyn, ed. Douglas Chambers and David
   Galbraith, 2 vols (Toronto, 2014)
London Revived: Considerations for its Rebuilding, ed. E. S. de Beer
   (Oxford, 1938)
Memories for my Grand-son, ed. Geoffrey Keynes (London, 1926)
Miscellaneous Writings, ed. William Upcott (1825). This contains
   reprints of most of Evelyn's writings and so is a useful
   compendium, though it too tends to be held in rare-book
   collections
A Panegyric to Charles the Second, plus *An Apology for the Royal Party*,
   The Augustan Reprint Society, no. 28 (Los Angeles, CA, 1951)
Particular Friends: The Correspondence of Samuel Pepys and John Evelyn,
   ed. Guy de la Bédoyère (Woodbridge, Suffolk, 1997)

Secondary Reading

Batey, Mavis, ed., *A Celebration of John Evelyn: Proceedings to Mark the
   Tercentenary of his Death* (Goldalming, 2007)
Bowle, John, *John Evelyn and His World* (London, 1981)
Chambers, Douglas D. C., *The Planters of the English Landscape Garden*
   (New Haven, CT, and London, 1993)
Darley, Gillian, *John Evelyn: Living for Ingenuity* (New Haven, CT, and
   London, 2006)
Greengrass, Mark, Michael Leslie and Timothy Raylor, eds, *Samuel
   Hartlib and Universal Reformation: Studies in Intellectual Communication*
   (Cambridge, 1994)
Harris, Frances, *Transformations of Love: The Friendship of John Evelyn and
   Margaret Godolphin* (Oxford, 2002)
—, and Michael Hunter, eds, *John Evelyn and his Milieu* (London, 2003)

Hunt, John Dixon, *Garden and Grove: The Italian Renaissance Garden in the English Imagination, 1600–1750* (London, 1986; Philadelphia, PA, 1996)

Hunter, Michael, *Science and the Shape of Orthodoxy: Intellectual Change in Late Seventeenth-century Britain* (Woodbridge, Suffolk, 1995)

Impey, Oliver, and A. MacGregor, eds, *The Origins of Museums: The Cabinet of Curiosities in Sixteenth- and Seventeenth-century Europe* (Oxford, 1985)

Laird, Mark, *A Natural History of English Gardening, 1650–1800* (New Haven, CT, and London, 2015)

Leslie, Michael, and Timothy Raylor, eds, *Culture and Cultivation in Early Modern England: Writing and the Land* (Leicester, 1992)

O'Malley, Therese, and Joachim Wolschke-Bulmahn, eds, *John Evelyn's 'Elysium Britannicum' and European Gardening* (Washington, DC, and Dumbarton Oaks, 1998)

Patrides, C. A., ed., *Sir Thomas Browne: The Major Works* (Harmondsworth, 1977)

Scurr, Ruth, *John Aubrey: My Own Life* (London, 2015)

ACKNOWLEDGEMENTS

I am much indebted to Michael Leslie, who has read and commented so usefully upon my first draft; to Mark Laird for his comments and help on garden matters; to Robert Williams for his careful copy-editing. To the Foundation for Landscape Studies I am grateful for funds to make one more visit to the British Library, to review their Evelyn manuscripts. For help at that Library and, more specially, for the assistance and help from John Pollack and his colleagues at the Rare Book collections at the University of Pennsylvania, I am always most grateful.

My interest in Evelyn, though, is long standing, and I should thus recognize the research I originally did for *Garden and Grove* (1986), and the Dumbarton Oaks symposium on John Evelyn's 'Elysium Britannicum', published in 1998, and notably to John Ingram, whose transcription of that manuscript was used by the contributors before it was published by the University of Pennsylvania Press in their Studies in Landscape in 2000.

Photo Acknowledgements

The author and publishers wish to express their thanks to the below sources of illustrative material and/or permission to reproduce it. Some locations are given here in the interests of brevity.

Ashmolean Museum, University of Oxford: 4; The Bodleian Library, Oxford: 5 (MS Aubrey 4), 30; The British Library, London (photos © The British Library Board): 2 (Evelyn estate papers, BL Add MS 78610 [H]),

3 (Evelyn estate papers, BL Add MS 78610 [I]), 8 (Evelyn estate papers, BL Add MS 78610 [C]), 10 (Add MS 78342-78344), 11 (Add MS 78342-78344), 18 (King's MS 43), 19 (BL Add MS 78628A), 21 (BL Add MS 78628B), 24 (Evelyn period, Box XI), 45 (formerly in the holdings of Christ Church College Library, Oxford, MS 45), 46 (formerly in the holdings of Christ Church College Library, Oxford, MS 45), 47 (formerly in the holdings of Christ Church College Library, Oxford, MS 45), 48 (BL Add MS 78610); The British Library, London, Map Library (photo © The British Library Board): 22 (K.Top. XVIII,17.3); Cambridge University Aerial Photography: 34; from Joshua Childrey, *Britannia Baconica; or, The Natural Rarities of England, Scotland, & Wales . . .* (London, 1661): 29 (photo The Library Company of Philadelphia); from Benjamin Cole, *London Restored; or, Sir John Evelyn's Plan for Rebuilding that Antient Metropolis after the Fire in 1666*, engraving after John Evelyn (London, [*c.* 1755]): 39 (photo University of Pennsylvania Libraries); from John Evelyn, *Diary and Correspondence of John Evelyn . . . Edited from the original Mss. at Wotton by William Bray*, vol. III (London, 1867): 36; from John Evelyn, *Elysium Britannicum* (British Library Add Mss 78342-78344): 10, 11, 17, 40, 41; from John Evelyn, *Kalendarium Hortense; or, The Gard'ners Almanac; directing what he is to do Monethly, throughout the Year* (London, 1664): 51 (photo University of Pennsylvania Libraries); from John Evelyn, *The Life of Mrs Godolphin*, ed. Harriet Sampson (London, 1939): 43; from *The Miscellaneous Writings of John Evelyn, now first edited, with occasional notes, by W[illiam] Upcott* (London, 1825): 20 (photo University of Pennsylvania Libraries); from [John Evelyn], *The State of France, as it stood in the IXth yeer [sic] of this present Monarch, Lewis [Louis] XIIII. Written to a Friend by I.E.* (London, 1652): 16; from [John Evelyn], *Sylva, or A Discourse of Forest-trees and the Propagation of Timber . . . By J.E., Esq. . . .* (London, 1664): 25; from John Evelyn, *Sylva: or, A Discourse of Forest-trees, and the Propagation of Timber . . .* (York, 1776): 26, 27 (photos University of Pennsylvania Libraries); from Roland Freart, *A Parallel of the Antient Architecture with the Modern, in a Collection of Ten Principal Authors . . . compared with one another . . . Written in French by Roland Freart, . . . made English for the benefit of builders . . . by John Evelyn . . .* 2nd edn (London, 1707): 38 (photo University of Pennsylvania Libraries); Harry Ransom Humanities Research Center, University of Texas at Austin: 33; Houghton Library, Harvard University, Cambridge, MA: 44; photos Houghton Library, Harvard University, Cambridge, MA: 13, 14, 44; National Gallery, London: 31; National Portrait Gallery, London: 15; from

INDEX